The Modern Association Playbook

Reimagining Strategy, Governance, and Value Creation

Sean M Johnson

Lakefield Drive Publishing
Townsville, Queensland

lakefield
drive

Revised Edition 2.0
Published 2025
by Lakefield Drive Publishing,
Lakefield Drive Pty Ltd
Townsville, Queensland, Australia

National Library of Australia Cataloguing-in-Publication Data
Johnson, Sean M. author.
The Modern Association Playbook: Reimagining Strategy, Governance, and Value Creation.
Townsville, Queensland, Australia: Lakefield Drive Publishing, 2025.
Includes bibliographical references.
Identifiers:
ISBN 978-1-7640727-3-1 (hardcover)
ISBN 978-1-7640727-0-0 (paperback)
ISBN 978-1-7640727-1-7 (ebook -PDF)
ISBN 978-1-7640727-7-9 (Kindle (EPUB))

Subjects:
LCSH: Associations—Management. | Business models—Nonprofits. | Governance—Associations and clubs. | Strategic planning—Membership organisations.

Classification:
LCC HD2741 | DDC 658.4, dc23
LC record available at N/A

Typeset in Georgia and Aptos by Lakefield Drive Publishing

For more information, visit: lakefielddrive.co
Connect with the Author: sean@lakefielddrive.co

For Nancy and Chasely

Preface

This book is the result of years of work, hard-won insight, and a belief that associations deserve more than inherited structures, tired strategies, and static governance. It is written for leaders who know their organisation holds more potential than it is currently realising.

The Modern Association Playbook brings together some of the most powerful ideas in economics and governance. It draws on theories such as platform economics, transaction cost theory, institutional design, and the economics of the commons. These models have shaped how businesses think and operate for decades, yet their application to associations has remained limited, often hidden behind academic language or confined to commercial contexts.

This book changes that. It translates those theories into practical tools for associations. It is both diagnostic and directional. It helps leaders understand where they are and supports them in navigating toward something stronger, more adaptive, and more relevant.

Above all, this is a response to what I have heard across boardrooms. A shared frustration with models that no longer match the complexity or ambition of the world around us. I have written this for association Chairs and CEOs, for Company Secretaries, for governance professionals, and for anyone shaping policy, services, and member value in an era defined by uncertainty and increasing demands.

This is a playbook in the truest sense. It is not prescriptive. It is practical. It offers strategy without jargon, governance without inertia, and a vision of leadership that is bold, future-focused, and grounded in purpose.

If you are ready to challenge convention and design something better, this book is your invitation.

Sean M Johnson

Disclosure

This book reflects the author's original intellectual frameworks and professional experience in supporting associations through change. Digital tools, including AI platforms such as ChatGPT (OpenAI) and Perplexity, were used under human supervision to support research collation, editing, and visual generation. These tools did not replace professional judgement, conceptual development, or strategic analysis.

All ideas and frameworks remain the intellectual property of the author. Third-party materials are cited in the Bibliography, and case studies are either anonymised, used with permission, or based on public sources.

This book was independently published by Lakefield Drive Pty Ltd, with editorial and design oversight by the author.

Structure of the Playbook

From Membership to Orchestration

Associations stand at a crossroads. Once central to professional development and sector coordination, many now face a stark choice: evolve or risk irrelevance.

The traditional model, built on annual dues, fixed benefits, and scheduled events, was designed for a time of institutional authority and limited information. That time has passed. Today, professionals engage in real time through decentralised, peer-driven platforms that offer value without formal membership.

This is not a temporary disruption. It reflects deeper structural change. As outlined in *Chapter 1*, associations are being reshaped by forces such as declining trust, skills disruption, distributed innovation, and the collapse of information scarcity.

The question is no longer whether associations matter, but how they stay relevant in a platform-enabled world.

Why Platform Thinking?

This playbook introduces platform thinking as a strategic response. It positions associations not just as service providers, but as value enablers, hosting ecosystems of learning, collaboration, and innovation.

This shift is structural and philosophical:

- From services to **orchestration**
- From internal delivery to **ecosystem impact**
- From static models to **networked participation**

At its heart is a generative question:

What if an association's primary role was to enable others to create value, ethically, inclusively, and at scale?

The Role of the APSF

The ***Association Platform Success Framework*** anchors this playbook. It integrates three core pillars:

- **Data, Technology, and Security**, Build trust, insight, and interoperability
- **Strategic Pathways**, Align participation, revenue, and service design
- **Governance and Leadership**, Support complexity, inclusion, and adaptive decision-making

Each chapter unpacks these pillars with applied tools for transformation.

Book Structure

Part	Title	Core Focus
I	The Shift	Structural drivers of change and the case for platform thinking
II	The Case for Platform Thinking	Reframing associations as orchestrators of value
III	Becoming a Platform-Based Association	Tools for business models, participation, and monetisation
IV	Digital Transformation and Governance	Infrastructure, insight, and agile governance
V	Implementation and Capability	Building strategic culture and leadership readiness
VI	Implementation and Measuring Success	Metrics, scorecards, and ecosystem evaluation
VII	Tools for Change	Diagnostic tools, implementation guides, and scenario frameworks

A Method, Not a Model

This playbook offers a **method**, not a formula or a model. It is designed as a playbook to help associations design, govern, and evolve with clarity and purpose in an era of complexity.

About the Author

Sean M Johnson is a governance advisor, strategy consultant and researcher, with an extensive career spanning law, policy, education, and digital transformation. He has worked with national associations, not-for-profit boards, professional bodies, regulators and industry peak organisations to rethink governance, develop future-focused strategy, and implement change with impact.

A Fellow of the Governance Institute of Australia, Sean combines practical boardroom experience with deep expertise in law, risk, regulation, and strategic innovation. His approach is grounded in a wide theoretical lens, including law, systems thinking, complex adaptive systems thinking, institutional economics, and informed by real-world practice.

Table of Contents

Part I. The Shift

The journey to platform-driven success begins with understanding the shifting landscape in which associations operate. In this section we outline some of the macro level drivers of transformation. These lay the base for why associations should be commencing a strategic journey of transformation.

Chapter 1. Shift Happens when Structures Change

Associations are not dying; they are being reborn. But only those who transform from institutions of provision to engines of participation will thrive in the platform era.

Standing at the Inflection Point

The associations of today are approaching a strategic inflection point. For decades, many associations have operated on relatively stable institutional models, member lists, committee structures, conferences, journals, and a blend of advocacy and service delivery. But those foundations are shifting.

The evidence is mounting across technological disruption, workplace decentralisation, societal re-prioritisation, and an evolving skills economy that are reshaping the assumptions upon which associations were built. This chapter lays out seven structural shifts transforming the environment in which associations will have to operate, what can be referred to as the *Platform Era Shifts*. These shifts are not temporary, they represent the new ground upon which all future strategy will have to be constructed.

From Belonging to Utility (and Back Again)

The social contract between members and associations is evolving. The historical rationale, professional solidarity, shared norms, and status through affiliation, is being nudged towards more instrumental logics of value. Members are asking:

- *What do I get for my fee?*
- *Can I access what I need when I need it?*
- *Is this community actively helping me grow?*

Yet at the same time, the need for belonging is resurging. The pandemic accelerated not only digital transformation but also a widespread re-evaluation of human connection and community. As physical isolation, remote work, and digital fatigue set in, individuals began to seek out more meaningful and values-aligned spaces where they could feel part of something bigger than themselves. This has reignited interest in trusted communities of practice, cause-oriented affiliations, and networks that offer psychological safety and shared purpose.

Associations, long positioned as stewards of professional identity and sector-wide coherence, are uniquely placed to meet this renewed appetite for connection, but only if they adapt. Belonging can no longer be assumed in being a member; it will have to be actively cultivated through inclusive governance, co-designed experiences, and engagement structures that reflect the lived realities of members. The future of belonging is participatory, contextual, and dynamic.

Associations will have to now straddle the demands of relational depth and transactional clarity, and shared identity and personalised services.

This is not a pendulum, it's a continuum of engagement logic.

The 2024 Member Value Studies (e.g. MCI, ASAE) show rising member churn among younger cohorts unless continuous, visible value is delivered. Generational research (McCrindle, Deloitte) indicates trust in traditional institutions is waning, but affinity for peer networks and causes is increasing.

The Collapse of Information Scarcity

Information is no longer a scarce asset. Platforms, AI, and open access tools have driven search and discovery costs toward zero. This fundamentally undermines the historical value proposition of many associations built around journals and gated publications, expert lists, and exclusive access to updates or tools.

Curation, interpretation, and community validation now matter more than ownership of content. Associations will have to become context enablers, not just content distributors.

The recent World Economic Forum data show 80% of professionals use generative AI for knowledge tasks, with accelerating uptake in legal, education, and health sectors. The rise of Stack Overflow, Substack, and LinkedIn Learning as real-time, networked knowledge systems reflects this shift.

Innovation disrupted

Innovation has decentralised. It no longer relies solely on startups or top-down institutional breakthroughs. According to Eric von Hippel's theory of user innovation, solutions are increasingly co-created by frontline users, peers, and micro-networks.

Associations that historically defined themselves as solution providers will have to now become solution enablers. The role will be to foster open collaboration, shared infrastructure, supportive IP frameworks, and participatory experimentation.

There are numerous case studies from open science, global health (e.g. COVID-19 research consortia), and citizen-led innovation (e.g. maker labs, design jams, policy labs) supporting these shifts. The research from MIT Sloan and the OECD confirms increasing returns from participatory design vs centralised R&D in professional fields.

The Skills Economy is Fracturing

By 2030, now less than five years away, the majority of core workplace skills will have shifted. The World Economic Forum, LinkedIn, and McKinsey all forecast skill obsolescence of 30–50% across most knowledge jobs.

Core 2030 skills include:

- AI and big data,
- Systems thinking,
- Emotional intelligence,
- Curiosity and lifelong learning,
- Resilience, flexibility, and ethical reasoning.

Associations will have to act now to become the platform through which skills are developed, refreshed, and recognised, not in siloes, but across networks.

Figure 1.1 The WEF *Future of Jobs Report* (2024) shows recent and well publicised shifts expected in the work requirements through to 2030. 44% of workers' core skills expected to change by 2028. Lepaya and McKinsey studies warn organisations that fail to embed continuous learning risk losing productivity and innovation capability.

Work Is Decentralising

We are moving from workplace to work-networks. The rigid, centralised office model is giving way to:

- Hybrid collaboration,
- Autonomous project teams,
- Peer-led initiatives.

Governance, culture, and strategic leadership models will have to adapt. Associations should model networked governance internally to maintain legitimacy and relevance externally.

The Accenture and PwC research finds that over 60% of knowledge workers prefer hybrid or distributed work models. Academic studies (Oxford, Cambridge, Washington) confirm self-managed teams outperform traditional ones in engagement, retention, and innovation.

Figure 1-1 **Share Of Employers Considering as a Core Skill - 2025 v 2030 (%)**

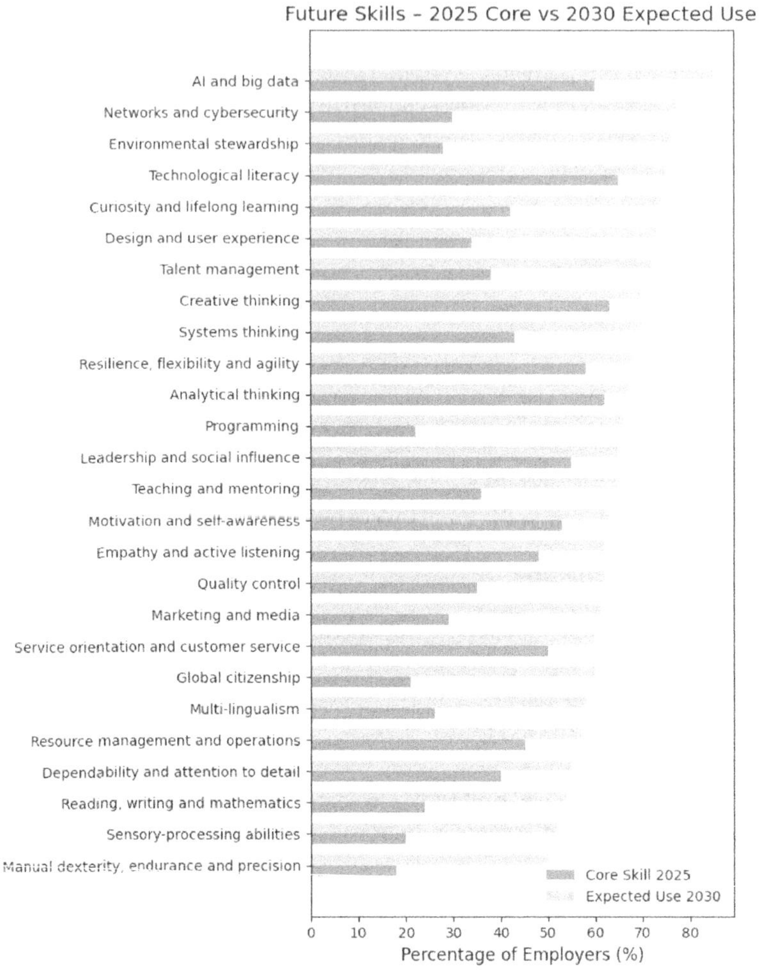

Data Source: World Economic Forum, Future of Jobs Survey 2024.

What we have been doing is not good enough for the future.

Ecosystem Value is the New Competitive Advantage

Organisations are shifting from siloed competition to ecosystem collaboration. Association relevance is increasingly determined not by what it owns or controls, but by the partnerships it sustains, the value it enables, and the problems it convenes people to solve. This demands new operating models, value metrics, and trust infrastructure where ecosystem collaboration as critical to long-term growth.

Trust Built From Within

In an era of declining institutional trust, legitimacy is no longer conferred by status, it will have to be earned through behaviour. Associations can no longer rely on historical credibility or sectoral dominance. Instead, trust will have to be continually renewed through transparency, reciprocity, and responsiveness.

This demands that associations actively govern data ethically and with clear consent frameworks, embed participatory practices in policy development, program design, and governance, and reframe power and representation to reflect the lived realities and diverse voices of their evolving membership.

Strategic governance is now a matter of legitimacy stewardship.

The 2024 Edelman Trust Barometer showed that while NGOs and professional bodies continued to score above business and government in overall trust, this standing was fragile among Gen Z and young professionals, who increasingly seek demonstrable values alignment, ethical purpose, and accountability beyond rhetoric.

By 2025, the global picture had darkened further. Edelman reported a broad collapse in trust, with the global average falling below 50 and 70% of people believing that business, government, and media leaders actively mislead the public. Australia slipped into the "distrust" category, with more than 60% of respondents expressing grievance-based disaffection, believing institutions serve the powerful rather than the public. This represents not just a reputational risk, it is a governance crisis in the making.

Against this backdrop, the guidance embedded in ISO 37000 (Governance of Organisations) becomes even more urgent. It identifies ethical purpose, stakeholder inclusion, and adaptive accountability as cornerstones of governance fit for the complexity and pluralism of modern institutions.

Associations that can reorient their governance frameworks to build trust by design, through inclusive decision-making, open reporting, and ethical infrastructure that aligns with both community expectations and organisational integrity increase their chances of being successful though the eyes of members.

Conclusion: The Strategic Mandate for Associations

To respond effectively, associations will have to Rethink identity: from provider to platform, Reframe governance: from compliance to strategic stewardship; Rebuild infrastructure: from siloed systems to interoperable networks; Redefine value: from internal delivery to ecosystem impact.

This is not about following trends. It is about future-proofing purpose.

The question is no longer *whether* change is needed. It is *how* associations will lead it. Chapter 2 begins that journey by tracing the evolution from Association 1.0 to 2.0, and setting the stage for bold, deliberate, and platform-enabled transformation.

Part II: The Case for Platform Thinking

The journey toward platform-enabled success begins with understanding the changing environment in which associations now operate. This section provides the strategic foundation for what follows, exploring the rise of platform models and their growing influence across every sector, from learning and advocacy to commerce and professional services.

Platform thinking offers associations a new way to organise value, foster engagement, and build sustainable impact. It reframes the association's role, not simply as a service provider, but as a convener and enabler of ecosystems.

In these chapters, we examine the key drivers of digital transformation, the evolution of member expectations, and the shifting economics of participation. Together, they establish why platform thinking is not just relevant, but essential.

This section sets the stage for the introduction of the *Association Platform Success Framework* and provides the context leaders need to rethink their strategy, structure, and purpose in a platform-shaped world.

Chapter 2. From Legacy to Leverage

Example 1. The Wake-Up Call[1]

Following the board's strategy retreat and with the review of the Edelman Trust data, the urgency of change felt real. This morning, Claire Evans, CEO of the Professional Network Association, gathered her executive team for a focused conversation.

"We're doing everything we've always done, and better, so we think. We do networking events, quarterly magazines, even the annual conference, but the members want more." the CEO, Claire Evans begins.

Heads nod around the table.

The marketing director adds, "We've tried to launch a community app, but uptake is slow. Our website can't keep pace with the tools people are used to. Every pivot feels like patchwork."

Beneath the surface, a shared anxiety lingers; how to meet evolving member expectations in a digital-first world. The challenge isn't just technology; it's fundamentally rethinking how value is delivered. And time is running out.

This book presents a comprehensive framework for orchestrating that evolution. Over the coming chapters, we'll explore how to:

- Redesign membership and engagement for true collaboration.
- Build multiple revenue streams beyond dues and conventional sponsorships.
- Develop a modern governance structure that is transparent, responsive, and member-centric.
- Adopt technology and data-driven strategies to sustain relevance and impact.

Now is the time for decisive action. Simply updating a membership platform or adding a mobile app will not suffice. Adopting a *platform-oriented mindset* is no longer optional, it's central to the association's survival and future prosperity. The chapters ahead introduce an *Association Platform Success Framework* that will help associations not only navigate these changes but flourish in the digital era.

[1] Throughout the book we use fictional vignettes to demonstrate application of concepts. Most are based on real cases and some are developed to demonstrate the concepts.

The Strategic Imperative for Change

As outlined in Chapter 1, associations today stand at the convergence of multiple structural shifts, from the collapse of information scarcity to the decentralisation of work and the erosion of institutional trust. These are not transient disruptions; they are foundational reconfigurations of the environment in which associations operate. The assumptions that once made the traditional association model stable and successful have eroded. What worked reliably in the 20th century, centralised service delivery, exclusive content, and uniform membership tiers, now delivers diminishing returns in a world of digital abundance, diversified professional identities, and dynamic ecosystems.

The challenge facing association boards and executives is no longer *whether* to change, but *how quickly* they can lead that change, and in which direction.

This chapter marks the shift from diagnosis to strategy. Where Chapter 1 explored the forces reshaping the terrain, this chapter begins to define the strategic response: a decisive pivot from Association 1.0, built for predictability and control, to Association 2.0, designed for adaptability, co-creation, and ecosystem enablement.

In this new landscape, members are not passive recipients of benefits, they are collaborators, contributors, and co-creators. They do not compare their experience to other associations, but to the seamless personalisation of Netflix, the relevance of LinkedIn, and the immediacy of Slack. Associations that meet these expectations are not merely digitising services; they are reimagining value creation altogether.

The strategic imperative, then, is clear: to move beyond legacy models and embrace a platform-based approach that enables interaction, participation, and sustained relevance.

Association 2.0 is not a technology upgrade or a communications refresh. It is a transformation in how associations think, operate, and govern, anchored in platform economics, adaptive governance, and shared value. The remainder of this chapter sets out the contours of this new model and introduces the mindset and design principles needed to realise it.

Association 1.0

The word "association" in this context refers to a broad spectrum of professional bodies, industry groups, community-based organisations, unions, and not-for-profits organisations. Each entity has a distinct history and purpose, yet they share a foundational goal: to serve their members or their target client base, through services, professional support, advocacy, and network-building.

Over the decades, many associations have embodied what we might call "*Association 1.0.*" This traditional model, though it continues to evolve, was built for stability. Its governance structures are largely hierarchical and top-down, with decision-making resting in boards or committees that convene periodically. Services follow a transactional pattern, offering a bundle of benefits, annual conferences, printed journals, and professional certifications, in a one-size-fits-all manner.

Predictability is the hallmark of Association 1.0. Membership often defined by little more than paying dues and receiving a set of standard entitlements. Engagement, rather than being continuous, revolves around an annual cycle of digital newsletters, events, and limited networking opportunities. Members rely on their association as gatekeepers to industry knowledge and career development.

Financial sustainability under Association 1.0 hinges heavily on membership fees, supplemented by sponsorships, advertising revenue, and event income. This approach was effective when members had few alternatives, and associations enjoyed considerable influence. However, with the advent of online platforms, open-access research, and digital professional networks, these 'bread and butter' revenue streams face intense pressure.

Another characteristic of Association 1.0 is its insular design. Traditionally, such organisations were built around discipline-focused silos, with minimal external partnerships. While this created strong professional identities, it also made them slow to adapt to broader shifts, be they technological, economic, or societal. In a landscape where professionals can easily access global knowledge and communities, relying on loyalty purely due to a shared professional identity is no longer sufficient. Today, people expect immediate relevance, responsiveness, and the ability to form meaningful connections within and across industries.

Although the model of Association 1.0 once provided stability and structure, it increasingly lags what the modern professional demands. Shifting to an "Association 2.0" framework does not require abandoning past strengths. Rather, it involves building on that heritage while embracing more dynamic, collaborative, and innovative practices, ensuring ongoing influence and sustainability in a rapidly changing world.

What Is Association 2.0?

Association 2.0 is not a communications refresh or technology upgrade. It is a fundamental redefinition of how associations operate, create value, and deliver impact. Instead of acting as service providers delivering a fixed bundle of member benefits, Association 2.0 organisations become platforms, enabling interaction, collaboration, and innovation across their ecosystems.

This shift builds on the best of traditional associations: purpose-driven identity, professional stewardship, and member trust. But it adapts those strengths to meet new expectations for personalisation, participation, and co-creation. Members are no longer passive recipients of services. They are active contributors, collaborators, and value creators in their own right.

To succeed in this environment, associations will have to reimagine how they engage members, structure their teams, generate income, and design services. Table 2.1 outlines the core characteristics of the Association 2.0 model.

Table 2-1 Key Characteristics of Association 2.0

Key Characteristic	Description
Platform Thinking	Associations evolve from being service providers to enablers of interaction between members, stakeholders, and external partners.
Personalised Engagement	AI-driven insights allow tailored experiences, shifting from mass communication to meaningful, individualised interactions.
Diverse Revenue Streams	Moving beyond dues-based funding to data monetisation, partnerships, sponsorships, and premium digital services. Perhaps whole new offerings.
Agility & Innovation	Adopting emerging technologies (AI, blockchain, VR) to streamline operations and enhance member experience.
Inclusivity & Sustainability	Ensuring equitable access and fostering cross-sector partnerships to address societal challenges.
Rethink Membership	Opening membership up to new classes of members who would add to and receive value from being in a networked ecosystem.

From Association 1.0 to 2.0: A Strategic Shift

The transition to Association 2.0 is more than digitising legacy systems. It involves redesigning purpose, structure, and engagement logic. Where Association 1.0 models were built for centralised control and predictable services, Association 2.0 enables dynamic interaction and shared value creation.

This shift affects every part of the organisation, from governance to technology, from finance to culture. Table 2.2 outlines how these shifts play out across key dimensions.

Table 2-2 Evolution Map

Dimension	Association 1.0	Association 2.0
Purpose	Serving members through centralised services.	Empowering ecosystems through shared value creation.
Structure	Hierarchical, siloed departments and committees.	Networked, modular teams with flexible governance.
Value Creation	Organisation as producer and distributor of benefits.	Platform as enabler of value co-creation among members and partners.

Dimension	Association 1.0	Association 2.0
Revenue Model	Subscription dues and event sponsorship.	Diversified revenue: digital products, data services, partnerships, marketplaces.
Engagement	Periodic engagement via newsletters and events.	Continuous, dynamic engagement via platforms, apps, and AI-driven content.
Technology	Association Management System centric limited integration or interoperability.	API-first, interoperable tech stack with real-time data and automation.
Governance Mindset	Compliance-focused, risk-averse, slow decision-making.	Adaptive governance: responsive, risk-informed, innovation-oriented.

Platform Thinking as the New Strategic Logic

Associations that adopt the Association 2.0 model do not abandon tradition. They build on it with modern tools, networked governance, and participatory logic that meet the moment.

This model repositions associations as orchestrators of value, not gatekeepers; enablers of ecosystems, not siloed service hubs; and drivers of shared outcomes, not only institutional outputs.

Association 2.0 is not about incremental improvements, it is about redefining how associations create and sustain value. By adopting these key characteristics, associations shift from transactional service providers to ecosystems that thrive on collaborative value creation.

Members increasingly want to shape their own networks and professional journeys, and they're willing to do so in communities that share control and insight. This underscores why Association 2.0 isn't just an upgrade, but a fundamental redefinition.

Example 2. Static Membership To Sector Influence

The CIPD has shifted its focus from static member benefits to sector-wide influence by deploying a content platform strategy. It now offers digitally personalised learning journeys, public access to research, and peer mentoring, effectively scaling its impact across both paying members and non-members (CIPD, 2022). [2]

[2] Case studies and examples of elements will be introduced through out the book, including hypothetical examples to demonstrate what is possible.

This approach exemplifies Association 2.0 thinking, expanding the association's value beyond membership walls and embracing platform dynamics of co-creation and open access.

The shift from Association 1.0 to 2.0 involves a fundamental reimagining of purpose, structure, and strategy. The following high-level comparison sets the scene for the practical transitions outlined in the above Table.

Rethinking Purpose: From Serving Members to Empowering Ecosystems

Traditional associations were often established to serve their members through representation, professional development, and access to exclusive benefits. While these remain important, they are no longer sufficient. Associations will have to now ask: *What is our systemic contribution?* and *Whom do we enable beyond our membership base?*

Example 3. ***American College of Cardiology* (ACC)**

A compelling illustration of this mindset shift is the American College of Cardiology (ACC), which repositioned its purpose from serving members to transforming cardiovascular care. This redefinition led to significant investments in health system registries, research data infrastructure, and policy co-creation with external partners. The ACC's purpose now centres on ecosystem stewardship rather than institutional preservation, enabling it to engage beyond traditional boundaries and deliver measurable sectoral impact (ACC, 2023a, 2023b, 2023c).

Consider other scenarios, say, a national arts association that once focused solely on member events and awards. Under the Association 2.0 lens, it could evolve into an innovation platform, running digital grant-writing workshops open to all creatives, curating a public mentorship exchange, and hosting cross-sector labs with funders and producers. The value shifts from internal membership servicing to enabling broad, systemic value creation.

Redesigning Structure: From Hierarchical to Networked

Association 1.0 governance is often centralised, slow, and protective of legacy norms. Association 2.0 requires more responsive, distributed structures that push decision-making closer to members and partners. This shift does not mean abandoning coordination or strategic direction. Instead, it requires enabling localised value creation within a shared framework.

Engineers Australia (EA) has embraced this model, empowering technical societies and regional groups through digital infrastructure and governance redesign. EA invested in member platforms, local advisory structures, and greater autonomy, enabling relevance and responsiveness at the network's edge while maintaining national coherence (Engineers Australia, 2022).

Imagine a national sporting body or a disciplinary peak body moving from top-down planning to orchestrated autonomy. Regional chapters could run their own events, manage data dashboards, and co fund pilot programs. This is not tokenism with a brief to drive membership recruitment but enabling. Empowering hubs to acts as a facilitator, curating insights, setting shared standards, and enabling interoperability across the system.

Redefining Metrics of Success: From Static to Dynamic Impact

In Association 1.0, success is typically measured by internal indicators, membership growth, event attendance, CPD hours. While these are still useful, they do not reflect external impact or ecosystem influence.

A modern association should assess value through the lens of contribution, not just consumption. This may include the uptake of shared tools or data by non-members. The volume and impact of innovations co-developed through member collaboration, how policy outcomes are enabled by cross-sector partnerships and overall improvement in outcomes for communities or industries served.

Consider a health association that moves from measuring CPD volume to tracking how its open data tools are used in state health planning, or how many co-designed service models emerge from member-partner collaborations.

In this new paradigm, relevance is not assumed by size or tradition. It is earned through systemic utility and measurable contribution to shared challenges.

A Call to Action: Embracing Association 2.0

The future of associations, in Australia and globally, demands urgent, strategic transformation. Reliance on older models with minimal digital interactivity, single-source revenue, and slow-moving governance is untenable in a world where professionals can easily find more dynamic communities online. Recent research from the Governance Institute of Australia also underscores how boards and executives are embracing agile risk management, data analytics, and AI, factors that associations should consider a master to remain credible in members' eyes.

The Pressures on Traditional Association Models

The structural forces reshaping the operating environment for associations are many. These macro-level shifts inform the design principles and strategic frameworks that underpin this playbook and help explain the shifts already occurring across the association landscape.

As outlined in Chapter 1, the core functions once monopolised by associations, including industry knowledge, credentialing, and member connection, are being rapidly disintermediated. Professionals can now access real-time insights, peer networks, and learning pathways without relying on institutional gatekeepers.

The traditional value proposition, anchored in exclusive publications, periodic events, and a fixed bundle of member benefits, is increasingly misaligned with the expectations of modern professionals. Static membership tiers and slow-moving service models can no longer compete with dynamic, user-driven alternatives like LinkedIn, Coursera, or Slack.

Recent research (Moore, 2024) reinforces what many association leaders already sense that the threat is not competition from within the sector, but the digital-native behaviours of their own members.

The implications are clear; without urgent and strategic change, associations risk becoming peripheral, relevant only by tradition, not by impact. Retaining the traditionalists and loosing the ne wave of potential members.

These structural shifts are not just background context, they are the drivers of urgency and relevance for every strategic conversation happening in association boardrooms today. The old logic of service delivery, static metrics, and top-down governance no longer matches the pace or complexity of the external environment.

To stay relevant, associations will have to move from awareness to alignment, from recognising these shifts to actively reshaping their organisations in response. That is the work of Association 2.0.

The remainder of this book will guide that transition, starting with the introduction of the *Association Platform Success Framework* in Chapter 2, a strategic model designed to help associations navigate complexity, enable participation, and design for impact.

Table 2-3 Structural Shifts and Strategic Implications

Structural Shift	Strategic Implication
From Belonging to Utility (and Back Again)	Membership models will have to offer both personalised utility and emotionally resonant, participatory community experiences.
Collapse of Information Scarcity	Associations will have to evolve from content gatekeepers to trusted curators and sensemakers, enabling context, not just delivering content.
Innovation is Now Distributed	Position the association as a facilitator of member-led experimentation by investing in

Structural Shift	Strategic Implication
	open platforms, shared IP infrastructure, and participatory innovation frameworks.
The Skills Economy is Fracturing	Become a central node in skills development ecosystems, offering modular, stackable, and cross-sector learning aligned with future-of-work demands.
Work Is Decentralising	Shift internal governance and service delivery toward more agile, distributed, and member-empowered models that reflect post-hierarchical work realities.
Ecosystem Value is the New Competitive Advantage	Redesign organisational value propositions around convening power, partnership enablement, and ecosystem impact rather than siloed service delivery.
Trust Will have to Be Rebuilt from Within	Rebuild institutional trust through ethical governance, stakeholder inclusion, transparent practices, and values-led leadership.

A Declining Value Proposition

Professionals no longer ask "*Which association should I join?*" but increasingly "*Do I need to join one at all?*"

Cherry picking and/or freeriding.

Where once associations offered privileged access to curated knowledge and networks, members can now access both through open digital platforms, peer-led communities, and on-demand media. This has eroded many of the perceived benefits of dues-based membership.

Platforms such as LinkedIn Learning, Substack, and MeetUp provide fluid alternatives to structured CPD programs and networking calendars. Associations that cannot clearly demonstrate personalised value, relevance, and opportunity for influence will see continued drops in retention, especially among younger cohorts.

The Fragmentation of Professional Development

The monopoly associations once held over CPD is dissolving. Learners now pursue diverse, portable learning opportunities, from microcredentials to AI-enhanced upskilling, offered by vendors, platforms, and employers themselves.

MOOCs (Coursera, edX), vendor certifications (AWS, Microsoft), and peer-driven learning communities have evolved, while integral in redefining what counts as legitimate professional development, the landscape was comllete upended with the access to large language model AI like ChatGPT. In contrast, many association-run CPD programs are often perceived as static, inflexible, or out of touch.

To remain relevant, associations will become learning ecosystems, brokering partnerships, curating agile learning pathways, and embedding CPD within everyday practice.

The Risks of Maintaining the Status Quo

Associations that fail to adapt face more than stagnation, they risk strategic irrelevance. The traditional model is under pressure from the three converging risk domains below:

Financial Instability

As dependence on dues, event income, and sponsorships becomes more fragile, the absence of diversified, digitally-enabled revenue streams exposes associations to volatility. Burritt, Guthrie, and Evans (2016) anticipated this shift nearly a decade ago, warning that business models built on knowledge control would erode in the face of digital democratisation. Their insights are proving prescient.

To survive future shocks, associations will explore new commercial models, data-driven services, subscription platforms, ecosystem partnerships, and more.

Declining Member Engagement

Static engagement models no longer resonate. Members, especially younger ones, expect interaction, visibility, and influence. Research confirms generational shifts in value expectations, from tangible benefits to symbolic recognition, purpose, and networked opportunity.

Without adaptive strategies, associations will see declining relevance not because their mission is flawed, but because their engagement logic no longer aligns with how people learn, work, and connect.

Governance and Reputational Risk

Legacy governance structures often inhibit rather than enable responsiveness. Slow decisions, poor digital governance, and opaque processes undermine member trust, especially in an era of growing concern over data ethics and institutional transparency.

Rebuilding legitimacy requires more than compliance. It demands participatory governance, ethical infrastructure, and open accountability aligned with ISO 37000 and public expectations.

Unless associations act boldly to realign their business models, engagement strategies, and governance practices, they risk drifting into irrelevance, not because their purpose has disappeared, but because their structure can no longer support it.

The Shift to Platform Thinking

As associations face declining membership engagement and increased competition from digital alternatives, a shift in strategic thinking is required. Traditional associations have operated using a service-based model, where value is delivered through static benefits, such as conferences, newsletters, and exclusive industry reports. However, the emergence of digital-first professional communities, AI-driven learning platforms, and peer-to-peer networking spaces has disrupted this model. Many associations are launching digital engagement models, but they often digitise traditional media and models.

Digital transformation is no longer optional for associations seeking to remain relevant in a digital world. Most have progressed to adoption of virtual events, personalised content, and interactive online engagement which is now essential in meeting the evolving expectations of members. Associations that fail to adapt risk losing members to more dynamic, user-driven platforms that offer on-demand professional development, niche networking, and collaborative knowledge sharing.

While digital transformation enhances engagement, it is only part of the solution, and to be honest, most associations are still way behind in the digital revolution. To achieve long-term sustainability, associations will have to move beyond digital tools and adopt a platform-based ecosystem approach.

Unlike the traditional model, where associations act as service providers, a platform-based association facilitates interactions between members, industry partners, and other stakeholders, creating a scalable and adaptive environment. This shift mirrors trends seen in the broader economy, where many organisations have had to transitioning from linear service delivery models to multi-sided platforms that enable value co-creation.

In a platform-based association, members are no longer passive consumers of content, they become active contributors, co-creators, and collaborators within the professional ecosystem. This model fosters continuous engagement, diversified revenue streams, and stronger industry influence.

This playbook expands on the idea of customised digital engagement, introducing a structured roadmap for platform-driven transformation, integrating governance agility, AI-driven decision-making, and financial sustainability strategies.

For associations to successfully embrace Association 2.0, they will have to not only implement digital engagement tools and reimagine their role as facilitators of dynamic industry ecosystems.

The next chapter introduces the *Association Platform Success Framework*, a structured model designed to help associations make this transition effectively.

Example 4. Digital Ecosystem Building

The American Institute of Architects (AIA) has transitioned from a traditional membership association to a digital-first professional hub for architects, offering multiple ways for engagement beyond static membership benefits.

Platform-Based Transformation:

- ***Dynamic Interaction****: The AIA launched a Knowledge Communities platform, where members, firms, and industry partners engage in ongoing discussions, share research, and co-develop resources.*
- ***Scalable Value Creation****: Its AI-powered continuing education (CE) platform personalises recommendations for architects based on their career stage, interests, and state licensing requirements.*
- ***Revenue Diversification****: Beyond dues, AIA generates income through sponsored webinars, digital learning subscriptions, industry partnerships, and AI-driven member data insights.*

Instead of simply delivering services, the AIA now facilitates collaboration among professionals, fostering an ecosystem where members continuously contribute and benefit. (American Institute of Architects. 2020, 2023, 2024)

Example 5. Australian Institute of Architects

The Australian Institute of Architects (AIA) has also introduced similar initiatives:

- ***Digital Platforms:*** *The AIA has launched several digital initiatives, including the "Community" member networking platform, which enables architects to connect, share resources, and participate in discussions online. This mirrors the Knowledge Communities approach seen in the US.*
- ***Online CPD and Contracts:*** *The AIA offers a comprehensive online Continuing Professional Development (CPD) platform and has digitised contract management through the ABIC Digital platform, streamlining processes for members and industry partners.*
- ***Resource Libraries:*** *Members have access to a digital resource library and online store, supporting ongoing professional learning and collaboration.*

Rise of the Platforms

In response to evolving member expectations, financial pressures, and digital disruption, forward-thinking associations are moving away from static, transactional membership models. Instead, they are embracing platform-based ecosystems that foster continuous engagement, innovation, and scalable value creation.

> *A platform-based association is more than just a digital extension of traditional services, it represents a fundamental shift in how associations interact with members and stakeholders.*

This approach enables dynamic, real-time interactions between members, partners, and industry stakeholders, scalable value creation through digital engagement, on-demand services, and network effects and new revenue streams beyond membership fees, leveraging digital products, data insights, and strategic partnerships.

Rather than simply delivering services, platform-based associations act as facilitators, enabling continuous collaboration, professional development, and industry advancement. This shift ensures long-term sustainability, growth, and relevance in a rapidly changing world.

Key Characteristics of Platform-Based Associations:

1. **Network Effects:** Value increases as more members engage, strengthening the association's influence and reach.
2. **Monetisation Beyond Memberships:** Digital tools, data-driven insights, and virtual or hybrid events provide additional revenue opportunities.
3. **Agile Governance:** Flexible decision-making structures allow associations to respond quickly to emerging industry trends and member needs.

Many leading associations have already started adopting platform-based models, leveraging technology and data to drive deeper engagement and long-term financial resilience. Those that fail to evolve risk declining member relevance, financial instability, and reduced industry influence.

This transformation is not an incremental improvement, it is a strategic necessity for associations aiming to thrive in the digital era.

While the shift to platform-based ecosystems offers significant advantages, there will always be a place for more traditional, slow-evolving association models. Some industries, particularly those with deeply established professional traditions, regulatory requirements, or long-standing governance structures, may continue to operate effectively within conventional membership frameworks. These associations provide stability, trusted expertise, and institutional continuity, which remain highly valued by certain member segments.

However, even these organisations will have to consider gradual adaptations to remain relevant. Incorporating selective digital enhancements, fostering stronger peer-to-peer connections, and exploring hybrid engagement models can help traditional associations bridge the gap between legacy structures and emerging expectations, ensuring they continue to serve their members effectively in a changing landscape.

Figure 2-1 **Strategic Drivers for Platform Thinking**

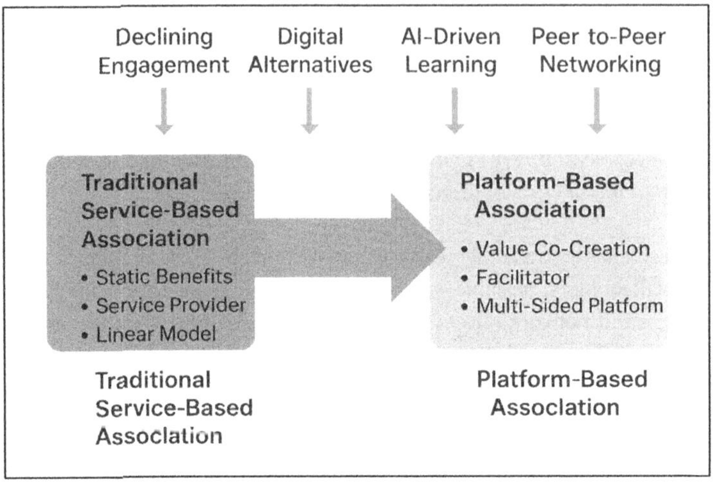

Example 6. From Conferences to Engagement[3]

***The Challenge**: Declining Relevance of Annual Events*

A hypothetical national industry association, traditionally known for its high-profile annual conference, faced a growing problem namely, the declining attendance, shrinking sponsorship revenue, and disengaged members. Once a flagship event that attracted thousands, the conference was struggling to compete with on-demand digital learning, corporate-led training programs, and online networking platforms.

Members, particularly younger professionals, expressed frustration that waiting a full year for networking and professional development no longer aligned with their needs. The association realised that to stay relevant, it needed to transition from a once-a-year touchpoint to a continuous engagement model.

Virtual Communities and Continuous Learning

The association shifted beyond annual events, creating always-on digital forums for networking, mentoring, and industry Q&As. The conference became a year-round experience through monthly webinars, workshops, and virtual roundtables.

---

3 The case studies are learning exercises designed to demonstrate how the concepts can be adopted or integrated.

Personalised Engagement

AI-driven profiling recommended relevant content, tailored CPD, and connected members with shared interests.

Hybrid Strategy

The flagship conference remained central but was integrated into a broader cycle of pre-event networking, digital previews, and post-event follow-ups.

The Results

Within two years, member engagement is projected to rise by 35 per cent, virtual attendance by 20 per cent, and sponsor interest to grow with more digital touchpoints. Engagement is no longer a single transaction but a continuous cycle of connection, learning, and value creation.

Lesson

Annual conferences alone are no longer sufficient. Associations must adopt platform-driven ecosystems that enable ongoing, personalised engagement.

The Future of Platform-Based Associations

The future of associations depends on decisive, strategic transformation. Organisations that cling to outdated models will be outpaced by digital-first, network-driven alternatives that deliver value through interaction, co-creation, and adaptability. The shift is not optional, it is existential. This book presents a structured roadmap for this transition. Through strategy, governance tools, and applied case studies, association leaders are equipped to redesign membership and engagement to align with modern expectations, diversify revenue beyond dues and events, strengthen governance through digital and data capabilities, and lead change intentionally, ethically, and systemically.

Table 2-4 Key Transformations from Association 1.0 to 2.0

Legacy Model (Association 1.0)	Platform Model (Association 2.0)
Serving individual members	Empowering ecosystems and shared value
Centralised, hierarchical governance	Distributed, adaptive, and agile structures
One-way service delivery	Member-led participation and co-creation
Standardised metrics (e.g. retention, revenue)	Dynamic indicators (e.g. engagement, contribution, impact)

Chapter 3. The Association Platform Success Framework

Example 7. The Turning Point

Claire Evans, CEO of the Professional Network Association (PNA), sat with her board reviewing a grim financial report. Membership was declining. Revenue was flatlining. Member feedback was lukewarm at best. Words like "disconnected" and "irrelevant" echoed across surveys. Attempts to modernise, discounted membership campaigns, glossy brochures, even a new app, had not shifted the dial.

During the meeting, Sophie, a tech entrepreneur on the board, finally said what others were thinking: "We're still operating like a service provider when the world has moved on. Platforms are winning because they connect people, not just deliver services."

That comment marked a turning point.

Claire began researching multi-sided platforms, business models like Airbnb, LinkedIn, and Coursera that succeed not by controlling value, but by enabling it. She saw a new role for PNA: not as a provider of pre-packaged services, but as a platform for participation, learning, and connection.

Claire's story is not unique. Across sectors, associations are waking up to the limits of the legacy model. This chapter introduces a structured alternative: the *Association Platform Success Framework*.

Introduction: From Services to Systems

Professional associations are at a crossroads. Many have modernised incrementally, updating websites, digitising events, adopting new tools. Yet beneath these updates, most still operate with a logic inherited from the industrial age: linear service delivery, centralised authority, and a tightly gated membership experience.

But the environment has changed. Members no longer rely on associations as their sole source of professional insight, connection, or development. The most pressing challenge facing associations today is not operational, it is strategic. It is a question of how value is created, exchanged, and experienced in a world shaped by networks, data, and participation.

To respond, associations will shift from being service providers to becoming platform enablers, institutions that orchestrate ecosystems of value, empower member-to-member exchange, and enable participation at scale.

This requires a new strategic lens.

From Pipelines to Platforms: A New Economic Logic

Traditional associations operate like pipelines. Value flows from the organisation to the member through newsletters, events, and services. Platform-based models flip this. They facilitate interaction between multiple actors, members, partners, learners, employers, creating value through connection.

Table 3-1 Core Economic Principles of Platforms

Concept	Strategic Insight for Associations
Network Effects	The more people who use the platform, the more valuable it becomes. For associations, this means that every new mentor, learner, or contributor increases the value for others.
Two- or Multi-Sided Markets	Platforms serve multiple user groups simultaneously, such as members and employers, educators and learners, and will balance their needs and incentives.
Cross-Side Subsidies	Some user groups (e.g. students, job seekers) may be subsidised to attract others (e.g. training providers, sponsors).
Marginal Cost Reduction	Digital platforms scale with minimal incremental cost, enabling new revenue streams without linear cost growth.
Data as an Asset	Platforms generate real-time data on member preferences, behaviours, and interactions, which can be monetised through insights, benchmarking, or tailored offerings.

These principles, network effects, two-sided markets, marginal cost leverage, and data monetisation. They represent a structural shift. They change how associations operate, fund themselves, and sustain impact.

This is not just a technological change. It is an *economic transformation*. Platforms don't merely make service delivery more efficient; they redefine what an association is for.

An economic transformation that reshapes the value proposition of associations from one of service delivery to value facilitation, positioning the association as an ecosystem leader rather than a sole provider.

In Ecosystem Economics for Modern Associations, the companion book to The Modern Association Playbook, we unpack the economics of value creation.

This new logic challenges not only how associations deliver value, but how they are designed. The shift from service pipelines to participatory platforms demands more than digital upgrades, it requires a new operating model grounded in capability, trust, and co-creation.

That model is the *Association Platform Success Framework.* It provides a strategic lens through which associations can reimagine themselves as enablers of ecosystems, not just deliverers of services.

Strategic Reframing: From Legacy Logic to Platform Leadership

Understanding this new logic is essential. But insight alone is not enough. Association leaders need a structured way to turn this awareness into action.

The *Association Platform Success Framework* provides this structure. It reimagines association strategy as a layered, adaptive system built on core goals, enabling capabilities, integration pathways, and design principles. APSF is not just a blueprint for digital maturity, it is a model for *strategic reinvention.*

In the next section, we introduce the APSF in full: its pillars, its purpose, and how it transforms the way associations create value, with, not just for, their communities.

Associations Need a Reframe

Transformation in associations is rarely hampered by a lack of ideas. What is often missing is integration and commitment of leadership. Digital projects proliferate, apps, webinars, portals, but without a cohesive strategic model, these remain fragmented. The risk is that associations invest heavily in technology while failing to rethink their core value proposition.

The APSF offers a structured roadmap to avoid that trap. It guides associations from legacy models to platform-based strategies by aligning:

- Strategic purpose (why we exist)
- Organisational capability (what we can do)
- Delivery systems (how we create value)

It enables associations to move from service provision to ecosystem enablement.

Associations Platform Success Framework (APSF)

Most associations are not suffering from a lack of ideas, they are struggling with fragmentation, legacy structures, and shallow transformation efforts that fail to stick. When digital projects proliferate without strategic coherence, the result is often fatigue, not momentum. What is missing is not just innovation, but integration.

The *Association Platform Success Framework* responds to this challenge. It provides a practical, strategic model to guide associations as they shift from delivering services to enabling ecosystems. It helps boards and executives cut through complexity, align around purpose, and design a future-ready operating model that reflects platform-era dynamics.

This chapter introduces the APSF in full, from its structural layers to the design principles and strategic tools that bring it to life. Rather than a rigid template, the APSF is a flexible architecture. It offers a unifying language for strategy, governance, and capability-building, helping association leaders translate aspiration into action, and

Each section includes case examples, guiding questions for leaders, and practical implications for boards and executives. The chapter positions APSF not just as a framework, but as a mindset, a method that enables associations to act with integrity, agility, and strategic coherence.

As platform transformation becomes a board-level imperative, the APSF equips associations to lead with clarity, not just in the boardroom, but across their entire ecosystem.

Why APSF Matters for Boards

As associations embrace platform logic, boards face new questions: *What does value look like when members are co-creators, not just consumers? How do we govern distributed ecosystems, not just internal programs?* And *What capabilities do we need to build trust, adapt, and scale impact?*

The APSF equips boards and executives to answer these questions. It ensures that transformation is not just a collection of digital projects, but a sustained shift in organisational identity and strategic posture.

Table 3-2 **Layers of the APSF**

Layer	Purpose
Core Goals	Define the strategic outcomes of transformation
Core Pillars	Identify the capabilities that enable sustainable, platform-based maturity
Integration Pathways	Operationalise those capabilities through systems, governance, and experience

These layers are brought to life through Design Pillars, the practical lenses that translate capability into real-world association delivery models. This separation of framework and expression ensures both strategic clarity and design flexibility.

This chapter will unpack each layer in turn, starting with the **Core Goals** that define platform-era success.

Figure 3-1 **Associations Platform Success Framework**

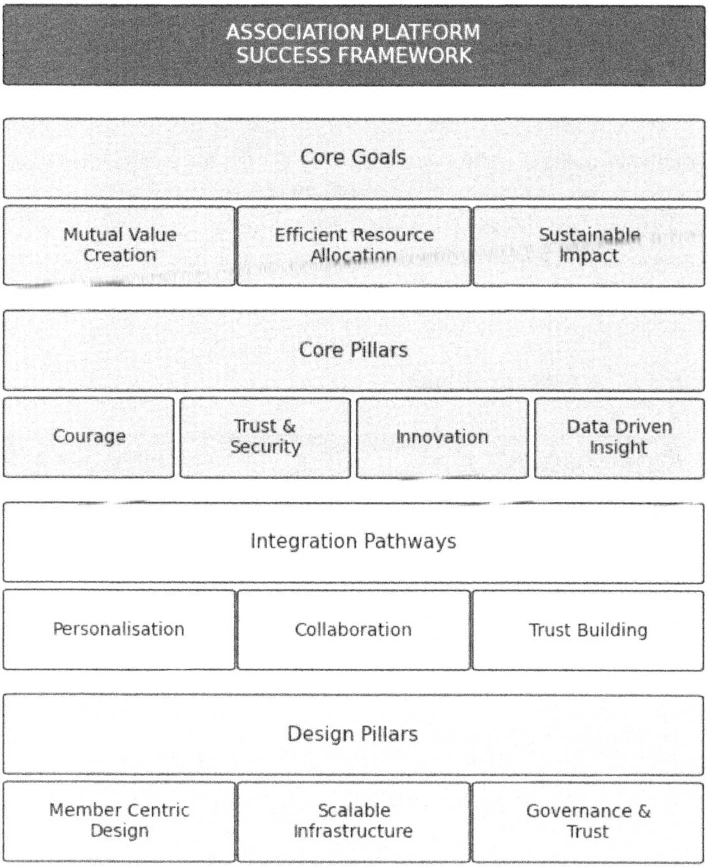

Each element of the APSF will be unpacked throughout this book. For now, we begin with the strategic rationale: why platforms, why now, and why associations will embrace this shift.

The next section explores:

- **Core Goals** – The strategic outcomes that define success in a platform-enabled world: mutual value creation, efficient resource allocation, and sustainable impact.
- **Core Pillars** – The enduring capabilities that enable these outcomes: innovation, courage, data-driven insight, and trust.
- **Integration Pathways** – The mechanisms that translate internal capability into external value: personalisation, collaboration, and trust-building.

- **Design Pillars** – The practical lenses that guide implementation, ensuring transformation is felt, not just planned: member-centric design, scalable digital infrastructure, and governance and trust.

Core Goals: Redefining Success

Traditional metrics, retention rates, attendance figures, compliance scores, no longer capture what matters most in an ecosystem-driven environment. Associations focused solely on outputs risk missing the deeper systemic impact they can have.

The *Association Platform Success Framework* redefines success through three *Core Goals*. These are not abstract ideals; they are strategic outcomes that guide every design, governance, and performance decision across a modern association.

Figure 3-2 APSF – Core Goals

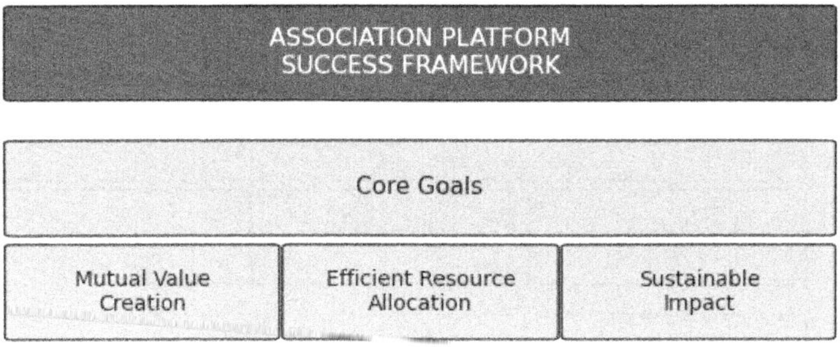

Table 3-3 Core Goals of Platform-Era Associations

Core Goal	Expanded Definition
Mutual Value Creation	Value is not delivered top-down by the association to passive recipients. It is co-created by all actors, members, partners, funders, and contributors, through meaningful, facilitated exchange across the ecosystem.
Efficient Resource Allocation	Platform strategies favour shared, interoperable infrastructure over siloed delivery. Financial, human, and digital resources are deployed to maximise shared utility and reduce duplication through scalable tools and leveraged partnerships.
Sustainable Impact	Transformation should generate long-term contributions, not just short-term metrics. This includes financial resilience, social legitimacy, and adaptive governance aligned with public trust and sector-wide capability uplift.

These three goals function as the *north star* for association leaders navigating platform-based transformation. They are not abstract aspirations, they are the core evaluative criteria for design decisions (e.g. whether to build or partner, which features to prioritise), governance oversight (e.g. what the board monitors and how it defines success) and performance evaluation (e.g. how value is tracked, reported, and evolved).

When implemented correctly, they shift the association's operating logic from delivering programs to enabling participation, from owning content to fostering ecosystems, and from reacting to disruption to orchestrating systems-level value.

Boards and executives can use these goals to

- **Interrogate investments**: Does this initiative enable mutual value, or reinforce top-down delivery?
- **Prioritise projects**: Are we scaling tools that support others to create and exchange value?
- **Assess results**: Are we measuring what matters, long-term contribution, not just activity?

Why These Goals Matter

Adopting these goals prompts a fundamental shift in the operating logic of modern associations. Rather than positioning themselves primarily as service delivery vehicles, associations are now being called to act as enablers, supporting participation, contribution, and value creation across their ecosystems. This shift moves the focus from transactional exchanges to deeper engagement and from a model centred on content ownership to one of ecosystem orchestration, where the association becomes a trusted facilitator of shared value.

These strategic goals have far-reaching implications for organisational design, governance, and performance. For example, they inform key design decisions such as whether to build capabilities internally or form strategic partnerships. Governance oversight will also evolve to ensure boards and executives are measuring what truly matters, tracking long-term contribution and ecosystem health rather than just outputs or activities. In this context, performance evaluation requires new metrics that prioritise impact over volume, enabling a more nuanced understanding of organisational effectiveness.

Boards and executive teams can use targeted questions to ground their strategic decisions in these principles. They should ask: does this initiative enable mutual value creation, or does it reinforce outdated, centralised delivery models? Are we investing in tools that empower others to contribute and connect, or simply extending our control? And critically, are we measuring engagement and ecosystem vitality, not just programmatic metrics, to reflect our broader purpose and value to members and stakeholders? These questions can anchor strategy in a participatory, future-oriented logic that strengthens the association's role as a platform for collective success.

The Core Goals of the APSF are not only consistent with good corporate governance, they deepen it. They extend governance beyond compliance metrics to a systemic, participatory, and impact-oriented model, making them highly relevant for modern associations operating in platform-based environments.

Mutual Value Creation

In the traditional association model, value is created centrally by the organisation and delivered to members in standardised, largely one-directional formats, such as newsletters, CPD events, or compliance-focused tools. While these services may meet basic expectations, they reinforce a passive consumption mindset among members and restrict opportunities for innovation, collaboration, and shared ownership of outcomes.

By contrast, the platform model reframes value as something that is co-created across the association's ecosystem. Members are not merely recipients of services, but active participants, generating content, sharing knowledge, leading initiatives, and contributing to governance. This inclusive model invites partners, contributors, and other stakeholders to engage in meaningful, multidirectional value exchange, resulting in greater relevance, adaptability, and collective impact.

As foreshadowed, the key shift is from service provider to value enabler; from segmenting members into predefined categories to empowering member agency; and from broadcast communications to peer-to-peer engagement models. These changes carry strategic implications for how associations design and operate. They will build systems that facilitate interaction, such as discussion forums, collaborative content platforms, and real-time feedback loops. Staff roles will evolve from service deliverers to facilitators and curators who nurture participation and insight. Crucially, associations will also recognise and reward member contributions, not just their attendance, to foster a culture of shared value creation.

For example, a mentoring platform that connects early-career professionals with senior peers; member led research initiatives, peer-curated resource libraries, or working groups can dramatically extend the association's impact and reach, without increasing its internal operational load. These participatory models demonstrate how co-creation and distributed agency can transform the association from a provider into a platform for collective success.

Efficient Resource Allocation

Most associations face increasing pressure to do more with less, they have more engagement, more services, more personalisation and all within static or shrinking budgets. Legacy models struggle because they allocate resources program by program, creating duplication, silos, and diminishing returns.

In the platform model, value is scaled not by adding effort, but by building shared, reusable infrastructure. Efficiency is not just about saving money, it's about strategic leverage.

Key Shifts:

- From duplication → to shared systems
- From internal build-everything → to modular partnerships
- From short-term delivery → to long-term infrastructure

Strategic Implications:

- Invest in *interoperable* platforms (e.g. integrated LMS/CRM) that serve multiple functions
- Outsource or *partner* where others can deliver better or faster
- Use *feedback loops* and member data to continuously optimise value delivery

Instead of developing multiple separate portals for CPD, events, and member services, a unified platform can reduce effort, increase member usability, and unlock cross-service data insights. Modular learning models and reusable microcontent improve ROI across audiences.

Sustainable Impact

Associations are custodians of professions, causes, and communities, yet many still measure success through short-term indicators: webinar attendance, click-through rates, or annual renewals. These outputs matter, but they don't reflect whether the association is building long-term value.

Sustainable Impact means aligning operations with outcomes that endure: professional credibility, sector capability, social equity, environmental leadership, or innovation ecosystems.

Key Shifts

- From transactions → to outcomes
- From annual metrics → to longitudinal value
- From organisational survival → to ecosystem resilience

Strategic Implications

- Align programs with sector-wide goals (e.g. workforce readiness, standards development)
- Incorporate ESG, DEI, and public impact into value frameworks
- Design platforms to track engagement translation to real-world contributions

Example 8. Australian HR Institute (AHRI)

The Australian HR Institute offers a compelling example of how a national body can shift from a transactional service provider to a platform-based professional ecosystem. Responding to rising member expectations and an evolving HR landscape, AHRI undertook a multi-year transformation grounded in the principles of the Association Platform Success Framework.

Mutual Value Creation: *AHRI redefined its purpose from delivering discrete CPD events to enabling career-long learning and capability development. It launched HR Certification, a national credentialing framework supported by a digital platform offering stackable credentials,* *self-paced learning, and progress tracking tools. This positioned AHRI not as a course provider, but as a standards-setting platform.*

***Efficient Resource Allocation**: A unified member portal consolidated CPD, event registrations, microlearning, and certification tracking via single sign-on. Behind the scenes, staff were retrained in product management, digital content strategy, and UX design, building the internal capability to scale intelligently.*

***Sustainable Impact**: Governance was strengthened through the National Certification Council, appointed by the board to ensure CPD and education standards reflect professional realities. This model supports long-term sector alignment and public trust.*

Additionally, AHRI embedded APSF Design Pillars:

***Member-Centric Design**: Personalised learning pathways tailored by role, industry, and experience.*

***Scalable Infrastructure**: A modular platform architecture supporting real-time learning and progression.*

***Governance & Trust**: Clear roles for oversight and standardisation through inclusive governance mechanisms.*

(AHRI, 202,2023, 2024)

AHRI's transformation has delivered more than improved digital access, it has repositioned the institute as a sector-wide enabler of relevance, rigour, and reach. By aligning digital infrastructure with governance, member insight, and long-term sector needs, AHRI has become a benchmark in platform-era association strategy.

Example 9. Core Goals to Transformation

Facing declining engagement and stagnant revenue, the Professional Network Association (PNA) turned to the APSF Core Goals to reshape its strategic direction. These principles became the foundation for a deeper transformation, from service delivery to platform enablement.

***Mutual Value Creation**: PNA moved away from one-size-fits-all programming toward a participatory model. It launched peer-led workshops, supported member-generated resources, and co-developed research with industry partners. Members became contributors, not just consumers, increasing both engagement and perceived value.*

***Efficient Resource Allocation**: Fragmented systems were replaced with a unified digital platform, eliminating duplication and enabling cross-team collaboration. Rather than reinventing every offering, PNA partnered with existing EdTech providers to deliver modular learning more efficiently.*

***Sustainable Impact**: A new sector capability framework helped align programming with long-term workforce development. PNA shifted its focus* *from event attendance and satisfaction scores to tracking how members applied their learning, contributed to industry outcomes, and engaged in collaborative, public-good projects.*

Together, these shifts repositioned PNA from a service hub to a participation platform. Member satisfaction climbed, partner engagement grew, and the board began to focus less on calendars and campaigns, and more on ecosystem health and co-created value.

Core Pillars: The Muscles That Drive Change

Strategy without capability is theory. For platform transformation to stick, associations will develop enduring internal strengths, capabilities that are not tied to individual projects but embedded into how the organisation learns, decides, and evolves.

These are the Core Pillars of the APSF: the organisational "muscle groups" that sustain platform-era maturity. While each is powerful alone, they deliver the most impact when developed together, as an integrated capability system.

Figure 3-3 APSF – Core Pillars

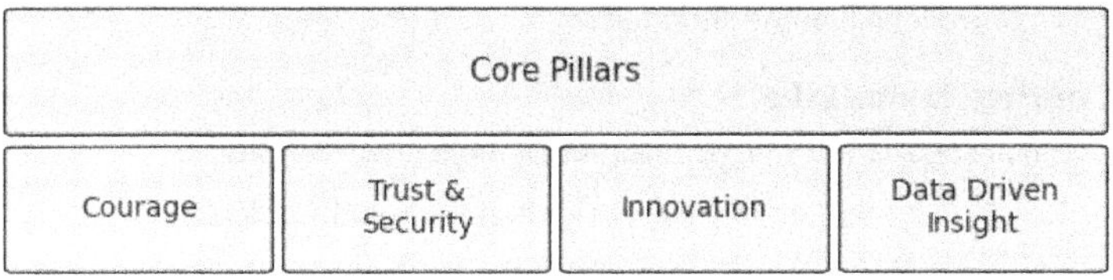

Table 3-4 Core Pillars

Pillar	Function
Courage	Emboldens governance and strategy to lead decisively
Trust & Security	Anchors all interactions in transparency, ethics, and safety
Innovation	Fosters experimentation and enables new engagement and business models
Data-Driven Insight	Leverages data to personalise, predict, and guide real-time decisions

These four pillars function like interconnected muscles. Innovation without data is guesswork. Data without trust can trigger backlash. Trust without courage leads to inertia. Courage without strategy can become unmoored.

Together, they empower associations to move beyond digital upgrades and toward strategic transformation.

Courage: Leading with Strategic Boldness

Courage is the most underestimated capability in association leadership.

In a market segment often dominated b y copying other's business models we see what is referred to as isomorphic landscape, with everyone looking like everyone else. There is safety "hiding in the pack" and not standing out. Many governance or executive leaders are deeply committed to the discipline and often have limited exposure to what is happening over the horizon. Courage is the attribute that ask leaders to decide what is best, not just what is safe.

Courage is not simply about taking more risks, but about challenging legacy assumptions, confronting institutional inertia, and stepping into new roles that may feel unfamiliar or politically uncomfortable.

Platform transformation requires associations to move away from long-standing practices, retiring underperforming services, sunsetting legacy committees, restructuring staff roles, and/or opening membership to new stakeholder groups. These are not operational decisions; they are acts of strategic will.

Courage enables boards and executives to lead ahead of certainty. It allows leaders to act on member signals before all the data is perfect, and to defend long-term decisions that may be controversial in the short term.

What Courage Looks Like

- Saying no to legacy programs that no longer deliver value
- Redefining membership categories to reflect platform logic
- Making early commitments to data ethics or inclusion, before external pressure
- Investing in uncertain but high-potential initiatives

Strategic Payoff

Table 3-5 Courage Capability payoff

Outcome	Description
Strategic Clarity	Focus on what matters, not what is familiar
Cultural Signal-Setting	Staff and members follow when leaders act decisively
Accelerated Reform	Faster decision cycles and strategic alignment
Stakeholder Respect	Trust is earned when leaders act with integrity and vision

Key Questions for Boards and Executives

- Where are we holding on to legacy practices that no longer deliver value?
- Do our governance processes support bold decisions or dilute them?
- How do we respond to strategic discomfort – with retreat or redesign?

Trust & Security: The Foundation of Participation

In platform models, trust is not optional, it is infrastructure. Members will have to feel confident that their data is protected, their voice is respected, and their values are reflected in the systems they use.

Trust and Security encompasses cybersecurity, ethical AI, member consent, and transparent governance. But it also includes human elements: fairness, accessibility, and psychological safety.

What Trust & Security Looks Like

- Consent frameworks embedded in member onboarding and data use
- Independent audits of digital governance and ethical oversight
- Secure platforms for credentialing, CPD, and payments
- Public reporting on data ethics, inclusion, and impact

Strategic Payoff

Table 3-6 Trust Payoff

Outcome	Description
Confidence in Participation	Members share, contribute, and return more frequently
Ethical Resilience	Alignment with emerging standards reduces risk
Reputational Strength	Ethical leadership enhances brand and legitimacy
Inclusive Legitimacy	Diverse members see themselves reflected in governance and systems

Example 10. Digital Membership Transformation

Engineers Australia (EA), the national peak body for the engineering profession, was facing rising member expectations, so embarked on a multi-year transformation to modernise its digital service model and better engage its diverse membership.

***Innovation**: Through its Future Now program, they adopted an agile delivery model, enabling rapid iteration of digital services. New tools like EA On Demand emerged from low-risk pilots and member feedback loops.*

***Courage**: EA committed to redefining value, phasing out legacy events and investing in platforms that reflect contemporary learning habits and professional demands. Strategic discomfort was embraced, not avoided.*

***Data-Driven Insight**: The organisation expanded its analytics capability to inform everything from content recommendations to member segmentation.*

***Trust & Security**: EA reinforced its role as a trusted credentialing authority through digital badges, real-time credential verification, and improved member consent frameworks. Governance structures were updated to support oversight of digital ethics and inclusion.*

Together, these capabilities allowed EA to evolve from a traditional membership body to a professional enablement platform, without compromising its core integrity or regulatory responsibilities.

Where the *Core Pillars* give associations the capability to act with agility, integrity, and influence, the next section explores how these internal strengths are activated externally, through Integration Pathways that embed capability into systems, services, and experiences.

Innovation: Embedding a Culture of Experimentation

Innovation is the capacity to respond to complexity with creativity. For associations, this means moving beyond risk-averse programming and embracing a mindset of continuous exploration. Innovation is not about launching radical new products every quarter. It is about cultivating adaptive habits: small pilots, iterative design, member co-creation, and feedback loops that improve over time. Platform thinking demands this mindset because it shifts value creation from being centrally designed to emergent. Value comes from the edges: from members, collaborators, and partners experimenting within the ecosystem.

What Innovation Looks Like

- Small-scale pilots with clear feedback mechanisms
- Innovation labs or member incubators
- Agile teams working in sprints, not static plans
- Rewarding experimentation, not just success

Key Questions for Boards and Executives

- How often do we test new ideas before scaling?
- What barriers exist to experimentation in our culture or governance?
- Do we celebrate learning or only outcomes?

Strategic Payoff

Table 3-7 Innovation Payoff

Outcome	Description
Increased Responsiveness	Ability to pivot based on member signals or environmental change
Reduced Risk	Prototyping reduces the cost of failure and speeds learning
Member-Led Value	Solutions grounded in real needs, not internal assumptions
Strategic Confidence	Boards are more likely to back bold initiatives when innovation is routine

Data-Driven Insight: Turning Information into Intelligence

Data is not a back-office function. In a platform association, it is a *strategic asset*. It enables personalisation, impact evaluation, and predictive decision-making, if the organisation is equipped to collect, interpret, and act

What Data-Driven Insight Looks Like

- Dashboards tracking member engagement and sentiment in real time
- AI-powered content recommendations or event nudges
- Analytics-informed board papers and strategic reviews
- Metrics that link engagement to outcomes, not just activity

Strategic Payoff

Table 3-8 Data-Driven Insight Payoff

Outcome	Description
Personalised Services	Members receive timely, relevant, and valuable experiences
Responsive Governance	Boards see trends early and make better decisions
Continuous Learning	Every interaction improves the system
Strategic Precision	Investment and reform are insight-led, not instinctive

Integration Pathways: Turning Strategy Into Action

The Core Pillars of innovation, courage, insight, and trust define an association's internal strength. But to generate real transformation, these capabilities will have to show up where members, partners, and the public actually interact with the organisation.

That's the role of *Integration Pathways*, the strategic mechanisms that translate internal capability into external value. They are how transformation becomes tangible: in services, platforms, governance, and culture. These are not departments or workflows. They are cross-cutting disciplines that embed platform logic into the association's daily operating model.

These are not tactical projects, but strategic channels that ensure platform logic shows up where it matters: in services, governance, data use, and communication.

Table 3-9 Integration Pathways

Pathway	Description
Personalisation	Uses data and insight to tailor experiences, content, and services to the needs of individual members
Collaboration	Enables shared creation, learning, and leadership across members, partners, and networks
Trust-Building	Embeds ethical design, transparency, and security into every layer of the member experience

Personalisation: Designing for Relevance at Scale

In a noisy, fast-moving world, relevance is everything. Personalisation ensures members receive content, services, and experiences aligned with their roles, goals, and stages of development.

Personalisation is the pathway through which platform-based associations deliver tailored, meaningful, and timely experiences to members. It shifts engagement from a one-size-fits-all model to a dynamic, data-informed journey.

This pathway is not about vanity-level customisation. It is about ensuring that each member sees, receives, and contributes value in a way that reflects their role, goals, preferences, and participation style.

Key Practices in Personalisation

- **Segmented Pathways**: Using CRM and behavioural data to segment members by interest, career stage, geography, or learning preferences.
- **Dynamic Content Delivery**: AI-driven content recommendations based on past interactions, peer behaviours, or declared needs.
- **Personalised CPD**: Offering learning journeys that adapt to the user's pace, aspirations, and recognised prior learning.
- **Nudging and Notifications**: Automating reminders and prompts that support engagement and conversion, when they are most relevant.

Design Questions for Associations

- What data do we already have about member behaviours and preferences?

- Where can we use this data to enhance relevance without creating noise or privacy risks?
- How do our systems enable, or constrain, dynamic delivery and adaptive learning?

Key Practices

- AI-driven recommendations for CPD, events, or communities
- Customised learning journeys based on behaviour and preferences
- Segmented engagement strategies by region, industry, or career stage
- Context-sensitive nudges and notifications

Impact

When executed well, personalisation increases return visits, deepens engagement, and drives self-directed value creation. It also lays the groundwork for scalable co-creation, because it starts with knowing who your members are, and what matters to them.

Table 3-10 Benefits of Personalisation

Outcome	Description
Higher Engagement	Members return more often, stay longer, and engage more deeply
Improved Retention	Value remains visible and adaptable as member needs evolve
Self-Directed Value	Members can navigate their own journey without high admin friction

Collaboration: Enabling Co-Creation and Community

Platform-based associations thrive not by doing everything themselves, but by enabling others to create value through them. The Collaboration pathway focuses on designing systems that allow members, partners, and stakeholders to contribute, co-create, and connect, transforming the association from a service hub into a participation engine.

This is the heart of the platform model: enabling many-to-many interaction, not just one-to-many delivery.

Key Practices in Collaboration

- **Peer-to-Peer Platforms**: Member forums, mentoring exchanges, and co-learning communities that support reciprocal engagement.
- **Partner Ecosystems**: External contributors such as universities, vendors, and startups deliver services or content directly through the platform.

- **Project-Based Networks**: Temporary teams or working groups enabled by digital infrastructure to collaborate on standards, research, or innovation challenges.
- **Co-design:** Co-designed standards, research, or advocacy campaigns
- **Member-Led Content and Events**: Curation and delivery of CPD, case studies, or events by members themselves, with staff acting as enablers.

Design Questions for Associations

- Where in our current model are members already collaborating informally? How can we formalise or support this?
- What rules, rewards, and recognition systems do we need to encourage contribution?
- How do we manage shared IP, quality control, and participant safety across collaborative activities?

Impact

Collaboration changes the power dynamics of associations. It shifts the centre of gravity from staff-led delivery to distributed networks of contributors. When members are trusted and enabled to build together, programs, content, or connections, the association's reach, value, and adaptability grow exponentially.

Table 3-11 Benefits of Collaboration

Outcome	Description
Ecosystem Activation	Value creation expands beyond staff-led programs
Innovation at the Edges	Members generate novel insights and offerings
Scaled Impact	Participation multiplies the reach and influence of the association

Trust-Building: Embedding Ethics and Safety by Design

Trust is no longer a reputational bonus, it's a design requirement. This pathway ensures the association's systems are ethical, secure, and transparent, and that members feel seen, heard, and protected. Without trust, members will not share data, contribute content, or participate meaningfully. The Trust Building pathway focuses on embedding ethical, secure, and transparent practices into the platform's architecture and governance.

It is the invisible infrastructure that supports every other element of transformation.

Core Design Features of Trust Building

- **Data Governance and Consent Frameworks**: Members understand what data is collected, how it is used, and can manage their preferences.
- **AI and Algorithmic Oversight**: Use of machine learning or personalisation tools includes transparency protocols, fairness checks, and audit trails.

- **Open Governance Channels**: Members can see how decisions are made, raise concerns, and access regular reporting on impact and performance.
- **Security and Resilience Standards**: Platforms will have to meet high standards for cybersecurity, uptime, and contingency planning, especially when credentials, financial transactions, or member data are involved.

Key Practices

- Consent-based data governance and clear privacy settings
- Ethical AI protocols and human oversight in decision systems
- Public reporting on performance, inclusion, and governance
- Secure digital credentialing, verification, and feedback channels

Design Questions for Associations

- What baseline ethical standards govern how our platform collects, uses, and shares data?
- How do members know they can trust our algorithms, decision-making, or moderation practices?
- Are we publishing meaningful metrics on performance, inclusion, and risk?
- Who has the right to question or change how the system works, and how is that operationalised?

Impact

Trust enables participation. Members will only engage deeply with an association platform if they feel safe, heard, and respected. Trust building requires proactive investment in governance, communication, and design, not as a compliance task, but as a strategic enabler of growth, innovation, and legitimacy.

Table 3-12 Benefits of Trust

Outcome	Description
Confidence to Participate	Members share data and ideas more willingly
Risk Resilience	Legal and reputational risk is reduced
Ethical Differentiation	The association leads on values, not just compliance

These Integration Pathways are the bridge between strategy and experience. They ensure the Core Pillars don't sit in isolation but are activated across systems and touchpoints.

Figure 3-4 APSF – Integration Pathways

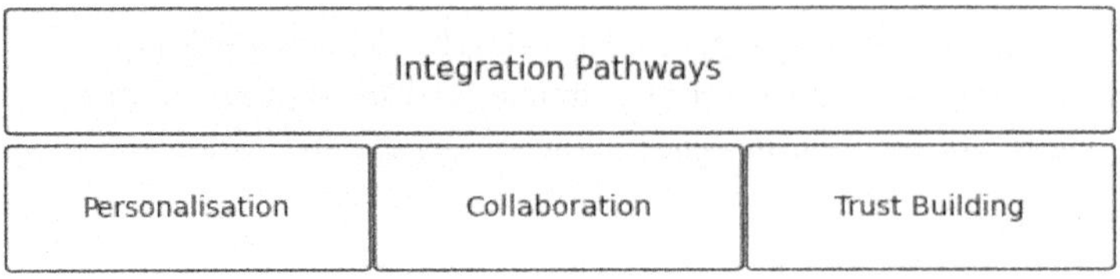

With these three Integration Pathways: Personalisation, Collaboration, and Trust Building, the Association Platform Success Framework becomes a living model, one that connects strategy to practice.

In the next section, we'll explore the Design Pillars, the lenses that guide how these pathways are implemented and experienced by members, partners, and the broader ecosystem.

Design Pillars: From Framework to Experience

The *Design Pillars* are not an additional structural layer within the APSF, they are *practical lenses* that guide how the framework is brought to life. They influence how the Core Pillars are expressed in practice and how the Integration Pathways are experienced by members, partners, and stakeholders.

These pillars shape how an association's core capabilities are embedded into its strategy, service design, and engagement architecture. They ensure that transformation is not just technically robust or strategically coherent, but visibly felt, in the quality of interactions, the relevance of offerings, and the consistency of experience.

Each Design Pillar activates and reflects the internal strengths of innovation, insight, courage, and trust, translating strategic intent into meaningful touchpoints. Without them, even well-designed systems can result in fragmented experiences, governance misalignment, or underused platforms.

In this way, the Design Pillars serve as filters and amplifiers, ensuring that platform logic is not just planned, but perceived.

Figure 3-5 APSF – Design Pillars

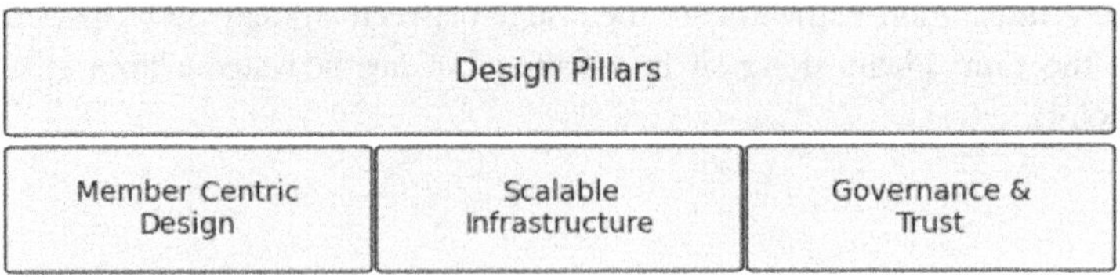

Table 3-13 Design Pillars – Focus Areas

Design Pillar	Focus Area
Member-Centric Design	Ensures products, services, and digital touchpoints are aligned to member journeys, needs, and life stages. Prioritises relevance, accessibility, and inclusion across all engagement tiers.
Scalable Infrastructure	Enables efficient, adaptive, and integrated systems that support growth, real-time data use, and personalisation at scale. Prioritises modular platforms, interoperability, and automation where appropriate.
Governance & Trust	Embeds ethics, transparency, and adaptive oversight into all transformation initiatives. Ensures decisions are inclusive, explainable, and aligned with both regulatory expectations and member trust.

Design Pillar 1: Member-Centric Design

A platform-based association does not start with content or committees; it starts with its members. Member-Centric Design is the first and most essential application of the APSF's core capabilities. It ensures that value is not just delivered to members but created with and through them. By shifting from top-down service delivery to participatory engagement, associations can unlock relevance, loyalty, and innovation.

This design pillar translates the Core Pillars of Innovation and Data-Driven Insights into actionable strategies that personalise, empower, and connect members across their career and life stages.

Design Principles

1. **Personalisation at Scale**

   Using AI, behavioural analytics, and user segmentation, associations can tailor the member experience - including content, communications, learning, and networking - based on individual interests, needs, and professional goals. The goal is not one-size-fits-all programming, but curated pathways that feel personal and valuable.

2. **Peer-to-Peer Engagement**

   Member-centric associations act as facilitators, not gatekeepers. They create the conditions for members to engage with each other, not just with the organisation. This includes communities of practice, discussion forums, working groups, and recognition systems that reward contribution and collaboration.

3. **Integrated Learning and Contribution**

   Rather than siloed offerings (e.g. events, CPD, mentoring), member-centric design integrates these into a cohesive experience. For example, a member might contribute to a knowledge hub, earn CPD points, and connect with a mentor - all through a single platform journey.

4. **Modular Design**

   The use of **modular product and service architecture,** allows members to choose, combine, or subscribe to components (e.g. learning modules, networking forums, certifications) based on their unique needs and willingness to pay.
   Modular design enables tiered access, transaction-based options, and the strategic bundling of value, critical capabilities for platform-based monetisation.

Key Design Considerations

- **What to Personalise**: Which elements of the member journey (e.g. onboarding, CPD, event invitations, content) can be dynamically customised without creating administrative burden?
- **Member Roles and Agency**: How can members move beyond passive recipients to active co-creators? What governance structures are needed to support moderation, feedback, and recognition?
- **Diversity and Inclusion**: How can design accommodate varying needs across member segments (e.g. early-career, rural, culturally diverse, First Nations)?
- **Technology Integration**: How will CRM, LMS, and analytics systems support seamless and ethical personalisation?

Table 3-14 **Pillar I Member-Centric Design Outcomes**

Outcome	Strategic Benefit
Increased Engagement	Members interact more frequently and meaningfully across the ecosystem.
Improved Retention	Members experience ongoing relevance and renewal of value.
Enhanced Satisfaction	Services feel responsive, tailored, and useful.
Higher Member Contribution	More members act as mentors, content creators, or community leaders.
Ecosystem Signal Strength	Member data reveals preferences, pain points, and innovation opportunities.

Design Pillar 2: Scalable Digital Infrastructure

Technology is not the answer, but it is a necessary enabler. Associations cannot deliver personalisation, peer collaboration, or data-driven trust without the right infrastructure. Scalable Digital Infrastructure is the second design pillar of the APSF. It brings the association's capabilities to life by ensuring that digital systems are integrated, responsive, and resilient.

In many associations, digital tools have evolved in silos, separate platforms for events, learning, communication, and billing. This fragmentation undermines the member experience. Scalable infrastructure, by contrast, creates a unified system where members move seamlessly between services, data is shared securely across platforms, and real-time insights drive smarter decisions.

To succeed, infrastructure will have to do more than just support operations, it will have to enable strategy. This includes modular architecture that allows for iterative development; APIs and integrations that connect CRM, LMS, and analytics platforms; and responsible AI systems that enhance rather than exploit user data.

Importantly, trust will have to be embedded in the infrastructure itself. Ethical use of data, transparency in algorithms, and robust privacy protocols are not compliance afterthoughts, they are design foundations.

Design Principles

1. **Integrated Systems Architecture**

   Infrastructure should support a unified member experience across functions - from CRM and learning management to community forums and billing. Integration allows for a 360-degree view of the member journey and enables real-time responsiveness.

2. **Data-Driven Automation**

   Intelligent use of data enables timely and tailored interactions - such as nudges to complete a course, reminders for lapsed engagement, or personalised content recommendations. Automation also reduces administrative burden on staff, freeing up capacity for strategy and service.

3. **Responsible Technology Governance**

   Associations will have to balance innovation with ethics. That means deploying AI and analytics responsibly, maintaining data privacy and cybersecurity, and ensuring platform accessibility for all members.

Key Design Considerations

These are decisions, which are often just assumed, e.g. build in-house v buy.

- **Build vs Buy**: Should the association develop proprietary infrastructure, adopt off-the-shelf solutions, or integrate with existing platforms?
- **Modularity and Scalability**: Can the infrastructure grow with the organisation? Is it flexible enough to support experimentation and change?
- **Data Strategy**: What are the data sources, standards, and stewardship practices? How are insights translated into action?
- **User Experience (UX)**: How intuitive and frictionless is the digital interface for members, staff, and partners?

Table 3-15 Pillar 2 Scalable Digital Infrastructure Outcomes

Outcome	Description
Operational Efficiency	Reduced manual work, lower tech maintenance burden
Seamless Member Journeys	Consistent, unified experience across touchpoints
Improved Data Quality	More complete, accurate, and actionable member data
AI-Enabled Personalisation	Smarter content, event, and learning recommendations
Enhanced Trust and Security	Confidence in the platform's ethical and technical foundations

Example 11. Digital Credentialing and CPD Tracking

The Australian Medical Association's (AMA) DoctorPortal Learning platform, which addresses many of the same challenges and solutions described in your hypothetical case.

The Challenge

Australian doctors, particularly general practitioners and specialists, faced significant administrative burden in tracking Continuing Professional Development (CPD), managing credentials, and meeting compliance requirements. Manual processes, fragmented systems, and evolving regulatory standards led to inefficiencies, errors, and member frustration.

The Transformation

The AMA responded by developing and launching the ***DoctorPortal Learning*** *platform, which provides:*

- ***Real-Time CPD Tracking:*** *Doctors can upload CPD documentation, track points across almost all specialties, and access their learning records 24/7 via a mobile-friendly interface.*
- ***Personalised Guidance:*** *The platform offers tailored guidance on CPD requirements for different colleges and specialties, helping members understand what is needed and when.*
- ***Automated Compliance Support:*** *Automated notifications and reminders help doctors stay on top of expiring certifications and upcoming renewal deadlines, reducing the risk of non-compliance.*
- ***Secure Document Management:*** *All CPD documentation can be uploaded and stored securely in one place, streamlining audits and verification.*

Results and Impact

- ***Reduced Processing Time:*** *The platform has significantly reduced the time required for certification and compliance reporting.*
- ***Improved Member Confidence:*** *Doctors report increased confidence in managing their CPD and credentials, with the platform providing a single source of truth for their professional development records.*
- ***Employer and Stakeholder Engagement:*** *Digital badges and certificates are easily shareable and verifiable, supporting new partnerships with employers and enhancing professional mobility.*
- ***Alignment with Legislation:*** *The platform is matched to new legislative requirements, ensuring ongoing compliance for members.*

Design Pillar 3: Governance and Trust

The platform model reshapes not only how associations operate, but also how they govern. As services become decentralised, and value is co-created with members, the traditional role of governance will have to expand. Governance and Trust, the third design pillar, reframes decision-making, accountability, and legitimacy for the digital age.

In platform-based associations, leadership no longer resides solely in boardrooms, it is distributed across communities, partners, and algorithms. Trust becomes both a cultural asset and a design imperative.

Design Principles

1. ***Agile and Distributed Governance***

   Traditional committee models often lack the speed or flexibility needed in fast-moving environments. Modern governance allocates decision rights closer to members, pilots distributed models (e.g. advisory panels, digital councils), and embraces networked accountability.

2. ***Transparent Decision-Making***

   Associations will have to earn trust, not just through intent, but through visibility. Publishing board decisions, ethics frameworks, partnership criteria, and performance dashboards signals openness and integrity.

3. ***Oversight of Digital and AI Systems***

   Governance will have to extend to platform operations, including algorithmic decision-making, data usage, and content moderation. Board committees may need new responsibilities for AI governance, cyber risk, or member data ethics.

4. ***Representation and Voice***

Governance systems should reflect the diversity of stakeholders they serve. This includes ensuring member insight informs strategy, elevating marginalised perspectives, and embedding participation into governance cycles.

Design Considerations for Boards and Executives

- Do our governance structures support timely decisions on platform innovation?
- Have we mapped accountability for AI, data ethics, and cyber resilience?
- How are member voices, especially from underrepresented segments, heard and acted upon?
- Are we proactively publishing decisions, performance data, and feedback responses?

Table 3-16 Governance & Trust Outcomes

Outcome	Description
Increased Member Trust and Confidence	Transparent and inclusive governance builds trust in decision-making and long-term institutional integrity.
Faster, Risk-Informed Decision-Making	Agile structures enable responsive action while maintaining ethical and operational oversight.
Ethical Resilience	Governance of digital systems, data, and AI ensures compliance, fairness, and alignment with evolving standards.
Member Representation at Scale	Members see their needs, identities, and perspectives reflected in strategic direction and platform governance.
Strategic Legitimacy	Governance becomes a visible asset that enhances the organisation's reputation and supports bold transformation.
Oversight of AI and Data Use	Boards are equipped to manage emerging risks and ethical challenges through structured, informed governance roles.
Member-Centric Transparency	Public access to decisions and performance strengthens member voice and reinforces accountability.

Example 12. Ecosystem Governance

1. *Have we mapped our full ecosystem of stakeholders, influencers, and participants?*
2. *Do we have a shared understanding of how our platform creates value beyond direct services?*
3. *Are our current board and committee structures equipped to govern AI, data ethics, and cross-sector engagement?*
4. *Are we creating the conditions for shared leadership, member-led innovation, and co-regulation?*

Ecosystem governance does not diminish traditional board duties, it enlarges them. It invites directors to think and act as stewards of a broader system of value, one that extends beyond the boundaries of the organisation and into the communities and professions it exists to serve.

Ecosystem governance challenges boards to shift from internal oversight to ecosystem stewardship. This demands new skills, structures, and accountability. This repositions governance as a *strategic enabler*, essential for supporting trust, inclusion, and innovation at scale.

Example 13. Hybrid Governance in a Legal Assoc.

As part of its digital transformation, a legal professional association redesigned its governance model to support continuous innovation while maintaining its fiduciary responsibilities.

The Transformation:

The association introduced a two-tier model:

- A traditional governing board retained oversight for strategy, risk, and compliance
- A Digital Advisory Council composed of members, partners, and external experts and shape priorities and offer real-time input on digital engagement, AI ethics, and user experience

This model allowed:

- Faster updates to platform features and CPD structures
- Early identification of digital inclusion risks
- More informed, data-driven decisions by the board

The Expected Results:

- Faster decision cycles on digital service updates
- Member trust scores improved in annual surveys
- New ethics guidelines adopted for AI use in member services

These pillars provide the foundational capability for platform transformation. In the next chapter, we explore how these capabilities are activated, and made real through integrated systems, experiences, and governance.

With the APSF structure now in place, from core goals through to operational pathways, the next step is diagnosis. How do you assess your current capabilities, identify gaps, and prioritise your transformation journey? Chapter 3 introduces the APSF Diagnostic Layer: a suite of tools that helps associations move from design to deployment with strategic precision.

Chapter 4. The APSF Diagnostic Layer

This chapter introduces the *Diagnostic Layer*, a suite of board-ready, practical tools designed to turn strategic intent into tangible action. Where previous chapters described what transformation looks like, this chapter shifts focus to how associations diagnose their current position, align on what matters most, and sequence the next steps on their platform journey.

The *Association Platform Success Framework* introduced in Chapter 3 provides a comprehensive blueprint for strategic renewal. But a framework alone cannot deliver transformation. Change happens when ideas become decisions, and decisions become systems. To bring the APSF to life, associations need tools that translate vision into governance, design into implementation, and ambition into measurable progress.

Built around the three Design Pillars, *Member-Centric Design, Scalable Digital Infrastructure, and Governance and Trust,* the Diagnostic Layer enables associations to move from conceptual alignment to operational momentum. It equips boards and executives with the insight needed to evaluate readiness, identify capability gaps, and set transformation priorities with confidence.

The pages that follow introduce the full suite of APSF diagnostic tools, outline their practical use in board and planning contexts, and provide a clear roadmap for how associations can embed them into governance cycles, strategic reviews, and performance measurement.

Together, these tools ensure that transformation is not just discussed in strategy papers but lived in practice.

Table 4-1 APSF Diagnostic Summary Grid

Design Pillar	Key Indicators	Assessment Focus	Associated Diagnostic Tools
Member-Centric Design	Participation, co-creation, experience depth	Value design, personalisation, contribution pathways	▪ Member Co-Creation Canvas ▪ Engagement Loop Designer ▪ Member Engagement Heatmap
Scalable Digital Infrastructure	Modularity, automation, platform enablement	Digital readiness, system integration, transformation logic	▪ Platform Readiness Diagnostic ▪ Technology Alignment &

Design Pillar	Key Indicators	Assessment Focus	Associated Diagnostic Tools
			Procurement Framework ▪ ROPI Readiness Checklist
Governance & Trust	Transparency, agility, ethical oversight	Strategic responsiveness, trust metrics, risk governance	▪ Governance Agility Scorecard ▪ Digital Trust Dashboard ▪ Insight Ecosystem Diagnostic

** For full tool details, see Chapter 15– Chapter 18.*

How to Use the Diagnostic Layer

- **As a Board Workshop Tool:** Use the diagnostics in retreats or planning meetings to identify blind spots and build a shared understanding of transformation maturity.
- **As a Strategy Input:** Link diagnostic outcomes to strategic priorities, investment cases, or pilot selection. Low-scoring areas often indicate where strategic experiments or capability building are most needed.
- **As a Progress Tracker:** Re-administer key diagnostics annually to monitor shifts in capability, culture, and governance alignment. Use colour-coded tracking (e.g. traffic light colour status by pillar) to communicate progress clearly.

Applying the APSF: From Framework to Action

The *Association Platform Success Framework* is designed to support strategic transformation, but frameworks do not implement themselves. For associations to realise the benefits of platform thinking, they will have to move from conceptual clarity to structured action. This section provides a practical roadmap for applying the APSF within diverse association contexts, acknowledging the constraints, readiness, and opportunities each organisation brings to the table.

Rather than a rigid sequence, the APSF roadmap offers a staged approach that can be adapted to different starting points. It supports associations in building capability over time, reducing risk, and generating quick wins to maintain momentum.

Table 4-2 Appling the Framework

Phase	Action	Strategic Purpose
1. Assess Readiness	Conduct organisational self-assessment using APSF diagnostics*	Identify capability gaps and transformation priorities
2. Pilot Engagement Models	Trial peer-led forums, AI personalisation, micro-events	Build internal confidence and surface scalable models
3. Align Governance & Finance	Update structures to support agility and diversified revenue	Strengthen institutional backbone for platform growth
4. Scale & Optimise	Invest in scalable infrastructure, analytics, and integrations	Drive member engagement, impact, and long-term value

* *For full tool details, see Chapter 15– Chapter 18.*

To guide this journey, the APSF includes a *four-stage implementation pathway*. Each phase offers a clear focus and tangible next steps:

Table 4-3 Four-Stage Implementation Pathway

Stage	Key Action	Strategic Outcome
1. Assess Readiness	Conduct an honest evaluation of your current member engagement model, digital capability, governance agility, and revenue resilience.	Identifies critical gaps and strategic opportunities. Creates a baseline for prioritisation.
2. Pilot Engagement Models	Launch low-risk, high-impact experiments, such as peer-led forums, AI-powered personalisation, or micro-events, to test new ways of interacting with members.	Builds internal momentum, gathers real-time feedback, and surfaces success factors before broader rollout.
3. Align Governance and Financial Models	Update decision-making structures and funding mechanisms to support agility, collaboration, and diversified income.	Ensures strategic alignment and sustainability. Reduces risk of siloed innovation or financial fragility.
4. Scale and Optimise	Extend successful pilots into scalable digital infrastructure and platform-based services. Use data insights to personalise experiences, grow participation, and improve outcomes.	Embeds platform logic into daily operations. Drives growth through network effects and adaptive learning.

This progression avoids common pitfalls of digital transformation, like overinvesting in underused tech or launching programs without governance support. Each stage builds on the last, ensuring associations move with intent, not haste.

Example 14. Putting the APSF into Practice

These fictionalised but realistic vignettes illustrate how each phase can be applied:

- ***Assess Readiness**: A national medical college runs a diagnostic across its member engagement systems. Results show strong CPD delivery but low peer interaction. The insight drives a strategy refresh prioritising digital community tools.*
- ***Pilot Engagement Models**: A regional science association experiments with a quarterly "Ask an Expert" video series on Zoom. Member participation exceeds expectations, leading to the development of a year-round knowledge hub.*
- ***Align Governance & Finance**: An industry certification body introduces a Digital Strategy Subcommittee and rewrites its delegation policy to fast-track innovation decisions while maintaining board oversight.*
- ***Scale and Optimise**: A mid-tier professional institute launches a data platform with AI-curated CPD, badge-based microcredentials, and member analytics dashboards. Member engagement triples over 12 months.*

Figure 4-1 **Implementation Pathway**

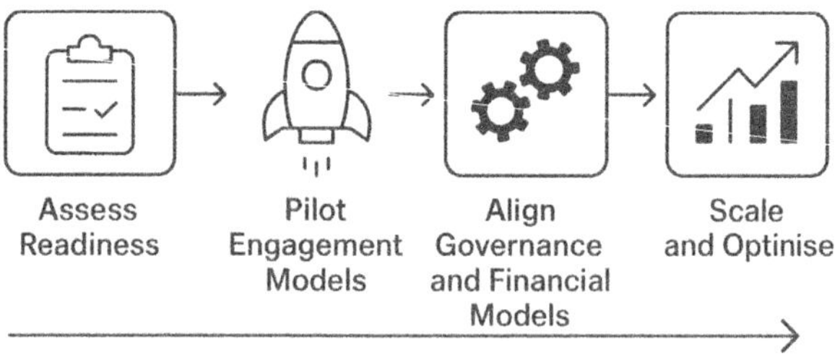

Key Implementation Principles

- Start small, but think big. Use pilots to validate strategic hypotheses while building the internal capability and trust needed for broader change.
- Sequence matters. Don't try to fix engagement, technology, and governance all at once. Focus on the next logical step in your unique context.
- Build momentum through results. Share early wins internally and externally. Demonstrated value creates buy-in and unlocks further investment.

- Measure what matters. Align metrics with APSF goals, from mutual value creation to resource efficiency and trust.

Table 4-4 Illustrative Mini-Cases by Stage

Stage	Example	Strategic Purpose
Start Where You Are	An education association reviews three years of email analytics and discovers members engage more with video summaries than long newsletters.	Generates evidence for shifting to micro-content delivery.
Pilot Engagement	A rural health organisation hosts a monthly, member-led virtual roundtable with 15 participants using free video conferencing tools.	Tests appetite for peer learning without upfront infrastructure investment.
Align Governance	A national industry group forms a Digital Strategy Subcommittee and includes a rotating member advisory panel.	Bridges the gap between board strategy and member expectations.
Scale and Optimise	A mid-tier certification body launches a modular learning platform with AI-curated CPD pathways and badge-based credentials.	Positions the association as an ongoing partner in career progression, not just a compliance provider.

Even the best frameworks can falter without a clear plan for action. The APSF's staged implementation pathway provides a practical roadmap to navigate uncertainty, build capacity, and generate early success.

This section anchors the APSF in reality, transforming it from an aspirational model into an operational strategy that associations can begin executing today.

Example 15. Platform-Centric Strategy

The Australian Computer Society (ACS) has redefined itself as more than a membership organisation. Through deliberate platform design, ACS now operates as a multi-sided credentialing and capability network, connecting members, employers, education providers, and government. With a strategic emphasis on digital badges, modular CPD, and skill recognition frameworks, ACS exemplifies how a professional body can evolve into an enabling infrastructure for a dynamic, technology-driven workforce.

Strategic Shift: From Member Services to Platform Enablement: *ACS's transition illustrates a deliberate pivot from Association 1.0's service* *delivery model to a platform-enabled strategy grounded in recognition, alignment, and capability-building. Key features include:*

- ***Digital Credential Ecosystem**: ACS issues microCredentials and SFIA-aligned digital badges that provide portable, stackable recognition of skills. These are hosted on the Credly platform, enabling real-time verification and sharing.*
- ***Modular CPD Framework**: Continuing Professional Development is now structured as modular, employer-aligned micro-learning units. This supports member autonomy, upskilling agility, and relevance to current and emerging tech domains.*
- ***Multi-Sided Certification Pathways**:*
    - *For Members: Professional pathways such as Certified Professional and Certified Technologist are scaffolded with micro-credentials and mapped to international frameworks.*
    - *For Employers: Skill verification tools support talent identification, workforce planning, and credibility assurance through real-time digital credentialing.*
    - *For Government: ACS is embedded in national skills strategies, playing a recognised role in migration assessment, digital workforce development, and national capability mapping.*

***Ecosystem Role and Capability Network Design:** ACS's platform model is anchored in broader ecosystem participation. It does not merely certify individuals; it coordinates a national capability architecture.*

- ***Collaborative Infrastructure**: Partnerships with industry, government, and academia position ACS as a convenor and translator of digital capability needs into credentialing frameworks and development pathways.*
- ***Real-Time Recognition**: The use of live, portable digital badges allows for granular, ongoing recognition of professional achievement, supporting mobility, career progression, and workforce matching in real time.*
- ***Public Value Contribution**: Through its assessment and advisory functions, ACS informs national skills policies, supports migration and employment pathways, and contributes to public digital literacy initiatives.*

Conclusion

ACS offers a leading example of what it means to build a platform association around capability and trust infrastructure. Its role spans credentialing, standard-setting, ecosystem coordination, and strategic workforce development. For associations grappling with how to remain relevant in fast-changing sectors, ACS shows that credibility and impact lie not in controlling knowledge, but in enabling its recognition, portability, and shared value.

Table 4-5 **Strategic Lessons for Associations**

Design Lever	ACS Application	Takeaway for Boards
Platform Thinking	ACS operates as a multi-sided skill platform	Redesign value from 'services for members' to 'interactions among participants'
Recognition Infrastructure	Micro-credentials and badges aligned to SFIA	Embed modular, verifiable credentials as part of your value proposition
Ecosystem Alignment	Deep partnerships with employers and government	Position your association as capability infrastructure, not just a convenor
Scalable CPD	Modular, stackable learning linked to real-time needs	Shift CPD from static compliance to agile, market-relevant learning pathways

Measuring What Matters: Feedback Loops for Platform Maturity

The APSF is designed to evolve with your association. That means defining success through metrics that reflect platform logic: value creation through interaction, resilience through diversification, and trust through transparency.

These metrics function as *feedback loops*. They help leadership monitor what's working, diagnose emerging risks, and make informed decisions about where to invest next. Importantly, they link strategic goals with operational performance, allowing boards and executives to stay focused on what matters most.

Table 4-6 **APSF Metrics Framework**

Metric Category	Indicator Example	Why It Matters
Engagement	Peer-to-peer participation rate	Signals whether members are active contributors, not just recipients
Trust & Transparency	Data privacy complaints, AI audit frequency	Demonstrates governance of digital risk and builds credibility
Revenue Resilience	% revenue from non-dues sources	Indicates diversification and business model health

Metric Category	Indicator Example	Why It Matters
Platform Stickiness	Return visits per member per month	Measures habitual engagement and platform value
Member-Led Contribution	% of content or learning generated by members	Reflects platform enablement and distributed value creation
Governance Adaptability	Delegation velocity or decision turnaround time	Shows how quickly governance can respond to change

Figure 4-2 **Example APSF Metrics Graph**

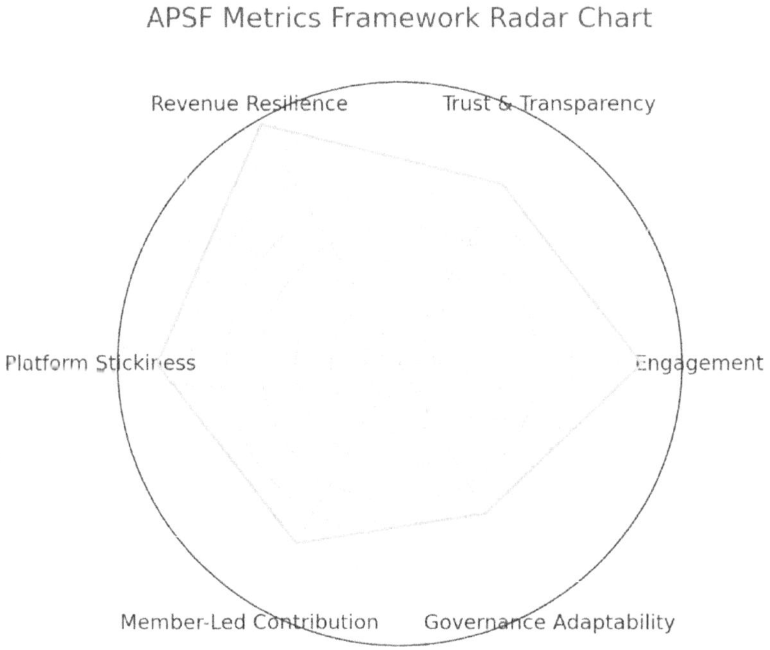

The next section will turn to Board Implications and the concept of Ecosystem Governance, explaining how platform-based associations will reimagine their board's role in overseeing complexity, shared authority, and ethical digital systems.

The Road Ahead

Example 16. From Traditional to Platform-Centric

Claire Evans, CEO of the Professional Nutrition Association (PNA), initially inherited a legacy model common to many associations. Member engagement was structured around annual conferences, quarterly newsletters, and fee-based professional development events. CPD was delivered as standalone webinars or in-person training, with little personalisation or data-driven insight. Member contributions were largely limited to committee participation, with few mechanisms for ongoing dialogue, co-creation, or system-wide learning. Revenue remained dependent on subscriptions and periodic event income.

This model served the profession's basic needs but struggled to remain relevant in an era of digital expectations, interdisciplinary practice, and on-demand education. The strategic question Claire faced, "How do we become an enabler of professional ecosystems rather than just a service provider?", marked the beginning of PNA's transition journey.

The *Association Platform Success Framework* is not a digital checklist or a technology upgrade plan. It represents a strategic reset. APSF introduces a new mindset for associations to think differently, lead with purpose, and evolve within an environment shaped by complexity, collaboration, and platform dynamics.

This framework repositions the association from being a service provider to becoming an ecosystem orchestrator. In this role, the association acts as a trusted convenor of people, knowledge, learning, and influence. APSF bridges the gap between traditional strengths and emerging needs by aligning strategic intent with operational capability.

At the centre of the APSF are four Core Pillars that define platform-era maturity:

- *Innovation* drives experimentation and supports ongoing relevance
- *Courage* empowers associations to make necessary structural and strategic shifts
- *Data-Driven Insights* enable personalisation, adaptability, and informed decision-making
- *Trust and Security* provide the ethical and operational foundation for sustained engagement

These pillars are activated through the three Design Pillars that shape how the framework is applied:

- Member-Centric Design ensures relevance and agency at every stage of the member journey
- Scalable Digital Infrastructure enables integration, responsiveness, and growth
- Governance and Trust embed transparency, ethical oversight, and inclusive leadership

Together, these elements transform strategy into measurable outcomes. They ensure that change is not only aspirational but grounded in everyday action and aligned to member experience.

Importantly, the APSF is not limited to national or well-funded associations. Its principles apply equally to regional organisations, federated networks, grassroots groups, and volunteer-led bodies. What matters is not organisational scale but the clarity of purpose and commitment to action.

This chapter has introduced the APSF's logic, structure, and diagnostic tools. The Diagnostic Layer provides more than assessment. It creates a shared lens for boards and executives to evaluate progress, identify risk, and lead transformation with focus and discipline.

Looking forward, the next strategic opportunity lies in reimagining the foundation of association life: membership. If associations are to thrive as platforms, the traditional model of membership will evolve. It will shift from a subscription to a system of participation, co-creation, and reciprocal value.

The next chapter explores this shift in depth. It outlines how associations can move beyond tiered access models and towards multi-sided, flexible membership structures that drive engagement, impact, and legitimacy in a platform context.

The platform era has already arrived. The question is not whether associations will adapt. The question is how prepared they are to lead with confidence and clarity.

As the book now turns to membership design, the APSF Diagnostic Layer stands as a vital tool for action. It ensures that strategic conversations do not stay theoretical. Instead, they become anchored in insight, guided by evidence, and focused on what will have to change.

Part III. Becoming a Platform-Based Association

With the case for platform thinking established, Part II turns theory into direction. This section introduces the practical design logic that underpins platform-based associations. It explores business models, value propositions, monetisation strategies, and ecosystem design. These chapters provide the tools and framing needed to build a future-ready association structure, one that supports participation, resilience, and strategic alignment. Whether starting from scratch or reconfiguring legacy systems, this is where transformation becomes design-led.

Chapter 5. Reimagining Membership Value

Example 17. Why would members pay?

Claire Evans, CEO of the Professional Network Association (PNA), scanned the latest retention report, flat growth, declining renewals, disengaged members. Despite marketing campaigns, event discounts, and referral incentives, nothing moved the needle.

At the last board meeting, the Chair of Membership, Ravi Patel, had been blunt: "We're competing with free. Why pay $750 when industry insights, networking, and training are available online at virtually no cost?"

Claire knew he was right. The one-size-fits-all membership model had worked for decades, but times had changed. Younger professionals wanted flexibility and choice, mid-career members engaged only when it suited them, and even loyal members questioned the value.

Sophie, a tech entrepreneur on the board, put it plainly: "People still want to belong, but they don't see why they should pay upfront. We need to rethink the model."

That night, Claire mapped out a new vision, one built on engagement, not transactions. The next morning, she asked her team: "What if membership wasn't a fixed fee, but an experience? What if members chose their level of involvement and paid for what they valued?" It was time to reimagine membership, not as a static subscription, but as a dynamic, evolving relationship.

Why Traditional Membership Models Are Failing

As explored throughout the earlier chapters of this book, the landscape for professional associations has shifted dramatically. The *Association Platform Success Framework* challenges associations to move beyond static organisational structures and reimagine themselves as dynamic ecosystems, fluid networks where participants engage in varied, value-driven ways. In this context, the traditional membership model is no longer fit for purpose.

For decades, annual subscription-based membership models have underpinned association revenue and strategy. These models assume that value can be packaged, priced, and delivered in a one-size-fits-all manner. Yet, as the needs and behaviours of professionals have evolved, this rigid structure is increasingly misaligned with how people want to connect, learn, and contribute.

The core problem lies in uniform pricing and benefits. A flat-rate membership presumes all members derive equal value, ignoring the diversity of roles, career stages, industries, and motivations. Some members may want leadership development, others networking or industry intelligence. Traditional models offer little room for differentiation or personalisation.

Further compounding this is the lack of flexibility in participation. Members are expected to pay for access regardless of whether they use the services provided. In today's on-demand, outcome-oriented economy, this feels both outdated and inequitable. The rise of accessible alternatives, such as free online communities, open educational platforms, and real-time knowledge-sharing via LinkedIn and Slack, means individuals can now fulfil their professional needs without tying themselves to a single association.

Perhaps most critically, the traditional model fails to deliver on engagement. Static benefits do not create dynamic relationships. Members increasingly expect a tailored, seamless experience that responds to their evolving needs. Many associations still deliver value through outdated, institution-centric processes that feel disconnected from members' professional realities. When this disconnect widens, engagement drops, and so does retention.

High attrition rates are not simply a symptom of poor marketing or changing preferences; they are a structural signal that the old model no longer meets expectations. Without meaningful, flexible pathways for participation, members question the value of their investment.

To remain viable, associations will have to shift from being gatekeepers of exclusive content and events to becoming platforms for participation. The solution is not merely to tinker with pricing tiers or add new benefits to the same model, but to reimagine the membership experience entirely. This means embracing modular, adaptive membership models that offer multiple levels of engagement and contribution, all supported by digital infrastructure that facilitates connection, learning, and co-creation in real time.

The APSF offers a structured roadmap for this transformation, from transactional membership models to engagement-led ecosystems. By leveraging platform thinking, associations can unlock new forms of value creation: communities that grow stronger the more they are used, services that adapt based on real-time feedback, and roles for members that go beyond consumption to include contribution and collaboration.

In short, to thrive in this new era, associations will have to stop trying to preserve outdated structures and instead build systems that reflect how professionals want to engage today: flexibly, meaningfully, and on their own terms.

Example 18. Two Diverging Paths

Imagine two similarly sized professional associations facing comparable challenges: falling renewals, declining event attendance, and growing competition from digital content providers. One association continues to rely on fixed-tier annual memberships, a quarterly journal, and a single flagship conference. Over time, engagement dwindles, especially among early-career professionals.

The other association rethinks its model, offering monthly subscription access, a freemium webinar series, and tiered pricing for microlearning. Over a few years, participation grows, younger members join, and new digital sponsors come on board.

While hypothetical, this scenario illustrates a real pattern seen across sectors: flexible, member-centred models consistently outperform static ones in attracting and retaining engagement.

Figure 5-1 **Membership Model Spectrum: Focus x Model**

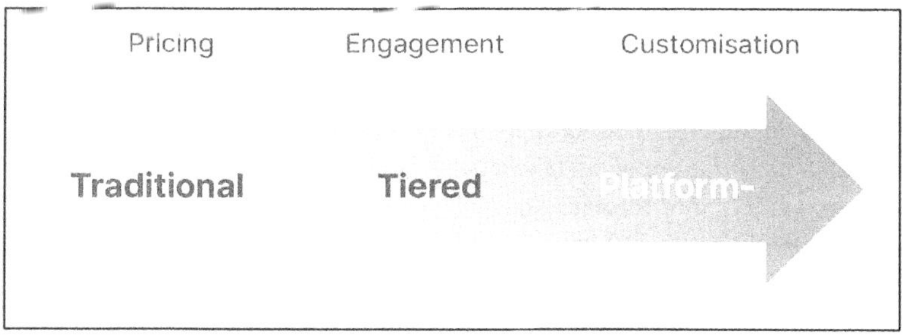

These failures are not just operational; they reflect a deeper misalignment between how associations define membership and how members define value. To address this, we will have to fundamentally reimagine what it means to belong.

This chapter draws heavily on the *Data-Driven Insights* pillar of the APSF illustrating how dynamic models of engagement are both possible and measurable.

Orchestrating Membership in an Ecosystem Model

The membership models of the past were designed for organisations that operated as service providers, delivering services to members. In contrast, platform-based associations operate as ecosystem orchestrators. This means their membership model will have to facilitate interaction, collaboration, and co-creation, not just access and provide services. The associations as orchestrator doesn't focus solely on delivering content or benefits, but on enabling a network of value exchange. This might involve members mentoring others, employers contributing resources, partners co-hosting events, or external bodies aligning their frameworks (or even service provision) within the association's platform. The membership model will have to become a gateway to participation, not a paywall to benefits.

Successful orchestration requires membership structures that are porous, participatory, and designed to scale engagement across diverse actors. Freemium models, marketplace dynamics, and tiered access are not just pricing tools, they are strategic levers for platform-based coordination.

If associations are to function as platforms, not silos, and extend their reach, they will have to first understand who is participating, how, and why they participate.

The following framework maps the ecosystem of modern professional engagement.

Membership: Uniformity to Ecosystem

One of the most powerful shifts associations will have to make in the platform era is a reconceptualisation of what "membership" means, and who qualifies as a member. The traditional assumption has been that "members" are individuals who pay annual dues in exchange for defined benefits and are part of a definable groups or discipline. This view may no longer serve the strategic needs of modern associations or the expectations of today's members.

In platform-based ecosystems, membership is no longer a singular, static category. Instead, associations will have to acknowledge that individuals and institutions engage at multiple levels, for different reasons, and in ways that shift over time. Membership is best understood as a *continuum of participation*, where value is exchanged in diverse ways: not just through fees, but through knowledge contribution, peer support, community facilitation, network access and strategic partnerships.

This is not simply a pricing innovation, it is a governance and identity innovation. Who gets to belong? Who gets recognised? Who contributes value, and how is that value defined and rewarded? These are strategic design questions, not just operational decisions.

Participation in a member or professional community need not be tied to traditional dues structures or titles. Each category has a distinct value logic, a unique role in the community, and different expectations for engagement. Rigid models that treat everyone the same, or that fail to recognise the bespoke value of contribution beyond payment, risk alienating key stakeholders and stifling innovation.

The following framework outlines key categories of participants within a platform-aligned association and explores how each contributes to, and derives value from, the ecosystem.

Table 5-1 Membership Categories

Category	Who They Are	Primary Value Exchange	Engagement Style
Core Members	Members in the field	Ongoing access to learning, networks, recognition	Recurring, embedded participation
Contributors	Speakers, authors, content creators	Knowledge sharing, thought leadership	Episodic but high-impact engagement
Non-Member Users	Students, public, prospective members	Access to open resources, events, or forums	Occasional, exploratory participation
Institutional Partners	Employers, universities, sponsors	Reach, branding, access to talent or research	Strategic collaboration
Adjacent Sector Actors	Members in related disciplines (e.g. HR tech, ESG)	Cross-pollination, partnerships	Edge engagement, opportunity-driven

By recognising and designing for these distinct categories, associations unlock new pathways for growth, legitimacy, and relevance. Flexible engagement strategies, adaptive pricing, recognition systems, and role-based contribution tools are no longer optional, they are essential to operating in a world where membership is not a gate, but a platform.

Designing flexible, data-driven membership models demands more than just pricing innovation, it depends on understanding the diverse roles members play within the association's ecosystem. Not all participants seek the same value, contribute in the same way, or engage with the same intensity. Successful associations will recognising this diversity and structure membership around it.

In a platform-based association, members are no longer a single, homogeneous group. Instead, they form a diverse ecosystem of participants who engage in different ways, contribute varying forms of value, and require tailored offerings. Understanding these categories helps design more flexible, personalised, and scalable membership strategies.

> *Associations are not their members. They are a separate entity whose objects should be to deliver value to their members. They need the skills and visions of platform orchestrators. If they fail, they lose members – it's that simple!*

Modern associations are increasingly recognising the limitations of treating membership as a uniform experience. Members engage at different levels and with varying expectations, ranging from deep content contribution to occasional participation in events or learning. Effective membership design now requires segmenting members not just by career stage, but by their role in the ecosystem, preferred mode of engagement, and value exchange preferences. They need new capabilities and tools that enable personalisation, like AI.

Example 19. Cross-Border Collaboration

Shared Infrastructure, Distinct Identities

Two professional associations operating in adjacent disciplines explored the possibility of merging to streamline operations, unify services, and amplify their impact. However, despite shared goals, they faced significant structural barriers: they served different geographic regions, operated under different legal and regulatory systems, and held unique governance traditions shaped by local contexts.

Rather than forcing a full merger, which risked compromising autonomy and compliance, they reimagined the problem through a platform lens.

The solution?

One association proposed to offer the other a "vanilla" platform model, offering the collaborator access to a shared infrastructure: event technology, digital learning environments, CRM systems, and core administrative services. This allowed both organisations to:

- *Retain independent governance and regional identity.*
- *Standardise user experience and service delivery where appropriate.*
- *And reduce duplication in operational investment.*

In effect, the larger association became a platform provider, enabling networked value creation without demanding structural integration.

This approach reflects the essence of platform strategy in the association sector: enabling participation and shared value through infrastructure and trust systems, without requiring uniformity or centralisation.

This example underscores a growing opportunity for associations to become infrastructure hubs, offering platform services to aligned organisations, local chapters, or international partners. For others it can focus on frontline engagement with the support of a back-office partner. Rather than controlling every node, associations can facilitate ecosystems, creating coherence through shared tools and protocols, not imposed governance.

From Gatekeeping to Platform Enabling

The origins of many professional associations lie in a fundamentally different world that where they find themselves today. Historically, associations were established to create and protect a shared identity around a discipline or core value, they formalised knowledge, established standards, and regulated who could participate. This was both a defensive function (safeguarding status, controlling entry) and a cohesive one (defining what it means to belong to a group of aligned others).

In this legacy model membership was as much about exclusion as inclusion. By drawing clear boundaries, between insiders and outsiders, qualified and unqualified, associations helped shape the legitimacy of an emerging field. This purpose was not only understandable; it was necessary in a time when disciplines were evolving with increased access to education and a more sophisticated consumer. They had to carve out their niche and justify their existence to protect their autonomy. This is a feature of many professional associations.

Today associations and their members operate in a digitally networked, interdisciplinary, and rapidly evolving work environment. Multi-disciplinary practice is becoming more prevalent and regulatory relaxation is supporting this transition with policy shifting towards consumer centricity. The boundaries that demarcated disciplines are becoming constraints. Rigid gatekeeping limits innovation, diversity, and relevance. It no longer reflects how people work, learn, or contribute to professional life.

Yet we will have to also recognise that the need for professional identity and cohesion hasn't disappeared. In fact, it may be more important than ever in a fragmented, reputation-driven digital economy.

The challenge is not abandoning the identity-forming role of associations, but to reframe it.

The "Both/And" Opportunity

While the historical role of associations as credentialing bodies and professional gatekeepers served an essential purpose, today's context demands a more expansive, inclusive, and flexible approach to participation. Importantly, this is not an argument against professionalism, standards, or identity, it is an argument for a pluralistic model of value and engagement.

Importantly, this evolution is not theoretical. Association leaders are increasingly recognising the limits of legacy structures and the need for adaptive models. As Moore (2025) observes in *Purpose Under Pressure*:

> *"Membership no longer means one thing. For some, it's about recognition and credentialing. For others, it's about connection, contribution, or simply having a voice in shaping the profession. Associations will have to learn to hold these multiple meanings at once." (p. 19)*

This insight marks a significant shift from a single, static definition of membership to a layered, role-based understanding of participation. In this model, associations retain the rigour and legitimacy of professional identity and embrace broader forms of engagement, from contributors and learners to institutional partners and adjacent sector actors.

This "both/and" logic is not a compromise. It represents a strategic evolution, a way for associations to remain credible and cohesive, while also expanding their reach, relevance, and capacity for innovation in a fast-changing landscape.

Rather than choosing between exclusive legitimacy and open participation, associations can now design for both maintaining rigorous pathways for professional recognition and standards and enabling broader participation, contribution, and community building across boundaries.

In a platform model, membership becomes porous, layered, and participatory. Associations can offer credentialed pathways for those seeking formal recognition, flexible engagement options for contributors, learners, partners, and adjacent sector actors and provide trusted infrastructures that allow professional identity to evolve through practice, not just policy.

This "both/and" approach directly supports the multi-role membership categories outlined earlier. It enables associations to protect what matters, professional ethics, quality assurance, and cohesion, while opening space for what's emerging: peer-led learning, interdisciplinary collaboration, and real-time co-creation.

> *Be wary of creating tiered memberships that overtly privilege one member type. No member wants to just be an "associate" that infers a class distinction .*

The future of associations is not less professional or cohesive, but it will be much more pluralistic and tolerant. It supports professional identity by participation, not just conferred through designation. It will support action, not just virtue signalling.

Member Value

Membership models are breaking under the weight of digital expectations. Once seen as a reliable foundation of association sustainability, traditional dues-based structures are now under strain, no longer aligned with how members discover value, form networks, or engage with their fields. Static benefits, annual renewals, and transactional logic are proving insufficient in a world shaped by real-time interaction, personalisation, and platform-based participation. The assumption that membership equals engagement will have to be challenged and recalibrated to offer a new model where belonging is earned through contribution, value is co-created, and associations act as orchestrators of shared purpose.

A platform-based approach to member value creation requires a shift in how associations define membership. Shifting from transaction to relational, where every member has an ongoing relationship at the individual level and engage enabled through multiple pathways.

The next section considers the benefits of flexible engagement strategies, and how associations can implement tiered, freemium, and marketplace-driven membership structures.

Defining and Measuring Member Value

What is Member Value?

Member value is the *perceived benefit* that individuals receive from being part of an association. Unlike traditional transactional models, where membership is a simple exchange of fees for access, modern membership models should be value-driven, providing tailored benefits that align with (each) members' evolving needs.

Member value is subjective, what a student values may differ from what a senior professional values. Associations that fail to articulate and deliver clear, differentiated value will struggle with engagement, retention, and revenue growth.

The Shift from Features to Value

Many associations focus on features rather than value when promoting membership. However, members don't pay for access, they pay for outcomes and experiences that improve their professional standing, network, or skills. The following are some examples of features and how they are interpreted through a value lens.

Table 5-2 Perceived Member Value

Feature	Perceived Member Value
Access to industry reports	Helps members stay ahead of trends and gain insights to advance their careers
Networking events	Provides meaningful professional connections that lead to job opportunities or collaborations
Advocacy efforts	Gives members a voice in shaping industry policies and standards
Discounts on conferences	Makes high-value learning experiences more affordable
Online community/forums	Creates a peer-support system for problem-solving and collaboration

Associations should consider moving beyond listing features and instead demonstrate how these features translate into tangible benefits and ultimately value for members.

> *Telling members of the value they receive is in ways that are meaningful to them seems so simple, and yet it is rarely done in an member-centric way.*

Reframing Value Through the Orchestrator Lens

As associations transition to platform-based models, the notion of value shifts from internal delivery to enabled outcomes. The most compelling associations will not only deliver value through programs, but they will also enable others in the ecosystem (members, partners, employers, educators) to create value collaboratively. In this orchestrator model, value is co-produced across the network: a job board is enriched by employer participation, CPD grows more relevant through member-led pathways, and advocacy is strengthened by partner alliances. Associations will have to learn to measure and communicate this ecosystem-enabled value, not just what they produce internally.

Measuring Member Value: Key Metrics

Associations need to track quantitative and qualitative indicators to assess whether they are delivering real value to members.

Table 5-3 Member Value Metrics

Metric	What It Measures	Rationale
Net Promoter Score (NPS)	% of members likely to recommend the association	A direct measure of perceived value and engagement
Engagement Rate	Logins, event attendance, content downloads	Indicates if members find the resources valuable enough to return
Retention Rate	% of members renewing annually	A strong signal of long-term perceived value
Upgrade Rate (Freemium Models)	% of free members upgrading to paid tiers	Shows if initial value convinces members to invest further
Revenue Per Member	Avg. spend per member (including non-dues revenue)	Demonstrates how well the association monetises engaged members

By tracking these indicators, associations can refine their membership models to ensure they are continuously improving member value.

Example 20. CIPD: Measuring Member Value

Measuring Member Value at the Chartered Institute of Personnel and Development (CIPD)

The CIPD in the United Kingdom provides a compelling example of how a professional association can move beyond traditional satisfaction metrics to deliver nuanced, actionable insights into member value. Recognising that a single satisfaction score could not capture the diverse needs and expectations of its broad membership, CIPD embarked on a journey to redefine how it measures and delivers value. This shift was driven by the realisation that value is multi-dimensional and context-dependent, varying significantly across career stages, professional roles, and geographic locations.

To address this complexity, CIPD developed a Member Value Index, *a dashboard that integrates behavioural analytics, persona mapping, and qualitative feedback. The Institute identified five key member segments: early-career professionals, HR generalists, senior HR leaders, academics, and international members. For each segment, CIPD tracked differentiated indicators such as app logins, CPD badge uptake, event attendance, and engagement with research platforms. This segmentation enabled the organisation to tailor its engagement strategies, identify under-served groups, and demonstrate a measurable return on membership in ways that were specific and relevant to each cohort.*

The implementation of the Member Value Index marked a philosophical shift within CIPD. Rather than simply asking members if they were satisfied, the Institute began to focus on whether it was delivering value as defined by the members themselves. This approach fostered a deeper understanding of what mattered most to different segments, allowing CIPD to adapt its offerings and communications accordingly. The result was a more empathetic, data-driven strategy that prioritised member experience and long-term engagement over generic satisfaction.

CIPD's experience demonstrates that meaningful value measurement in professional associations requires a multi-faceted, member-centric approach. By combining quantitative analytics with qualitative insights and segment-specific metrics, CIPD has set a benchmark for how associations can remain relevant and responsive in a rapidly evolving professional landscape. This case underscores the importance of designing value measurement systems that reflect the real-world diversity of member needs and aspirations, ultimately strengthening both organisational impact and member loyalty. (Corney 2021)

This example demonstrates that meaningful value measurement is both multi-dimensional and context-dependent, and will have to be designed with empathy for members' varying needs and career stages.

The Table 5-4 shows how the CIPD segmented their membership categories n measured value.

Table 5-4 CIPD's Five Key ember Segments

Segment	Primary Value Drivers	Measurement Approach
Early-Career	Mentoring access, CPD completion	App logins, CPD micro badge uptake, mentor-match success
HR Generalists	Practical tools and templates	Download rates, repeat usage, satisfaction with toolkits
Senior Leaders	Strategic insights, thought leadership	Event attendance, whitepaper downloads, Net Promoter Score
Academics	Access to research and publishing platforms	Journal contribution frequency, research engagement rates
International Members	Local relevance, remote access	Time-zone specific webinar participation, translated content use

The Shift to Dynamic Membership Models

As mentioned earlier, member value is the perceived benefits a member receives in exchange for their investment of time and money in an association. It is dynamic and varies across career stages, professional needs, and engagement levels.

A platform-based approach to membership moves away from fixed tiers toward a model that adapts to the needs of members over time. Dynamic membership models will incorporate multiple entry points, enabling broader participation to create network effects, the incremental benefits arising from having more people engaging together. It scales benefits based on member engagement rather than a rigid fee structure and facilitates ongoing interaction rather than limiting access to predefined benefits.

The goal is to provide members with options that align with their specific needs while maximising long-term engagement and financial sustainability for the association.

Chapter 6. Platform Era Membership Models

Example 21. CIPD: Measuring Member Value

Claire Evans, CEO of the Professional Network Association (PNA), leaned back as the finance director closed the budget presentation. "Dues renewals are steady," he said, "but growth is flat. Younger professionals are sampling our webinars, downloading free resources, and then moving on. They're not joining."

Around the board table, frustration was palpable. Ravi Patel, Chair of Membership, spoke first. "We keep adjusting the price point, offering discounts, even adding perks, but members want choice, not bundles. They don't all want the same thing, and they won't pay for what they don't use."

Claire nodded. She had just come from a call with a peer CEO overseas, who described how their association had shifted to a hybrid model: a freemium tier to draw in new participants, premium pathways for those who wanted more, and a marketplace where members could transact directly with each other. "It wasn't about lowering fees," the colleague had explained, "it was about widening the tent and letting value flow in different ways."

That conversation stayed with her. What if PNA could offer modular participation, say, a mix of free, flexible, and premium options, and recognise value wherever it emerged, not just in dues payments? What if the membership model itself could act as a platform, connecting professionals, partners, and contributors in ways that reflected the diversity of their needs and the fluidity of modern careers?

This was the challenge before the board: to move beyond a static, one-size-fits-all structure, and design a membership system that could adapt, scale, and sustain relevance in the platform era.

In this chapter a number of membership models will be considered: tiered, freemium, pay-per-service, and marketplace models. Each of the models reflects a shift from linear delivery to orchestrated participation. They enable associations to create more open, modular, and scalable value propositions, hallmarks of the orchestrator identity described throughout this book. The goal is not just to diversify revenue, but to activate the association's ecosystem, allowing members and partners to choose how they engage, contribute, and grow.

No single membership model fits all associations. The right structure depends on factors such as audience demographics, industry expectations, and long-term sustainability goals. All four models are adaptable to align with the needs of modern associations. The alternative membership models can support a more flexible and scalable approach offering different advantages depending on the association's goals, industry, and member demographics.

Tiered Membership Structures

A tiered model allows members to choose from different levels of access and engagement, each with its own pricing and benefits.

- **Basic memberships** provide access to essential resources such as newsletters, online content, and community discussions.
- **Mid-tier memberships** include additional benefits such as discounted event attendance, priority networking opportunities, and exclusive professional development content.
- **Premium memberships** offer the most comprehensive benefits, including personalised services, one-on-one mentoring, and strategic leadership programs.

This approach caters to diverse membership needs while ensuring those who derive greater value contribute more to the association's financial sustainability.

Tiered membership models allow associations to align offerings with different audience segments. A strong example of this is in the case below which demonstrates how redesigning a membership structure to better accommodate varying levels of engagement.

Example 22. The Tiered Membership Model

The American Marketing Association (AMA) provides a robust example of how a professional association can adopt platform thinking to revitalise member engagement and value delivery. Facing the challenge of serving a diverse and evolving membership, the AMA transitioned from a traditional, one-size-fits-all model to a tiered membership structure. This approach aligns with platform strategy principles, enabling multi-sided participation, modular offerings, and ongoing value exchange for members, employers, and partners.

The Transformation

The AMA's tiered membership model offers distinct pathways for different member segments:

- ***Student Membership:*** *Entry-level access for undergraduates, including collegiate chapter participation and discounted events.*
- ***Professional Membership****: Full access to national and local events, professional development, certifications, and networking.*
- ***Group Membership****: Discounted rates for organisations, supporting collective engagement.*

- ***Executive Marketer Community:*** *Exclusive benefits for senior marketers, such as strategy roundtables and leadership development.*

This structure allows members to select the tier that best matches their career stage and needs, with the flexibility to upgrade as their professional journey progresses. The AMA's digital infrastructure supports personalised content, targeted communications, and real-time access to resources, fostering continuous engagement and community building.

Platform Thinking in Practice

The AMA's model exemplifies platform thinking through:

- ***Multi-sided Value Creation:*** *Serving members, employers, and partners with tailored benefits and verification tools.*
- ***Modular, Scalable Offerings:*** *Tiered membership and add-ons (e.g., certifications, exclusive content) accessable as needed.*
- ***Personalised Engagement:*** *Data-driven curation of resources and events for different segments.*
- ***Continuous Value Exchange:*** *Year-round access to webinars, journals, and networking, not just annual renewals.*
- ***Ecosystem Facilitation:*** *Connecting members with chapters, interest groups, and industry partners for collaborative growth.*

Outcomes

- ***Broader Appeal:*** *The model attracts younger professionals and students who may not be ready for full membership, while providing advanced benefits for senior members.*
- ***Revenue Growth:*** *The flexible structure enables the AMA to capture a wider range of members and encourage upgrades.*

Limitation

While the AMA's tiered membership model demonstrates elements of platform thinking, it is not a fully open platform. Participation and value creation remain largely curated by the association itself, and the model's success relies on sustained investment in digital infrastructure, data analytics, and user-centred experience design. Although positive outcomes have been reported, specific quantitative data on engagement and retention improvements are not consistently made public, limiting the ability to directly attribute success to the tiered approach (American Marketing Association 2024; Mihelich 2023; Re:Members 2024).

The Australian HR Institute (AHRI) is another association that offers a clear example of tiered membership in action, from student and graduate levels through to certified professional and fellow status. This structure supports professional progression while maintaining strategic alignment with workforce development outcomes.

Freemium Membership Models

A freemium model reimagines the boundary between members and non-members by offering open access to core features while reserving advanced, high-value services for paying users. This design lowers the barrier to entry, allowing individuals to engage with the association without immediate commitment, building trust and demonstrating value before any transaction occurs. It is particularly powerful for associations aiming to grow visibility, nurture future members, or capture new market segments such as early-career professionals, adjacent fields, or international audiences.

In a freemium architecture, free-tier participants might gain access to curated resources, selected webinars, public forums, newsletters, and limited networking features. Meanwhile, *premium* members unlock access to exclusive learning modules, personalised career pathways, certifications, member-only events, advanced data tools, or leadership development programs. This structure aligns with the platform logic of progressive engagement: as users extract value and deepen their involvement, conversion to paid tiers becomes a natural next step, not a forced decision.

Freemium models rely on design excellence, the free tier will have to be valuable enough to engage, but incomplete enough to incentivise upgrading. When executed well, the model enables associations to expand their perimeter of influence while preserving premium pathways that drive meaningful revenue.

A standout example is the American Institute of Architects (AIA). AIA has shifted from a traditional gated-membership model to a tiered digital ecosystem, where both members and non-members can engage with selected resources, participate in discussions, and access professional content. Paid tiers offer enhanced learning experiences, credential tracking, and specialised toolkits aligned with licensure and career milestones. By positioning learning and engagement as modular and open-access, AIA has transitioned from an entitlement model to a value-first, platform-based experience, reinforcing its relevance while widening its reach.

This approach not only attracts a broader audience but builds momentum for deeper involvement. In doing so, it reframes the association's role: not as a gatekeeper of benefits, but as a curator of growth pathways. Importantly, it also creates a data-rich environment, enabling insight into member journeys, content resonance, and conversion drivers, all of which can be used to refine offerings and pricing strategies over time.

Pay-Per-Service or Transaction-Based Membership

A pay-per-service or transaction-based membership model allows members to access association services without committing to an annual fee. Rather than bundling value into a single dues-based package, this approach treats each offering, such as events, certifications, resources, or consultations, as a discrete, purchasable product. This model aligns with a broader trend in the digital economy: users expect customisation, flexibility, and the ability to pay only for what they use, when they use it.

In this framework, the association becomes a modular platform, allowing users to assemble their own value pathway. It can be particularly effective for associations serving diverse or transient member bases, such as consultants, contractors, international members, or early-career entrants who may be unwilling or unable to commit to traditional full membership.

For the association, the advantages include:

- **Increased participation** from outside the membership base
- **Expanded addressable market**, including non-members
- **Data-driven insight** into which services generate the most demand
- **Opportunities to upsell** or convert high-use participants into longer-term members or contributors

However, this model also presents challenges: it requires clear pricing, strong digital infrastructure, and a coherent customer experience that maintains strategic alignment even when participation is fragmented. Without these, the organisation risks commodifying its offerings or undermining the perceived value of full membership tiers.

A leading example is Engineers Australia (EA), which has begun moving away from an all-or-nothing membership model. Through initiatives like its *Future Now* strategy and digital badge ecosystem, EA enables members to access CPD modules, digital credentials, and content-rich engagement opportunities on a flexible, transactional basis. These services are open not only to full members but also to contributors and participants who may be engaging episodically or exploring new career transitions. EA's model supports stackable credentials and modular value, key features of a platform-oriented approach.

This shift allows EA to activate a broader professional ecosystem while maintaining trust and credential rigour, essential in a regulated profession. It also reflects a deepening maturity in its strategic design: rather than forcing commitment up front, EA enables participation first, then invites users into deeper engagement over time.

In platform terms, this model positions the association as a trusted broker and capability enabler, rather than a membership gatekeeper. It facilitates value creation through choice, unlocks new revenue through participation diversity, and aligns well with user-centric design principles in the platform economy.

Marketplace-Driven Memberships

This model requires high-trust infrastructure, clear rules for member-contributed value, and shared revenue or recognition pathways to maintain fairness and legitimacy.

In a marketplace-driven membership model, the association evolves from service provider to ecosystem orchestrator, enabling members to transact, collaborate, and exchange value with each other and external actors. Here, membership is no longer the endpoint of engagement but a gateway to a structured economic network. The association facilitates these exchanges, offering trust infrastructure, visibility, and curated access, while monetising the value flows rather than the gate itself.

Marketplace logic allows associations to generate revenue through platform-based mechanisms such as transaction fees, visibility boosts, reputation systems, or premium positioning. For example, a job board hosted by a health or engineering association might allow members to post or browse roles freely, while charging employers for priority listings or analytics access. A consulting association could support a services marketplace where members offer expert advice, short-term project delivery, or coaching, with the association earning a percentage of each transaction or providing escrow, compliance, or vetting services as value-added layers.

This model transforms the association's core function from one of provision to enablement, fostering trusted peer-to-peer or peer-to-market exchanges. It also helps associations surface latent member value: capabilities, experience, and assets that may otherwise remain untapped. Critically, this approach expands the association's role as an economic node in the sector, a convenor not just of dialogue, but of opportunity.

However, marketplace models require strong governance: rules for participation, dispute resolution, equitable exposure, and ethical pricing will have to be clearly established to preserve trust and platform integrity. Data ownership, algorithmic visibility, and fairness in access to demand are critical considerations. Done well, this model diversifies revenue while deepening member utility and relevance.

By contrast, freemium membership models focus on expanding the perimeter of engagement. They treat access as a spectrum, offering free or low-barrier entry to content, networks, or services, with monetisation introduced through advanced features, credentials, tools, or exclusive programming. This approach excels at attracting new audiences, building trust before conversion, and capturing attention in a crowded, digital-first world.

Example 23. Community + Marketplace Hybrid

Platform Type: *Community of practice (tech/design)*

IndieHackers and Dribbble stand as leading examples of digital platforms that successfully blend the features of a community of practice with those of a professional marketplace. While neither is a traditional association, both platforms serve technology and design professionals by enabling peer-to-peer learning, portfolio development, job discovery, and freelance collaboration in a decentralised, user-driven environment.

***Dribbble**, originally established as a portfolio-sharing site for designers, has evolved into a sophisticated hybrid platform. Today, it allows users not only to showcase their work and receive feedback from peers but also to access a thriving freelance marketplace. Designers can be hired directly by clients, participate in project bidding, and transact securely through the platform. Dribbble generates revenue through Pro memberships (which unlock advanced features and higher visibility), transaction fees on* *freelance work, and premium placement for employers and brands seeking talent.*

***IndieHackers**, meanwhile, functions as a vibrant online community for independent entrepreneurs, developers, and makers. It provides forums for discussion, knowledge exchange, and mutual support. Members share their projects, seek collaborators, and connect with potential partners or clients. While IndieHackers does not operate a formal job board or transactional marketplace to the same extent as Dribbble, it facilitates economic opportunity by connecting users with resources, advice, and visibility for their ventures.*

Both platforms perform many of the core functions traditionally associated with professional associations: supporting ongoing learning, enabling peer recognition, facilitating career advancement, and providing mechanisms for members to monetise their expertise. Their decentralised, user-driven models allow for continuous value exchange, with the platforms acting as facilitators and curators rather than central authorities.

For member associations, these models offer a blueprint for the future. By enabling verified member marketplaces, where members can offer freelance services, deliver CPD, provide coaching, or share intellectual property, associations can unlock new revenue streams and dramatically enhance member value. Monetisation can occur through infrastructure fees, premium placements, transaction charges, and value-added services such as reputation curation or analytics. Ultimately, the IndieHackers and Dribbble approach demonstrates how associations can evolve into dynamic, multi-sided platforms that foster learning, collaboration, and economic opportunity in a digital-first world. (Dribbble 2025; IndieHackers 2025).

Matching Models to Context

As associations explore more adaptive and platform-aligned approaches to membership, it's essential to evaluate each model not only for its strategic appeal but also for its operational viability. Table 6-1 compares four emerging membership models across three key dimensions: their strategic strengths, inherent risks or limitations, and the conditions required to implement them effectively. This comparison supports informed decision-making as associations seek to evolve from traditional subscriptions toward more flexible, engagement-centric ecosystems.

Table 6-1 Comparison of Platform-Aligned Membership Models

Model	Strategic Strengths	Risks or Limitations	Enabling Conditions
Tiered	Aligns with career stages; scalable pricing	Can feel hierarchical or exclusive	Clear value differentiation; credential logic
Freemium	Drives reach and lead generation	Low conversion if premium value unclear	Strong UX, onboarding, and content design
Pay-per-Service	Flexibility for members and non-members	Can undermine full membership value	Product quality, seamless purchase flow
Marketplace	Enables member-to-member value creation	Requires trust, moderation, and legal clarity	Platform infrastructure; governance rules

As associations move beyond the limitations of static, one-size-fits-all membership structures, a range of alternative models have emerged to better align with diverse member needs and contemporary engagement behaviours. These models prioritise flexibility, accessibility, and scalable participation, core principles of the Association Platform Success Framework. We explore four adaptive membership models, describing how each works, where it fits best, and offering real-world examples. While no single model suits all contexts, each provides a strategic pathway for transitioning from transactional subscriptions to more dynamic, engagement-led ecosystems.

Table 6-2 Fit of the Membership Models

Model	How It Works	Best For	Example
Tiered Membership	Members choose from different access levels with varying benefits	Associations with diverse audiences (students, professionals, executives)	National Marketing Association (NMA)
Freemium Membership	Free basic access with premium paid tiers for exclusive benefits	Organisations seeking to expand reach while monetising engagement	International Water Resources Association (IWRA)
Pay-Per-Service Model	No annual dues; members pay only for the services they use	Professionals who prefer flexibility over fixed costs	Certifications, event-driven associations
Marketplace Model	Members transact within an ecosystem; the association earns revenue from transactions	Industries with freelancers, consultants, or job-seekers	Job boards, consulting marketplaces

Flexible Membership Model

A flexible membership model moves beyond the rigid constraints of annual subscriptions and fixed-tier structures, allowing associations to offer modular, responsive, and member-centric participation options. Rather than forcing members into one-size-fits-all plans, flexible models are designed to accommodate varied needs, career stages, and engagement preferences, mirroring the personalised, on-demand experiences people now expect across all areas of professional and digital life. These models enable associations to function more like dynamic platforms, facilitating value exchange, enabling peer-to-peer contribution, and adapting in real-time to member behaviours.

The *Data-Driven Insights* pillar of the *Association Platform Success Framework* emphasises the use of real-time engagement analytics, member feedback, and behavioural data to inform strategic decisions. As a core component of APSF, this pillar enables associations to move beyond assumption-based planning and instead design offerings grounded in evidence. By understanding how members interact with services, what they value most, and where participation is lagging, associations can make informed choices about which elements to evolve, expand, or retire.

Applying this approach is essential when transitioning from a traditional subscription-based model to a flexible, platform-aligned membership structure. The process begins with analysing usage patterns, survey responses, and participation data to identify high-impact services and underutilised assets. The following steps outline how associations can implement a flexible membership model using this data-led, member-centric lens.

Associations should analyse engagement patterns, survey responses, and past participation trends to identify high-value services and underutilised benefits. The transition from a traditional subscription model to a dynamic, platform-based approach requires careful planning. Associations should follow a structured process to ensure a smooth transition.

Step 1: Assess Current Member Needs

Before introducing a new membership structure, associations should gather insights on what members truly value. This may include:

- Conducting surveys to understand preferred benefits and pricing flexibility.
- Analysing engagement data to identify underutilised services.
- Reviewing industry trends to benchmark against alternative membership offerings.

Step 2: Design a Membership Framework Aligned with Strategic Goals

A new membership structure should align with the association's broader objectives. Leadership should determine:

- The primary drivers of engagement and revenue.
- How different membership levels or options will be positioned.

- The balance between free and paid offerings to maximise both reach and financial sustainability.

Step 3: Pilot and Test New Models

Before fully implementing a new structure, associations should test different membership options with targeted segments of their audience.

- A soft launch can be introduced to a subset of members to assess interest and refine pricing strategies.
- Engagement and retention metrics should be tracked to identify potential improvements before a full rollout.

Step 4: Communicate and Transition Members

A clear communication strategy is essential to ensure members understand the value of the new model. This may include:

- Outlining the benefits of the new structure through webinars, emails, and personalised outreach.
- Providing transition plans for existing members to migrate to new membership levels.
- Offering incentives for early adopters to encourage uptake.

Example 24. Camplify

Camplify, an Australian peer-to-peer campervan rental platform, enables individuals to share underused personal assets with others seeking flexible travel experiences. Camplify doesn't own the vehicles, it creates the infrastructure for safe, trusted exchange: listings, ratings, insurance, and payments.

The association parallel? Knowledge, tools, leadership, and experience are often unevenly distributed across member networks. Much of it goes underutilised, locked in individual practices or local chapters.

If associations functioned more like Camplify, they would:

- Allow members to contribute expertise (e.g. templates, playbooks, local innovations),
- Enable others to benefit from that value, and
- Build trust infrastructure (e.g. peer review, credit systems, recognition) to manage the exchange.

This analogy helps reframe the association's role: not as the sole provider of programs, but as a facilitator of peer-powered value creation.

Just as Camplify enables unused assets to generate value through structured, peer-to-peer trust systems, associations can unlock latent member capability by redesigning for participation, not just service delivery.

Table 6-3 From Traditional Engagement to Platform Participation

Engagement Dimension	Traditional Association Model	Platform Participation Model (e.g. Camplify Logic)
Value Source	Staff-led programs and centralised expertise	Member-contributed tools, insights, and assets
Participation Role	Passive recipient or appointed volunteer	Active co-producer, peer reviewer, community host
Access to Resources	Gated by role, tenure, or committee structure	Open, modular, searchable contributions across the network
Recognition Mechanism	Titles (e.g. Fellow, Committee Chair)	Dynamic badges, contributor ratings, user feedback
Governance of Quality	Staff review and approval	Peer curation, trust scoring, and transparent contribution logs
Technology Use	Static portals, newsletters, PDF downloads	APIs, searchable platforms, real-time contributions
Network Effect	Limited to event participation or chapter involvement	Value grows as more users contribute and remix shared assets

Example 25. Flexible Membership Model

In response to evolving member needs and industry dynamics, the Australian Marketing Institute (AMI) recognised the necessity to move away from a traditional fixed-tier, annual dues-based membership structure. Engaging in extensive consultations with its diverse membership base, including individual marketers, corporate entities, and educational institutions, AMI sought to understand the varying requirements and preferences of its constituents.

Based on the insights gathered, AMI introduced a range of membership options designed to offer greater flexibility and value:

- ***Professional Memberships**: Catering to individual marketing professionals at different career stages, these memberships provide access to professional development programs, networking opportunities, and industry resources.*
- ***Corporate Learning and Development Memberships**: Tailored for organisations of varying sizes, from small consultancies to multinational corporations, these memberships offer benefits such as discounted training programs, professional indemnity insurance, and access to exclusive events.*

- ***Educational Institution Memberships***: *Designed for universities and other educational bodies, this category includes complimentary individual memberships for students, demonstrating AMI's commitment to fostering the next generation of marketing professionals.*

To further accommodate member preferences, AMI implemented flexible payment options, including monthly recurring payments, allowing members to manage their financial commitments more effectively.

This strategic shift not only enhanced member satisfaction by aligning services with their specific needs but also strengthened AMI's position as a forward-thinking and member-centric organisation within the Australian marketing community. *(Australian Marketing Institute, 2025)*

Example 26. Network Enabler

The Chartered Institute of Personnel and Development (CIPD) in the United Kingdom has undergone a significant transformation, evolving from a traditional, centralised content provider into a distributed, member-driven knowledge network. This shift reflects broader changes in the professional association sector, where digital disruption, member diversity, and rising expectations have prompted a move away from top-down delivery towards participatory, co-created engagement.

Historical Model

Traditionally, CIPD operated much like other legacy associations:

- *Produced research papers and standardised CPD pathways.*
- *Delivered centrally managed conferences and events.*
- *Maintained a top-down approach to content and learning, with staff or consultants developing materials and members participating as passive recipients.*

Key Participation Shifts

CIPD's transformation is characterised by several strategic shifts:

- ***Empowering Local Branches and Special Interest Groups:*** *Local entities now run their own events, discussion forums, and micro-learning opportunities, supported by central resources such as toolkits, templates, and governance protocols.*
- ***Co-Designed Learning Experiences:*** *Practitioners are actively involved in shaping CPD content and delivery, ensuring relevance and practical value.*
- ***Enabling Curated Exchange:*** *CIPD has moved from being a gatekeeper of expertise to an enabler of practitioner-led*

knowledge sharing, deepening engagement and democratising learning across the profession.

Strategic Insight

CIPD's journey demonstrates the power of "participation by design." By aligning governance frameworks, digital tools, and engagement principles, the Institute has unlocked distributed value creation, allowing members to contribute, collaborate, and lead.

Table 6-4 **Shift from Traditional to Platform Participation Model**

Design Element	Traditional Model	Platform Participation Model
Event Delivery	Centrally planned annual conference	Member-led micro-events and peer exchange
Learning Format	Set CPD curriculum	Modular, stackable, user-generated learning
Volunteer Role	Committee nomination, formal pathways	Micro-volunteering, peer mentoring, project-based
Content Development	Staff or consultants	Co-created with practitioner contributions
Feedback Mechanisms	Annual surveys	Real-time feedback loops, data analytics

Table 6-5 **Centralised Delivery vs. Networked Co-Learning**

Design Element	Traditional Learning Delivery	Networked Co-Learning Platform (e.g. CIPD)
Learning Model	Top-down, curriculum-led	Peer-led, modular, and adaptive
Content Ownership	Staff or consultants	Co-created with members and practitioners
Delivery Channels	Events, PDFs, LMS	Live forums, digital hubs, micro-events, threads
Recognition Mechanisms	Attendance certificates, CPD hours	Digital credentials, community validation, feedback
Member Role	Passive learner or attendee	Active co-creator, contributor, mentor
Support Infrastructure	Centrally controlled, compliance	Scaffolded resources for self-organisation
Feedback and Insight	Post-event surveys	Real-time insight loops, community analytics

Design Element	Traditional Learning Delivery	Networked Co-Learning Platform (e.g. CIPD)
Engagement Style	Episodic (event-based)	Continuous (embedded in practice)

Lessons for Associations

CIPD's evolution exemplifies the transition from broadcasting knowledge to enabling participation. The Institute's approach demonstrates that, as member needs and digital capabilities evolve, associations will have to move from static, centralised delivery to dynamic, co-created engagement. This model not only deepens member involvement but also ensures that learning and professional development remain relevant, adaptive, and embedded in everyday professional practice. (26 DX, 2024; Carr, A., 2023; Chartered Institute of Personnel and Development, 2025a, 2025b).

Strategic Insight:

CIPD's transformation illustrates the power of participation by design: governance frameworks, digital tools, and engagement principles deliberately aligned to unlock distributed value creation.

As associations shift from broadcasting knowledge to enabling participation, learning models will have to evolve from static, centralised delivery to dynamic, co-created engagement. CIPD's evolution exemplifies this transition, one that many associations are now poised to undertake.

Measuring ROI: Flexible Membership Models

Associations that successfully deliver high member value, through flexible models and ongoing engagement, experience higher retention, greater event participation, and increased premium upgrades. Freemium members, for example, are not just potential paying members; they represent a pool of engaged professionals who contribute through transactions, sponsorships, and referrals.

Table 6-6 Key Metrics for ROI Evaluation

Metric	What It Measures	Rationale
Conversion Rate	% of free members upgrading to paid tiers	Determines if freemium members see enough value to invest in premium options.
Engagement Rate	Frequency of logins, event participation, and content consumption	Higher engagement correlates with increased likelihood of renewal and upgrades.

Metric	What It Measures	Rationale
Churn Rate	% of members not renewing or downgrading	Identifies retention challenges and areas for improvement.
Average Revenue Per Member (ARPM)	Total membership revenue ÷ total members (including free and paid)	Helps assess whether a freemium model generates sustainable revenue over time.
Lifetime Value of a Member (LTV)	Revenue earned from a member over their lifetime with the association	A higher LTV indicates stronger member retention and recurring revenue potential.

Associations should conduct pilot programs and track these ROI metrics before fully transitioning to a new model. By doing so, they can make data-driven decisions about whether a freemium or tiered membership structure aligns with their long-term sustainability goals.

Table 6-7 ROI Potential: Freemium vs. Traditional Membership Models

Factor	Traditional Model (Fixed Annual Dues)	Freemium/Tiered Model
Barrier to Entry	High (requires upfront payment)	Low (free access attracts broader audience)
Revenue Dependence	Primarily on membership dues	Dues + upsells (events, certifications, sponsorships)
Retention Risk	Higher churn if members feel benefits aren't worth the cost	Lower churn if engagement is sustained through ongoing interaction
Scalability	Limited to those willing to pay upfront	Broader reach with monetisation at multiple levels

Table 6-8 Example Dashboard: Membership ROI Tracker

Metric	Target	Actual	Change	Commentary
Total Membership Revenue	$1.2M	$1.35M	▲ +12.5%	Driven by uptake of premium microlearning add-ons
Non-Dues Revenue (% of total)	30%	42%	▲ +12 pts	Increase from tiered CPD subscriptions
Member Retention Rate	78%	84%	▲ +6 pts	Most gains in <35 age segment
New Members (Q1–Q4)	1,200	1,425	▲ +18.75%	Growth due to monthly and student-friendly pricing

Metric	Target	Actual	Change	Commentary
Cost per New Member Acquisition (CPA)	$85	$62	▼ -27%	Lower costs due to referral-based onboarding
ROI (Net Revenue / Operating Cost)	2.1:1	2.8:1	▲ 33%	Improved cost-efficiency through automation

Note: Dashboard figures are fictional but reflect real-world ROI dimensions tracked by digital-first associations transitioning to platform strategies.

Dashboard: ROI on Flexible Membership Strategy

To move beyond anecdotal feedback and general satisfaction ratings, associations adopting new membership models should monitor ROI using an integrated dashboard that aligns engagement, revenue, and strategic impact. Below is a fictional example of what such a dashboard might look like over a 12-month period following the introduction of a flexible membership model.

Interpretation for Boards and Executives

This type of dashboard supports:

- *Board-level visibility* into ROI drivers
- *Quarterly decision-making* on where to invest further (e.g. onboarding UX, CPD libraries)
- *Narrative development* for funders, sponsors, and impact reporting

This dashboard aligns directly with the *Association Platform Success Framework*, enabling associations to move from *cost-centre logic* to a *value-creation mindset* grounded in measurable outcomes.

Governance Oversight in the Era of Dynamic Membership

As associations shift from static, entitlement-based membership models to dynamic, platform-enabled participation, the role of the board will have to also evolve. These emerging models, from freemium to marketplace, introduce new ethical, strategic, and operational considerations that require active oversight. Boards will have to move beyond reviewing fee schedules and renewal rates, and begin asking deeper questions about pricing fairness, data use in tiering and targeting, and the governance of value exchange between members, contributors, and third parties.

For example:

- How are pricing models aligned with member equity and accessibility goals?
- Are we unintentionally excluding early-career professionals or diverse contributors through monetisation thresholds?

- What safeguards are in place to ensure transparency and trust in marketplace or freemium tiers?
- How are member-contributed value (e.g. peer learning, content, mentoring) recognised or compensated?

These questions underscore the need for strategic governance frameworks that go beyond financial compliance, incorporating digital ethics, inclusive design, and participatory accountability. Later chapters will explore how agile governance, signal-based oversight, and stakeholder-centred policy structures can support this shift.

In short, membership models are no longer just marketing decisions, they are governance matters. And the future relevance of associations will depend on boards that treat them as such.

Example 27. Implementing a Freemium Model

Issue: Membership Accessibility and Engagement Barriers.

IWRA struggled with two key challenges:

- ***Accessibility**: High membership costs excluded early-career professionals and those in developing economics.*
- ***Engagement Decline**: Professionals were increasingly using free industry resources, questioning the value of paid membership.*

The International Water Resources Association (IWRA) faced a membership engagement challenge that is common among global professional associations. While IWRA provided valuable networking, advocacy, and research opportunities, it encountered two key barriers to growth. Limited accessibility for early-career professionals and individuals from lower-income regions: The cost of traditional membership structures restricted participation, particularly in developing economies where financial constraints limited engagement in international associations and declining engagement and retention with prospective who were hesitant to commit financially without first experiencing the value of membership.

Additionally, competition from free online communities and open-access research networks meant professionals were engaging elsewhere.

IWRA needed to restructure its membership model to remove financial barriers, attract a more diverse membership base, and ensure long-term sustainability.

Solution: A Freemium and Tiered Membership Model

IWRA introduced a three-tier membership model for individuals and also introduced Organisational Memberships:

- Silver Partner *($550/year): Small and non-profit organisations receive sub-memberships, access to the IWRA network, and job listing privileges.*
- Gold Partner *($1,500/year): Larger organisations gain visibility, advertising benefits, and sponsorship opportunities.*

Application: How the Model Works in Practice

- Lowering Barriers to Entry*: The Bronze tier allows unlimited free membership, ensuring broad engagement without financial commitment. This enables students, early-career professionals, and individuals in lower-income regions to participate.*
- Encouraging Upgrades*: The Silver and Gold tiers provide increasing levels of access and leadership opportunities, incentivising active members to upgrade.*
- Institutional Partnerships*: The Organisational Membership model provides incentives for universities, NGOs, and industry stakeholders to support IWRA while extending benefits to their staff.*

Conclusion: Positive Impact & Key Takeaways

- *Increased engagement across career stages, from students to senior leaders.*
- *Diversified revenue streams, reducing reliance on dues.*
- *Strengthened IWRA's influence in global water resource management.*

Key Takeaways:

- *Freemium models build trust and engagement before monetisation.*
- *A strong upgrade path ensures financial sustainability.*
- *Organisational partnerships add revenue stability while supporting professional development.*

(IWRA, 2024a, 2024b, 2024c)

Table 6-9 Membership Tiers

Tier	*Pricing*	*Key Benefits*
Bronze (Freemium)	Free	Newsletters, event updates, and limited participation in IWRA's Task Forces and Chapters.
Silver	$65/year	Access to most "members-only" content, voting rights, research publications (Water

Tier	Pricing	Key Benefits
		International), and eligibility for leadership roles.
Gold	$165/year	All Silver benefits + discounts on Congresses/Conferences, invitations to exclusive leadership events, and enhanced networking opportunities.

IWRA's transition to a freemium model demonstrates that lowering barriers to entry expands reach without compromising financial sustainability. By balancing free access with premium upsells and corporate partnerships, IWRA unlocked new revenue streams while maintaining strong member engagement.

Example 28. The Ecosystem Pivot

Claire Evans, CEO of the Professional Network Association (PNA), sat across from her strategy advisor, puzzled by a troubling yet familiar data point: despite a solid renewal rate among existing members, new member acquisition had plateaued. Worse, engagement rates across younger professionals, cross-sector contributors, and adjacent industries remained low, despite growing interest in PNA's public-facing webinars and online thought leadership.

Claire's insight came during a co-hosted virtual roundtable on Sustainable Work and Future Skills. Among the 400 attendees were not only professional members, but also policymakers, HR tech entrepreneurs, career coaches, and data ethicists. These contributors were adding enormous value to the discussion, but they weren't eligible to become PNA members under its existing bylaws. Nor were they actively invited to co-produce or curate knowledge.

With board support, Claire initiated a pilot program called PNA Collaborate, offering a lightweight affiliation model for adjacent stakeholders. Contributors could:

- *Publish insights on PNA's open platform,*
- *Earn verified digital recognition,*
- *Participate in community-designed sprints on workplace transformation.*

Importantly, these contributors were not classified as "members" but as ecosystem participants, each connected to PNA's mission but with different needs and offers.

The result was a shift in posture: PNA no longer saw value only in those who paid dues, but in those who generated momentum. Revenue models followed suit, some collaborators became sponsors or paid contributors; others referred their networks or co-hosted knowledge events.

By opening its platform and modularising its services, PNA:

- *Expanded its influence into adjacent markets,*
- *Deepened engagement with previously "invisible" actors,*
- *And developed a more resilient mission-aligned business model.*

Claire's core realisation: "It's not about growing membership. It's about growing relevance and reach."

Figure 6-1 **PNA's Evolving Value Network**

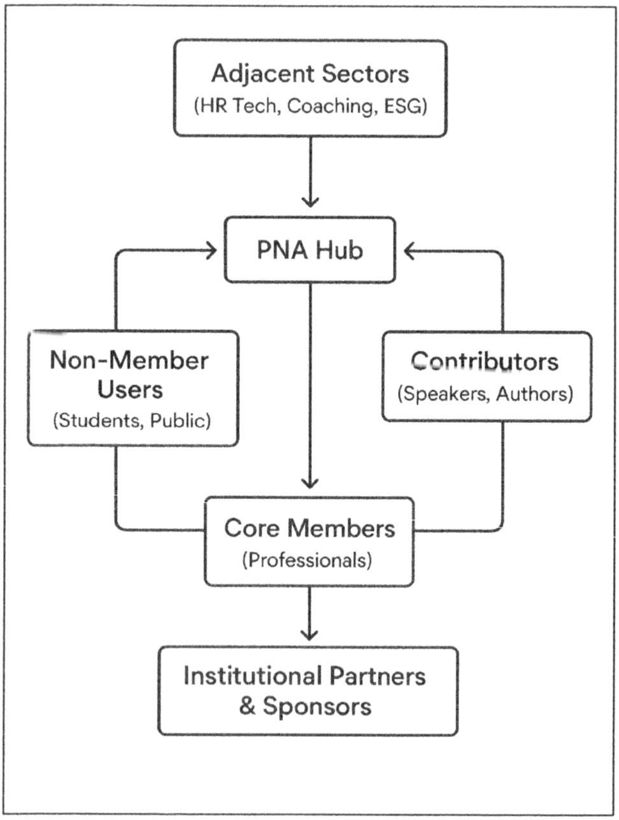

Operationalising a platform-based membership model

To operationalise a platform-based membership model, associations will have to distinguish between different types of participants, not all of whom are formal members.

The following table outlines the core participation nodes within the PNA network case and the typical pathways through which they engage with and contribute to the association.

Table 6-10 Participation Roles in the PNA Value Network

Node	Role in the Network	Participation Pathways
Core Members	PNA's traditional membership base	Access benefits, vote, contribute knowledge
Contributors	Subject matter experts, volunteers, writers, project leads	Co-create content, lead forums, moderate events
Non-Member Users	Individuals who benefit from open access (e.g. students, public)	Learn, attend public events, share resources
Adjacent Sectors	New audiences with aligned interests (e.g. tech, health, ESG)	Join as collaborators or project sponsors
Partners & Sponsors	Employers, funders, institutions	Fund initiatives, co-design programs

Aligning Membership Models to the APSF

Throughout this chapter, we've explored how associations can evolve from static, entitlement-based models to dynamic, platform-enabled membership ecosystems. These shifts are not superficial adjustments, they represent a deeper reimagining of participation, value creation, and organisational purpose.

To support this transformation, the Association Platform Success Framework provides a holistic lens. By aligning flexible membership models to the framework's core goals, pillars, integration pathways, and design principles, associations can ensure that innovation is not only bold, but also strategic, coherent, and sustainable.

The table below summarises how each adaptive membership model aligns with the APSF architecture, offering a blueprint for selecting and refining models that serve your mission, market, and member ecosystem.

APSF-Aligned Membership Models

Core Goals

Goal	Membership Model Contribution
Mutual Value Creation	Freemium, Marketplace, Pay-per-Service → Enable value exchange between members, contributors, and partners

Efficient Resource Allocation	Tiered and Transactional Models → Match service delivery to demand and willingness to pay
Sustainable Impact	Hybrid/Flexible Models → Encourage long-term engagement and diverse participation

Core Pillars

Pillar	Aligned Membership Model
Courage	Transitioning from legacy dues to dynamic models like marketplace or freemium
Trust & Security	Marketplace models (with clear governance), contributor roles
Innovation	Modular, role-based models; member-as-contributor logic
Data Driven Insight	Tiered, flexible, and freemium models optimised via engagement analytics

Integration Pathways

Pathway	Enabling Practice in Membership Models
Personalisation	Role-based access, dynamic pricing tiers, adaptive value delivery
Collaboration	Contributor roles, peer-to-peer services, co-created learning
Trust Building	Transparent recognition systems, verified contributor status

Design Pillars

Pillar	Membership Model Design Implications
Member-Centric Design	Members choose their path, by career stage, contribution type, or need
Scalable Digital Infrastructure	APIs, analytics, CRM integration for freemium and marketplace models
Governance & Trust	Ethical participation design, contributor policies, dispute resolution systems

As we move into the next chapter, we turn to the enabling conditions that will have to surround these models, monetisation, governance frameworks, digital infrastructure, trust systems, and agile leadership, that bring platform-based membership to life. The next chapter explores how the membership model itself will have to be reimagined to support this shift - moving from a transactional dues framework to a dynamic, multi-sided value relationship.

Chapter 7. Platform-Enhanced Business Model Canvas for Associations

Many associations jump straight to revenue without clearly articulating *how* value is created, *by whom*, and *under what governance conditions*. This often leads to monetisation misfires, models that either underperform commercially, damage trust, or erode long-term engagement.

The Platform-Enhanced Business Model Canvas is adapted for the association context. It replaces single-sided logic with a multi-actor, trust-aware, and governance-aligned framework for designing association platforms.

Table 7-1 Business Model Alignment Canvas

Canvas Area	Modified Focus	Strategic Prompt
Participant Segments	Multi-sided actors	Who are the key groups engaging with our platform (e.g. members, partners, employers, learners)?
Value Propositions	Multi-actor value	What value does each participant group receive or create? How does this value emerge?
Participation Pathways	Interaction channels	How do participants connect, contribute, and access value (e.g. portal, events, forums, co-design groups)?
Relationships & Trust	Trust, reciprocity, transparency	How do we build credibility, ethical governance, and engagement across diverse actors?
Revenue Streams	Actor-specific monetisation	How is revenue generated from or through each actor group? Is it direct, indirect, or blended?
Key Contributions	From members and partners	What do participants contribute (e.g. content, data, facilitation, reputation)? How is this supported and recognised?
Key Resources	Platform + relational infrastructure	What capabilities (tech, data, staff, systems) are required to support interactions and value creation?
Key Partnerships	Ecosystem and enablers	Who do we partner with to expand our impact (e.g. EdTech, government, industry, funders)?
Cost Structure	Operational, relational, governance	What are the core costs? Which costs are fixed vs variable? Where does governance effort sit?
Governance & Ethics	Oversight, inclusion, safeguards	How is the platform governed? Who has voice and decision rights? How is data used and protected?

Canvas Area	Modified Focus	Strategic Prompt
Risk & Reputational Zones (New)	Potential friction points	What parts of the model could backfire (e.g. paywalls, data use, partner alignment)? What safeguards are in place?

Table 7-2 Worked Example: PNA's CPD and Career Services Platform

Canvas Area	Example from PNA
Participant Segments	Early-career professionals, experienced members, mentors, employers, CPD partners
Value Propositions	Members gain CPD, networking, and career pathways; partners access a skills-aligned audience; mentors gain recognition and leadership exposure
Participation Pathways	Member portal with CPD dashboard, peer-learning circles, mentoring forums, job board
Relationships & Trust	Transparent recognition of contributions; open member feedback loop; consent-based data use
Revenue Streams	Premium membership tiers; micro-credential fees; employer partnerships, CPD partner licensing
Key Contributions	Members contribute lived experience (e.g. case studies), co-lead webinars, participate in peer-review
Key Resources	Modular LMS, CRM-integrated member portal, CPD credentialing framework, facilitation staff
Key Partnerships	Universities (micro-credential co-design), tech providers (platform stack), employers (job placement)
Cost Structure	Platform licensing, content development, governance costs (e.g. ethics review panel), staff time for moderation and support
Governance & Ethics	Board-approved Monetisation Charter; co-designed CPD standards; member advisory panel on pricing
Risk & Reputational Zones	Paywall backlash if essential CPD is locked; data use concerns; partner credibility risks, all mitigated by phased piloting and ethical review processes

How to Use This Canvas

- **Board Strategy Workshops**: Use this as a boardroom tool to map current vs proposed business models.
- **Revenue Planning**: Align proposed monetisation strategies with participant value and trust dynamics.
- **Governance Oversight**: Spot friction points and pre-empt reputational risks.
- **Pilot Design**: Choose one actor group and co-design with them first before scaling.

Chapter 8. Monetising the Platform Business Model

Example 29. The Revenue Pivot

Claire Evans, CEO of the Professional Network Association (PNA), faced a harsh reality, membership renewals had stalled, sponsorships were unpredictable, and expenses were rising. At the last finance committee meeting, Michael Chan, the Committee Chair, was blunt:

"Membership alone isn't going to sustain us anymore. We need to start thinking like a business, not just a professional body."

PNA's revenue model, built on membership dues, was failing. Younger professionals accessed free networking and training online, while sponsors demanded clearer ROI. The old approach was no longer enough.

That night, Claire mapped out PNA's untapped opportunities:

- ***Employers** needing a skilled talent pipeline.*
- ***Industry partners** seeking meaningful connections with professionals.*
- ***Members** willing to pay for premium, personalised experiences.*

The next morning, she gathered her executive team.

"What if we stopped thinking of ourselves as a membership club and started acting like a professional marketplace? Instead of just collecting dues, we build a platform where members, businesses, and industry partners transact, learn, and engage."

Her team knew this would be the biggest shift in PNA's history, but also its greatest opportunity.

Monetisation is one of the most misunderstood, and mismanaged, areas of association strategy. Too often, it is treated as a bolt-on activity, a pricing exercise or fundraising campaign rather than a system-wide design challenge. In a platform-based association, however, monetisation is deeply entangled with how value is created, who participates in the ecosystem, and which capabilities are embedded across the organisation.

This chapter reframes monetisation as a core design function. It explores how associations can generate sustainable, diversified revenue by creating valuable experiences, orchestrating multi-sided marketplaces, and enabling contributors, not just extracting fees from members. The goal is not to commercialise everything, but to monetise meaningfully, in ways that reinforce trust, extend mission impact, and reward participation.

This chapter will not only provide tools and frameworks but also build toward a fully worked example of how an association can craft a monetisation plan from strategy to execution.

Understanding Business Model Archetypes Before Monetising

Before designing new revenue streams, associations will have to first understand the economic engine they are operating. Monetisation is not a standalone act, it is the downstream expression of a business model. Without clarity on how value is created and exchanged, attempts to generate income risk being misaligned, ineffective, or even damaging to trust.

This section outlines four common business model archetypes in the association sector, and the implications of each for monetisation, engagement, and governance.

Table 8-1 Business Model Archetypes in the Association Landscape

Model Type	Value Logic	Monetisation Strategy	Risks / Considerations
Service Provider	Deliver defined programs to members	Fee-for-service, event income	Low scalability; easily commoditised
Subscription-Based	Membership bundles access to core services	Flat dues, limited tiers	Attrition risk if perceived value drops
Participation Platform	Enable value creation through interaction	Tiered services, data, sponsorship	High governance complexity, requires trust
Ecosystem Hub	Orchestrate multi-actor value at scale	Outcome-based, shared revenue, grants	Strategic alignment and ethical risk management

Choosing the Right Frame

Each model represents a different theory of value. A service-provider model assumes members are consumers. A subscription model assumes they value bundled access. A platform model assumes members want to participate, contribute, and co-create. An ecosystem model assumes value lies in network outcomes, not just transactions.

Before monetising, boards and executives should ask:

- *What kind of value do we enable, and for whom?*
- *Are we monetising access, interaction, or outcomes?*
- *Is our business model fit for the revenue models we are pursuing?*

Strategic Fit and Governance Implications

Monetisation without model alignment creates friction. For example:

- A platform-style monetisation approach (such as tiered CPD credits or data services) will struggle in a legacy service model where interaction isn't designed in.
- Ecosystem-level partnerships demand shared governance frameworks, not just contracts.
- Member contributions will have to be acknowledged and protected, otherwise monetisation can erode trust and participation.

The association's governance model will have to also evolve to match the business logic. Participation models require participatory governance. Ecosystem strategies demand adaptive oversight and cross-sector intelligence.

Tools to Support Business Model-Monetisation Fit

Several tools in this playbook and the companion *Economics of Modern Associations* can support this alignment:

- **Platform Revenue Model Matrix**: Maps revenue logic across direct vs indirect and association- vs member-generated value.
- **Monetisation Decision Matrix**: Evaluates ideas against criteria such as member impact, scalability, trust, and technical readiness.
- **ROPI (Return on Platform Investment) Framework**: Shifts financial analysis from traditional ROI to a platform-specific lens that captures alignment, engagement, and enablement outcomes.

Business models are not just about money, they are about meaning. They shape how members engage, how decisions are made, and how trust is earned. Getting the business model right is not a prerequisite to monetisation, it is its foundation.

Monetisation Through the APSF Lens

Monetisation in platform-based associations should not be seen as a bolt-on commercial function, but as a natural output of value orchestration. The *Association Platform Success Framework* provides the foundation for this. When implemented effectively, several key APSF pillars enable responsible, scalable, and member-aligned revenue generation.

The table below maps core APSF pillars to specific monetisation strategies, showing how each element supports long-term value capture through models such as freemium tiers, digital products, marketplaces, and affiliate services.

Table 8-2 APSF Pillars for Monetisation

APSF Pillar	Relevance to Monetisation
Scalable Digital Infrastructure	Enables delivery of revenue-generating services (e.g. learning platforms, job boards, data exchanges) at low marginal cost.
Governance & Trust	Legitimises monetisation models through transparency, ethical design, and reciprocal value exchange.
Data-Driven Insight	Unlocks revenue through segmentation, predictive analytics, and the curation of high-value products and services.
Member-Centric Design	Supports modular product structures, tiering strategies, and experience bundles aligned with user willingness-to-pay.
Personalisation (Integration Pathway)	Enables tailored recommendations, dynamic pricing models, and adaptive service access based on engagement signals.

Strategic Takeaway

These pillars form the operating conditions under which monetisation can be responsibly and strategically pursued. They also create the platform infrastructure for long-term value capture, through both traditional and emerging mechanisms, marketplace orchestration, content syndication, dynamic subscriptions, and data-informed product development.

Rethinking Revenue in a Platform Context

For decades, associations have relied on a relatively fixed portfolio of revenue streams: membership dues, event registrations, sponsorship packages, and perhaps a publication or training program. These models were grounded in a one-way value exchange - the association produced, the member consumed, and revenue was tied to access or attendance.

A platform model changes the logic of value creation.

In a platform-based association, value is no longer solely created by the organisation, it is co-created with and between members, partners, and external stakeholders. Members are not just recipients of services; they are contributors, collaborators, and in some cases, product owners. As a result, monetisation will have to move beyond selling access or content. It will have to capture value from interactions, reputation, contribution, and network effects.

This reframing requires boards and executives to ask what types of value are being created within our platform? Who is generating that value - and who benefits from it? What monetisation mechanisms are consistent with our purpose, trust obligations, and member expectations?

Rather than seeking a single "right" model, platform associations will have to evaluate multiple revenue strategies, sometimes concurrently, that reflect the diversity of interactions occurring across the ecosystem.

The Platform Revenue Model Matrix

To support this re-evaluation, the Platform Revenue Model Matrix provides a simple yet powerful framework for mapping monetisation approaches based on two key dimensions:

- **Value Origin**: Who is generating the value that can be monetised - the association or the members?
- **Monetisation Mode**: Is the value monetised directly (through payments, subscriptions, or transaction fees) or indirectly (through third-party sponsorships, partnerships, or data insights)?

Table 8-3 Platform Revenue Model Matrix

	Direct Monetisation	**Indirect Monetisation**
Association-Generated	CPD subscriptions Tiered memberships Digital event tickets	Institutional grants Corporate sponsorships Branded content partnerships
Member-Generated	Marketplace commissions Premium community access Micro-credential sales	Ad revenue from member-generated content Data licensing Affinity partnerships

This model allows boards to compare not just how money flows into the organisation, but also who is driving the underlying activity being monetised - and what that means for governance, risk, and member trust.

Strategic Takeaways:

- Association-generated/direct models offer high control but may have limited scalability without major investment.
- Member-generated/indirect models may be highly scalable but carry ethical and reputational risks if poorly governed.
- Blended models are not only common, but they are also often necessary to balance reliability, growth, and alignment with purpose.

This matrix also prompts a deeper governance question: "If members are helping to generate value, should they also share in the benefits - through influence, rewards, or reinvestment?"

Example 30. Broadening the Concept of "Member"

Smart Precinct NQ (SPNQ), based in Townsville, Queensland, Australia, demonstrates how associations and ecosystem actors can unlock new value by redefining their core community. Although not a traditional membership organisation, SPNQ operates as a platform for entrepreneurs, small businesses, researchers, and mentors. By providing programs, pitch events, co-working space, and capability-building activities, it facilitates high-value interactions between loosely connected actors.

SPNQ's approach challenges the idea that only paying members count. Value is created through the density and productivity of relationships across the ecosystem. Some contributors receive support, others provide funding or in-kind expertise, but all participate in the broader mission of regional economic development.

Strategic Insight: *SPNQ's model highlights the opportunity for associations to grow relevance and impact by shifting from "membership" to "ecosystem participation" as the primary unit of engagement.*

In the next section, we introduce a practical decision matrix to evaluate the suitability, scalability, and risks of each monetisation path.

Business Model Patterns in Association Monetisation

No single revenue model fits all associations - nor should it. As associations evolve into platform-based ecosystems, they require a **portfolio approach** to monetisation that reflects how value is created and exchanged across their networks.

This section introduces a set of practical business model patterns that align with the strategic realities of modern associations. These models differ in how they monetise value, who participates in generating that value, and what infrastructure or governance is required to support them. Most successful platform associations adopt a hybrid approach, blending two or more of these models to reduce dependency, expand impact, and scale sustainability.

Table 8-4 Business Models for Monetising

Business Model	Key Features	Monetisation Pathways	APSF Pillars Activated
Membership-Based Model	Traditional dues model with access-based tiers	Annual fees, tiered access, member benefits	Trust, Participation
Freemium Model	Free baseline access + premium paid features	Paid CPD, events, content subscriptions	Participation, Modular Design

Business Model	Key Features	Monetisation Pathways	APSF Pillars Activated
Transaction-Based Model	Members pay per service or interaction	Job listings, micro-credentialing, pay-per-course	Modular Design, Insight
Sponsorship/ Partnership	Corporate or sector partners fund engagement activities	Sponsored content, events, branded resources	Ecosystem Leverage, Trust Infrastructure
Digital Content Model	Monetising exclusive learning or research outputs	Online courses, whitepapers, learning bundles	Insight, Participation, Modular Design
Marketplace Model	Platform facilitates transactions between participants	Consulting services, listings, peer learning	Participation, Trust, Modular Design
Platform Ecosystem Model	Members, partners, and third parties co-create and exchange value	Third-party commissions, data licensing, collaboration fees	Ecosystem Leverage, Insight, Participation

Choosing the Right Model

Each model presents different trade-offs:

- **Membership-Based and Freemium Models** work best when there is strong demand for curated, high-trust knowledge and networking.
- **Transaction and Marketplace Models** suit associations enabling active peer-to-peer or professional services engagement.
- **Sponsorship and Content Models** are most effective where the association represents a clearly defined audience that is valuable to partners or advertisers.
- **Platform Ecosystem Models** are appropriate for mature associations that want to enable interactions and value creation across multiple stakeholder types - including members, vendors, and sector partners.

Associations do not need to choose one model - they need to choose the *right combination* for their purpose, membership profile, and digital capability.

The next section presents a decision matrix to help leaders assess which monetisation approaches best align with their strategic intent, member value proposition, and operational readiness.

Example 31. Monetising Member-Generated Value

Rather than producing all learning content internally, our learning example, PNA accredits experienced members and industry partners to develop and deliver workshops, online modules, and webinars. These offerings are hosted on PNA's central learning platform, with revenue shared between the presenter and the association. In effect, PNA acts as a trusted marketplace facilitator, curating quality, ensuring consistency, and generating income through:

- *Revenue share from member-delivered CPD*
- *Commission fees on partner-delivered content*
- *Tiered access pricing for different membership levels*

This approach expands PNA's CPD catalogue rapidly, encourages peer-led learning, and strengthens the value proposition for members who want to teach, earn, or build profile.

"Our members are not just consumers of education, they are contributors and collaborators. That shift has added both depth to our CPD and strength to our business model.": PNA CPD Program Lead

Strategic Insight: PNA's approach demonstrates how member-generated value can be monetised ethically and sustainably, transforming engagement into shared benefit and platform-enabled recognition.

This case illustrates the Marketplace and Content-as-a-Service revenue models in action and demonstrates how associations can unlock latent member value while building financial resilience.

Matching Monetisation Models to Association Types

Not all associations are positioned to implement every monetisation model with equal success. The right business model depends on the association's stage of maturity, member behaviour, digital capability, and strategic posture within its sector.

This section provides a practical typology to guide associations in selecting monetisation approaches that best fit their structure and strategic intent. It does not prescribe a single model - rather, it enables board and executive teams to match monetisation strategies to their operating reality, while identifying opportunities to diversify over time.

Table 8-5 Matching Monetisation Approaches to Association Types

Association Type	Best-Fit Monetisation Approach	Primary Revenue Drivers
Large, Established Professional Body	Sponsorship + Premium Content	Corporate partnerships, executive education, gated research
Emerging or Growth-Stage Association	Freemium + Pay-per-Service	Entry-level content access, paid CPD, career services
High-Engagement Niche Association	Subscription-Based Model	Tiered membership, expert forums, curated resources

Association Type	Best-Fit Monetisation Approach	Primary Revenue Drivers
Community-Led or Peer Network	Marketplace + Transaction-Based Model	Member-led services, coaching marketplaces, listings
Cross-Sector Federation or Umbrella Group	Platform Ecosystem Model	Licensing, third-party integrations, cross-sector value exchange
Cause-Based or Advocacy Organisation	Partnership + Grants	Sponsored research, advocacy campaigns, philanthropic funding

Example 32. Examples of Models

CPA Australia: *Tiered, access-based membership and static CPD pricing.*

Engineers Australia: *Modular CPD, stackable credentials, member-led content contributions.*

Governance Insight: *One optimises for stability, the other for participation and scale.*

Strategic Factors to Consider

Choosing the right monetisation model isn't simply a financial decision, it's a strategic design choice that will have to align with an association's purpose, infrastructure, and community dynamics. As associations diversify revenue streams and explore platform-based models, it becomes critical to evaluate internal readiness, member expectations, and market positioning. The following factors provide a decision-making lens to help boards and executives assess which monetisation approaches best fit their current state - and where investment may be needed to support future readiness.

- **Member Expectations**: What are members willing to pay for? What do they expect to be free, subsidised, or sponsored?
- **Digital Infrastructure**: Is the association technically equipped to support personalised access, transactions, or third-party integrations?
- **Market Position**: Does the association hold influence that attracts partners, funders, or sponsors?
- **Engagement Model**: Are members primarily content consumers, co-creators, or contributors in a broader ecosystem?
- **Risk Tolerance and Governance Maturity**: What level of commercial activity can the association ethically and operationally manage?

Moving Toward a Hybrid Model

In practice, most associations will find that no single monetisation model can serve all purposes or member segments. The diversity of member needs, partner opportunities, and strategic priorities often calls for a blended approach. Hybrid models allow associations to balance predictability with growth, and accessibility with sustainability - all while staying aligned to their core mission. The following examples illustrate how different combinations can be tailored to suit an organisation's strategic posture, infrastructure, and stakeholder expectations; A professional body may combine tiered subscriptions with sponsorship of executive learning; A peer-led association may offer free access and monetise career services or peer review programs; A cross-industry alliance may monetise data insights while offering core services freely.

The goal is not to "monetise everything", it is to design a revenue model that reinforces trust, supports strategy, and reflects the association's unique role in its ecosystem.

In the next section, we explore the principles of value-first monetisation, ensuring that every revenue decision enhances member experience and long-term sustainability.

Example 33. Freemium Membership for Growth

The Challenge

The Association of the United States Army (AUSA), a major professional body supporting soldiers, families, and supporters of the US Army, faced the challenge of expanding its reach and relevance in a changing environment. Traditional paid membership models limited access, particularly for early-career professionals, families, and those hesitant to commit financially without first experiencing the association's value. As with many global associations, AUSA needed to lower barriers to engagement and demonstrate value to a broader audience while maintaining a sustainable business model.

The Solution*: AUSA's Freemium Membership Model*

AUSA introduced a two-tiered membership structure:

Basic (Free) Membership:

- *Open to anyone interested in supporting or learning about the US Army.*
- *Provides complimentary access to:*
- *AUSA events and professional networks*
- *Podcasts, newsletters, and advocacy campaigns*
- *Job boards, discounts, and family programs*
- *Chapter affiliation and community engagement opportunities*

- *Designed to allow prospective members to experience the association's value at no cost, increasing inclusivity and reach.*

Premium (Paid) Membership:

Includes all Basic benefits, plus:

- *Subscription to ARMY magazine*
- *Discounted event registration and tickets*
- *Access to digital publication archives*
- *Eligibility for scholarships and special programs*
- *Free legal document services and additional exclusive resources*
- *Premium members underwrite core governance and access high-value services, sustaining the association's operations.*

Impact and Outcomes

- ***Broader Engagement:*** *The free Basic Membership tier significantly increased new registrations and event participation, especially among younger professionals, families, and those previously unengaged with AUSA.*
- ***Diversity and Reach:*** *The model enabled greater diversity in regional and demographic participation, strengthening AUSA's role as a national voice and community hub.*
- ***Sustainable Growth:*** *Premium memberships, supported by the vibrancy of the free tier, continued to fund core activities and exclusive offerings, ensuring financial sustainability and ongoing value for committed members.*
- ***Enhanced Legitimacy:*** *By opening its doors to a wider audience, AUSA increased its influence, advocacy impact, and ability to form new partnerships, mirroring the legitimacy gains seen in the IWRA case above.*

Key Takeaways

- ***Freemium models can drive both reach and resilience*** *for professional associations, especially when aligned with mission-driven values and a clear upgrade path.*
- ***Free tiers build trust and engagement*** *before monetisation, while premium tiers sustain core operations and exclusive benefits.*
- ***Inclusivity and accessibility*** *are enhanced, supporting greater diversity and legitimacy in the association's field.*

Table 8-6 AUSA Freemium Membership Structure

Tier	Cost	Key Benefits	Target Audience
Basic	Free	Events, networks, newsletters, discounts, job board	Prospective members, families, early-career, supporters
Premium	Paid	All Basic benefits plus magazine, discounts, scholarships, legal services	Committed professionals, leaders, long-term supporters

Value-First Monetisation Framework

A common pitfall in monetisation strategy is starting with revenue targets and working backwards. In a platform-based association, this approach risks undermining member trust and long-term value creation. Instead, associations should adopt a value-first monetisation mindset - asking not “What can we sell?” but “What value are we enabling, and how might that value be monetised ethically and sustainably?”

This mindset reframes monetisation as an extension of the association’s mission and platform engagement strategy.

Three Principles of Value-First Monetisation

In platform-based associations, sustainable monetisation will have to begin with member value - not revenue targets. A value-first approach ensures that pricing, access, and commercial partnerships are aligned with trust, equity, and impact. Rather than monetising everything that moves, value-first monetisation focuses on enabling broad engagement while creating clear, ethical pathways to revenue. The following three principles provide a foundation for designing models that are both financially viable and strategically aligned with member outcomes:

1. **Deliver Core Value for Free** - Ensure members can access essential knowledge, networking, and community benefits without financial friction. This builds engagement, loyalty, and inclusion - especially for emerging professionals.
2. **Monetise Transformational Experiences** - Charge for premium experiences that offer significant professional impact - such as certifications, mentoring, deep learning, or exposure to influential networks.
3. **Align Revenue with Member Success** - Monetisation should track with value delivered. Members should feel they are paying for outcomes - such as career advancement, recognition, or business growth - not access or obligation.

Applying the Framework

Use this framework to evaluate existing and proposed revenue streams:

- Does this offering support or enhance a core member journey?
- Is the pricing proportional to the value created?
- Are we offering alternatives for members unable to pay?
- Does this model strengthen - not strain - member trust?

By placing value at the centre of monetisation strategy, associations can avoid commodifying services and instead foster a more sustainable, member-aligned revenue portfolio.

Example 34. Trust and Scale in Professional Learning

The Australian Psychological Society (APS) provides a compelling example of how a large professional body can scale monetisation of member-relevant services, while navigating the ethical obligations of a trust-based profession.

Recognising shifts in how psychologists access, consume, and value professional learning, APS restructured its CPD offerings to enable:

- *Members to access a broad catalogue of paid and free learning resources;*
- *Accredited partners and recognised experts to publish their own workshops and modules on the platform with APS endorsement;*
- *Flexible pricing models that supported both early-career and established professionals.*

This platform-enabled approach created clear monetisation pathways, including:

- *APS approved partner-provided CPD;*
- *Tiered pricing for premium content;*

However, APS was careful not to treat CPD as a commercial commodity. It maintained high ethical standards by:

- *Vetting all third-party content for psychological safety and scientific validity;*
- *Involving members in co-designing evaluation criteria;*

***Strategic Takeaways**:*

APS shows how associations can scale CPD through platform models without eroding trust, provided governance, transparency, and member participation are built into the design. The success of their marketplace also highlights the value of member-contributed services that align with professional standards. (Australian Psychological Society, 2025).

This case embodies the *Marketplace and Content-as-a-Service* models described in this chapter, and reinforces the APSF principles of trust infrastructure, participation, and modular delivery.

Example 35. Monetisation Decision Matrix

At the quarterly strategy meeting of the Professional Network Association (PNA), CEO Claire Evans presented three potential revenue streams for consideration as part of their platform transition:

- *Premium Job Board Access for Recruiters*
- *Corporate Sponsorship of CPD Webinars*
- *Member Data Analytics for Partner Insights*

Using the Monetisation Decision Matrix, the board and executive team assessed each option against the five governance lenses in Table 8-7

After structured discussion, the board endorsed the premium job board and a pilot CPD sponsorship model with clear content standards. The third option, selling anonymised data, was ruled out pending development of a stronger ethical and governance framework.

The decision reinforced APSF's emphasis on revenue as design, not just dollars, but alignment, legitimacy, and impact.

Table 8-7 Application of the Monetisation Decision Matrix

Governance Lens	Job Board	CPD Sponsorship	Member Data Sales
Strategic Alignment	Strong fit: supports career pathways	Moderate: depends on sponsor alignment	Weak: mission drift risk
Member Value Creation	High: improves visibility and access	Medium: quality varies with sponsors	Low: value not clear to members
Reputation & Trust	Neutral to positive	Mixed: needs vetting & transparency	High risk: potential backlash
Revenue Potential	Moderate to high	High if scaled	High: but reputationally sensitive
Execution Complexity	Low: job board already exists	Medium: requires sales and moderation	High: legal, privacy, comms overhead

Governance and Ethics in Monetisation

In the platform era, monetisation is no longer a straightforward pricing question, it is a governance challenge. Decisions about *how* to monetise, *who* benefits, and *what is traded* (data, attention, participation, insight) will have to be made transparently and strategically. Revenue innovation, if pursued carelessly, can erode member trust and damage the platform's legitimacy. In this context, ethics and trust are not constraints, they are enablers of durable commercialisation.

Rather than applying a blanket 'yes' or 'no' to new revenue models, associations should assess monetisation opportunities using a tiered set of ethical and strategic filters. The table below condenses the principles discussed earlier and provides a practical decision tool for boards and executives:

Table 8-8 Strategic and Ethical Filters for Monetisation

Test	Key Question	Description	Alignment
Mission Fit Test	Does this model advance our core purpose?	Avoid mission-drift by ensuring alignment with member needs and organisational identity.	APSF Pillar 1: Mission-Driven Value
Trust & Transparency Test	Would members be surprised, alienated, or uncomfortable if they knew how we monetised this?	Ensures informed consent, data transparency, and clarity on revenue-sharing.	APSF Pillar 2: Governance & Trust
Reciprocity Test	Does the member receive fair value in exchange?	Guards against extractive or exploitative models by emphasising value parity.	APSF Pillar 3: Ecosystem Engagement
Digital Stewardship Test	Are we using data and AI responsibly and securely?	Assesses ethical data use, third-party partnerships, and AI model explainability.	APSF Pillar 4: Data & Infrastructure
Resilience Test	Does this model create long-term value or dependence?	Encourages sustainable, diversified revenue planning and risk awareness.	APSF Pillar 5: Strategic Agility

This diagnostic can be applied to any monetisation idea, from paid subscriptions and tiered CPD products to data partnerships and affiliate revenue. By embedding these filters into board deliberations and commercial planning processes, associations can systematically evaluate new ideas without defaulting to outdated heuristics (e.g. "members won't pay", "grants are safer", etc.).

Associations that take the time to build and protect monetisation legitimacy gain more than revenue. They create an ecosystem where contributors, partners, and members participate willingly, because the value exchange is transparent, strategic, and grounded in shared purpose.

Example 36. Data Monetisation Misstep

In 2020, the Royal Dutch Lawn Tennis Association (KNLTB) sold personal data of 350,000 members to two sponsors for direct marketing purposes, resulting in a €525,000 fine from the Dutch Data Protection Authority (AP). The KNLTB's actions were deemed a violation of privacy regulations, as the commercial interest did not justify the infringement on members' privacy rights. This incident underscores the critical importance for associations to align monetisation strategies with ethical data practices and member expectations to maintain trust and compliance. (European Data Protection Board, 2020).

Building a Multi-Revenue Model

Thriving in a platform environment requires associations to move beyond dependence on a single income stream - particularly legacy reliance on membership dues. A future-ready revenue model is adaptive, diversified, and aligned with how value is created and exchanged across the association's ecosystem. This doesn't mean launching every monetisation idea at once. Instead, it means designing a revenue portfolio that reflects the organisation's strategic posture, member behaviours, and market leverage. The following steps outline a practical pathway for building a multi-revenue strategy that is scalable, ethical, and aligned with the *Association Platform Success Framework*.

Five Steps to a Multi-Revenue Strategy

1. **Audit Existing Revenue Streams** - Identify risks, over-reliance, and under-monetised assets (e.g. trusted brand, community expertise).
2. **Identify Monetisation Opportunities** - Map potential new models against the APSF: Where does member engagement, data, or partner demand create scalable value?
3. **Pilot High-Potential Streams** - Start with low-risk, high-value initiatives - such as professional development courses, job boards, or sponsored research hubs.
4. **Build the Enablers** - Ensure legal structures, financial governance, and insurance coverage are in place to support commercial risk management.
5. **Measure, Learn, and Iterate** - Monitor revenue performance, engagement impacts, and reputational effects. Adjust pricing, access, and messaging in real time.

Table 8-9 Common Hybrid Models

Model Combination	Description
Freemium + CPD Marketplace	Open access + paid learning content or micro-credentials
Subscription + Sponsored Content	Tiered membership access + partner-funded research or media
Community Platform + Job Board	Free peer network + paid career services
Licensing + Data Insights	Content created by members + anonymised insights for third parties

Associations should aim for a revenue portfolio that balances predictability (subscriptions), scale (sponsorship), and flexibility (transactional services).

Spin-Outs and Strategic Ventures

As associations mature their platform strategy, some may find themselves sitting on underutilised assets, capabilities, data, infrastructure, or intellectual property (IP), that can be commercialised beyond the bounds of traditional membership. These spin-out opportunities allow associations to create adjacent revenue streams, often with broader market appeal, while protecting the integrity of the core mission.

Spin-outs are not side hustles, they are deliberately structured commercial ventures, usually managed under separate governance or through subsidiary entities. They enable associations to:

- **Enter new markets** (e.g., industry-wide services, sector education platforms)
- **Build equity-generating businesses** from grant-funded pilots or high-performing programs
- **Licence proprietary tools or data products**
- **Partner with venture collaborators**, corporates, or startups without compromising not-for-profit status

Table 8-10 Spin-Out Structures

Spin-Out Type	Description	Example Application
Commercial Subsidiary	A fully owned, profit-generating arm	Online learning platform or job board
Licensing Model	IP used by third parties for a fee	Data tools, diagnostics, or standards
JV/Partnership Venture	A shared venture with external stakeholders	Co-branded credential or insights platform
Foundation-Owned Entity	Used where philanthropic control is desired	Social enterprise or impact vehicle

Example 37. Data or Diagnostic IP as a Spin-Out Asset

An association that develops a successful governance toolkit, workforce benchmarking platform, or AI-based CPD planner could license it to other organisations, creating ongoing royalty or fee-for-service income. Alternatively, it could spin the asset into a jointly governed digital venture in partnership with a university or EdTech firm.

Governance and Risk Considerations

Spin-outs require careful planning. Boards will have to:

- *Ensure mission alignment and brand integrity*
- *Ringfence risk exposure, especially legal, financial, or reputational*
- *Establish clear oversight frameworks, including separate reporting, conflict-of-interest protocols, and return-to-purpose mechanisms*

Consider equity-sharing models that benefit both the commercial arm and the broader association community

Strategic Insight: *Spin-outs work best when they emerge from validated core activity, serve a market need, and reinforce the association's role as a sector enabler and knowledge broker.*

Example 38. Benchmarking Platform Spin-Out

The Royal Australasian College of Surgeons (RACS) provides a strong real-world example of an association developing and commercialising a digital asset, its Morbidity Audit and Logbook Tool (MALT). Originally created as an internal benchmarking and quality improvement platform for surgical training and professional development, MALT has evolved into a sophisticated data and diagnostic tool with sector-wide impact.

The Spin-Out and Commercialisation Process

- ***Asset Development:*** *RACS invested in building MALT as a secure, cloud-based platform for recording, auditing, and benchmarking surgical procedures and outcomes. The tool supports both individual CPD and system-wide quality assurance.*
- ***External Licensing and Partnerships:*** *Recognising the broader value of MALT, RACS began licensing the platform to other medical colleges, hospitals, and health networks across Australia and New Zealand. This created a new, ongoing revenue stream through licensing fees and service contracts.*

- ***Collaborative Ventures:*** *RACS has partnered with universities and health technology firms to further develop and adapt the platform for research, education, and workforce planning. These partnerships have included co-governance arrangements, shared IP, and joint ventures to expand the platform's reach and functionality.*

Governance and Risk Management

- ***Mission Alignment****: RACS ensured that all commercialisation activities aligned with its mission to improve surgical standards and patient outcomes. The platform's use is restricted to organisations that share these values.*
- ***Risk Ringfencing****: The College established separate legal and financial structures for the MALT platform, protecting its core operations from commercial risk and ensuring compliance with privacy and data protection laws.*
- ***Oversight and Reporting****: Dedicated governance committees oversee the platform's development, licensing, and partnerships, with clear protocols for conflict of interest, reporting, and return-to-purpose mechanisms.*
- ***Equity and Benefit Sharing****: Where joint ventures are involved, RACS negotiates equity-sharing and revenue distribution models that benefit both the College and its broader membership, ensuring that commercial success translates into sector-wide value.*

Strategic Impact

- ***Sector Enablement****: The MALT platform has become a benchmark for surgical audit and quality improvement, reinforcing RACS's role as a sector enabler and knowledge broker.*
- ***Sustainable Revenue****: Ongoing licensing and partnership income support the College's educational and advocacy activities, reducing reliance on traditional membership dues.*
- ***Reputation and Influence****: By successfully spinning out a validated, mission-aligned digital asset, RACS has enhanced its reputation for innovation and sector leadership.*

Key Takeaways

- *Spin-outs are most effective when they build on validated core activities and serve a clear market need.*
- *Robust governance, risk management, and mission alignment are essential for protecting the association's integrity and public trust.*

- *Equity-sharing and return-to-purpose mechanisms ensure that commercialisation benefits the entire professional community.*

(Royal Australasian College of Surgeons, 2023, 2024, 2025)

Example 39. From Advocacy to Enterprise

In the early 1960s, a South Australian pharmacist, Alan A. Russell, recognised a critical gap in professional protection after learning of a hairdresser facing litigation without adequate insurance. He envisioned a similar risk for pharmacists and proposed the idea to the National Council of the Federated Pharmaceutical Services Guild of Australia (now The Pharmacy Guild of Australia). This led to the establishment of Guild Insurance in 1963, providing specialised insurance cover against the risks of running a pharmacy.

Strategic Evolution: *Guild Insurance began as a member-focused initiative to protect pharmacists but evolved into a multifaceted insurance provider. Over the decades, it expanded its services to include business insurance, professional indemnity, home and contents, and car insurance, catering to a broader range of professionals.*

Diversification and Growth: *Beyond insurance, the Guild Group established several subsidiaries to meet the diverse needs of its members:*

- ***GuildSuper (1994):*** *Offering superannuation solutions tailored for the allied health and childcare industries.*
- ***Meridian Lawyers (2004):*** *Providing legal services in insurance law, health law, corporate and commercial law, among others.*
- ***Vets Choice (2019):*** *A pet insurance product endorsed by the Australian Veterinary Association, extending the Guild's reach into veterinary services.*

Governance and Structure: *Guild Insurance operates as a wholly-owned subsidiary of Guild Group Holdings Ltd, which is under the umbrella of The Pharmacy Guild of Australia. This structure ensures that the commercial ventures remain aligned with the association's mission while allowing for operational independence.*

Impact and Recognition: *Guild Insurance has been recognised for its innovation and commitment to professional communities. In 2021, it was awarded the ANZIIF Small General Insurance Company of the Year.*

Strategic Insights for Associations:

- ***Mission-Aligned Commercialisation:*** *Guild Insurance exemplifies how associations can create commercial entities that serve both financial sustainability and member needs.*

- ***Leveraging Core Competencies:*** *By building on its understanding of professional risks and needs, the Guild successfully expanded into related services.*
- ***Governance Structures:*** *Maintaining a clear governance framework ensures that commercial ventures support, rather than detract from, the association's core mission.*

(Guild Group, 2023; Guild Insurance, 2025; The Pharmacy Guild of Australia, 2025)

Boardroom Questions to Explore Spin-Out Readiness

- What capabilities or programs are attracting external demand?
- Have we created tools, platforms, or partnerships that could sustain value outside membership?
- Do we have the governance maturity and risk appetite to pursue spin-out pathways?
- How would we balance profit, purpose, and control in a commercial entity?

Monetisation as Strategic Design

Monetisation is not a financial afterthought,
it is a deliberate act of strategic design.

When approached thoughtfully, strategically designed monetisation strengthens the association's mission, funds investment in member outcomes, and signals long-term relevance. When mishandled, it can undermine trust, fragment the value proposition, and expose the organisation to reputational and financial risk.

By applying the *Association Platform Success Framework* and leveraging tools such as the Revenue Model Matrix, Monetisation Decision Matrix, and Value-First Principles, associations can shift from simply funding the organisation to fuelling a dynamic, member-aligned ecosystem.

In the platform era, the most sustainable associations don't begin with the question:

"How can we charge more?"

They begin with a better one:

"What new value are we enabling - and how can we share in that value responsibly, transparently, and in alignment with our purpose?"

The following table outlines the strategic tensions that boards and executives will have to navigate when balancing mission, market dynamics, and value design in a platform context.

Table 8-11 Strategic Tensions

Strategic Tension	Traditional Association Logic	Platform-Era Opportunity
Member vs Market	Prioritise members exclusively	Serve adjacent markets and latent contributors
Mission vs Monetisation	Mission will have to be protected from revenue	Revenue can fuel mission-aligned growth
Service vs Ecosystem Enablement	Deliver value to members	Enable value across interconnected systems
Internal vs External Legitimacy	Internal credentials and hierarchy	External partnerships and ecosystem credibility

Table 8-12 Revenue Enablement Conditions: APSF Link Map

Revenue Design Condition	Strategic Question	Aligned APSF Pillar
Digital Delivery at Scale	Can we deliver and monetise value digitally, repeatedly, and efficiently?	Scalable Digital Infrastructure
Ethical and Transparent Practice	Is the monetisation approach designed to build and retain trust?	Governance and Trust
Insight-Driven Targeting	Do we understand what members and users value enough to price, tier, or package accordingly?	Data-Driven Insight
Flexible Experience Packaging	Can our products and services be configured to match diverse user needs and price points?	Modular Products and Experiences
Contributor Enablement	Are we enabling others in the ecosystem to monetise or contribute to shared revenue?	Ecosystem Participation & Network Effect

Monetising the platform business model is not simply a commercial design task, it is a test of the association's digital maturity, governance discipline, and ability to orchestrate multi-sided value creation. Sustainable revenue models require more than compelling products; they depend on interoperable systems, trustworthy data practices, and scalable platforms that can deliver differentiated experiences across user types. In the next chapter, we shift focus to the enabling technologies and infrastructure, exploring how associations can embed digital capability for long-term success, while safeguarding trust and agility as the foundations of platform growth.

If your members help generate value, how will you ensure they share in the return?

Example 40. PNA: Applying the Playbook

To translate monetisation theory into action, this section presents a fully worked application of the platform monetisation playbook in practice. The case of the Professional Network Association (PNA) offers a structured, stepwise illustration of how a modern association can design and implement a diversified, ethically sound revenue strategy aligned to purpose and member value.

Background and Strategic Context

In 2023, PNA's Board faced an inflection point. Membership income had plateaued, fixed costs were rising, and the value expectations of members, especially younger professionals, were shifting rapidly. The Board had also committed to transitioning PNA into a platform-oriented model over a three-year horizon. To support this transformation and reduce over-reliance on legacy funding models, it endorsed the development of a structured monetisation plan.

The Board's guiding question was simple: How can we generate sustainable new revenue streams that enhance member value and trust, not erode it?

Monetisation Model Design

Following the platform monetisation framework outlined earlier in this chapter, the PNA team identified four primary revenue pillars, each with a clear design rationale, implementation pathway, and governance controls.

1. Tiered Membership Model

PNA introduced a three-tiered membership structure to better align value with price and create a growth pathway for more engaged members.

Each tier included digital and community features that enhanced platform engagement. Importantly, the Premier tier generated margin while deepening the association's strategic relationship with its highest-value members.

2. Ethical Data Monetisation

Leveraging aggregated, anonymised workforce intelligence from the member base, PNA developed benchmark reports and sector dashboards for employers, regulators, and government agencies. Products were offered on a subscription basis or licensed for single-use.

Privacy and trust were paramount. All data products were opt-in governed, de-identified to rigorous standards, and overseen by a Member Data Ethics Committee that included independent experts. Revenue from this stream exceeded expectations in Year 1, with a 42% conversion rate among pilot members and a foundation client base of 17 paying institutions.

3. Corporate Partnerships and Sponsorships

A new sponsorship framework was introduced with three tiers ($3K, $7K, and $15K p.a.), designed not as transactional exposure packages but as value-aligned partnerships. Offers included co-branded resources, thought leadership opportunities, and access to strategic roundtables.

An internal Sponsorship Governance Panel reviewed each partnership to ensure alignment with PNA's values and strategic intent. Sponsor transparency registers were published online to reinforce legitimacy and mitigate perceived conflicts.

4. Value-Added Digital Services

The PNA team built a suite of modular digital products, including:

- *Paid CPD modules (microcredentialed);*
- *Customisable career planning tools;*
- *Access to the "Network Futures" dashboard, enabling members to map their position in the national ecosystem and benchmark against peers.*

Services were offered on a freemium model, basic versions included in Professional membership, with premium access available as individual or organisational upgrades.

Governance and Implementation

To support implementation, the CEO appointed a Monetisation Taskforce reporting to the Board. Key governance features included:

- *Sponsorship Register: Public, quarterly updated;*
- *Data Ethics Charter: Adopted by Board resolution, published on the PNA website;*
- *Member Feedback Loop: Embedded into the member dashboard to monitor concerns and improve offers in real time;*

***Impact Review**: Twelve-month independent evaluation against trust, inclusion, and financial KPIs.*

The team applied a five-phase rollout:

- *Platform Stabilisation and Merger Completion*
- *Tiered Membership Pilot and Feedback Collection*
- *National Launch and Partner Engagement Campaign*
- *Sponsor Onboarding and Offer Expansion*
- *Impact Review and Next Iteration Design*

Financial and Strategic Outcomes

In the first 12 months post-launch, the plan generated a positive ROI achieved in less than 18 months. Over a three-year outlook, projected *returns exceed $1.6 million net, with capacity to scale without significant additional fixed investment. Strategically, the PNA Board reported a shift in how monetisation was understood, not as a commercial compromise, but as a design challenge to better meet member needs while reducing fragility.*

Table 8-13 Membership Tiers

Tier	Annual Fee	Included Benefits
Basic	$50	Access to the digital member hub, monthly newsletter, and discounted event registration.
Professional	$150	All Basic benefits, plus access to toolkits, live and on-demand webinars, career services, and a CPD tracking dashboard.
Premier	$500	All Professional benefits, plus full access to data dashboards, curated insight briefings, and exclusive invitations to strategic roundtables.

This example illustrates the principle that ethical, trust-aligned monetisation is not only possible but highly advantageous when built on platform foundations. For associations navigating similar transitions, the PNA model provides a replicable pathway from aspiration to execution.

Monetisation Maturity

The Monetisation Maturity Ladder in Table 8-14 outlines how associations can progress from transactional pricing models to participatory, ecosystem-enabled revenue systems. It integrates platform economics, trust governance, and value co-creation into a practical tool for evaluating strategic fit and ethical posture.

Table 8-14 Monetisation Maturity Ladder: From Access to Co-Creation

Level	Label	Core Characteristics
1	Flat-Fee Access	Uniform membership pricing; all members pay the same; little linkage to service usage.
2	Segmented Subscription	Basic segmentation (e.g. student, retired); no behavioural or engagement-based pricing.
3	Tiered Offerings	Multiple tiers of access (e.g. premium CPD); optional upgrades; some value alignment.
4	Dynamic Pricing & Modular Value	Services priced individually; usage-based value; pay-per-interaction.
5	Ecosystem Monetisation	Revenue from members and non-members; marketplace participation; income from co-created value.
6	Trust-Based Monetisation	Members co-produce value and are recognised; data, access, and contribution monetised; ethical governance and transparency embedded.

Boardroom Debrief: Five Questions to Guide Revenue Strategy":

- Where are we creating untapped value?
- Which stakeholders are helping to generate revenue, and are they sharing in the return?
- What governance is in place for trust, equity, and risk?
- Do we have pricing models aligned with member outcomes?
- What should we stop, start, or scale?

Part IV. Digital Transformation and Governance

The success of a platform-based association is not just about strategy, it depends on robust digital infrastructure, data-driven decision-making, and agile governance. Part III focuses on the intersection of technology, governance, and risk management, exploring how AI, automation, and cybersecurity can support associations in scaling their impact while ensuring compliance and trust. This section also addresses governance agility, highlighting how boards and executive teams can adapt governance models to enable platform innovation. Through real-world case studies, this section provides actionable strategies for associations to build a resilient, technology-enabled governance framework.

Chapter 9. Embedding Technology for Long-Term Success

Example 41. Technology Roadblocks at PNA

Claire Evans, CEO of the Professional Network Association (PNA), had spent the last six months leading the shift to a platform-driven membership model. The Board had approved new engagement strategies, and members showed strong initial interest in networking and CPD marketplaces. But the transition was proving more complex than expected.

At a recent executive meeting, the Head of Digital Operations, Alex Carter, voiced a concern:

"We have great ideas, but our tech is holding us back. Our systems don't talk to each other, our website is outdated, and members expect AI-driven personalisation, not generic email blasts. If we don't rethink our digital infrastructure, all our work on engagement and monetisation will fail."

Claire knew Alex was right. Associations like PNA couldn't afford to see technology as an afterthought, it had to be embedded into their core strategy. But the board was still cautious about investing in digital transformation.

"Let's map out exactly where technology adds value, to members, to sponsors, and to our financial model. If we frame this as an investment in engagement and revenue, not just another software upgrade, I think we can make this work."

The next day, Claire and her team outlined a phased approach to digital transformation, ensuring that PNA's tech investment aligned with its platform strategy and monetisation goals.

Introduction: Technology as a Strategic Enabler

As explored in the previous chapter, a successful association can move beyond membership dues and adopt diversified revenue models. However, achieving this level of financial sustainability requires a solid digital infrastructure. Without technology to support personalisation, engagement, and transactional capabilities, monetisation strategies remain theoretical rather than practical. This chapter explores how associations can embed technology to enable and sustain these revenue streams

Digital transformation is no longer optional for associations seeking to remain competitive. While associations have traditionally been slow to adopt new technologies, the shift to a platform-based model requires a deliberate and strategic approach to digital integration.

Technology is not simply a tool for efficiency; it is an enabler of new business models, deeper member engagement, and stronger governance structures. However, many associations struggle with technology adoption due to resource constraints, where budget and expertise limit implementation, resistance to change, particularly among leadership teams and long-standing members, and a lack of a clear digital strategy, leading to fragmented adoption of tools without long-term sustainability.

This chapter explores how associations can embed technology effectively, ensuring that digital infrastructure supports engagement, governance, and financial sustainability.

Digital Maturity Looks Like ...

Technology is no longer a back-office function. In platform-based associations, digital infrastructure underpins engagement, trust, scalability, and revenue innovation.

Technology decisions are not infrastructure choices alone, they are the operational reflection of your business model. A well-designed platform business model defines how value flows between participants, how contributions are enabled, and how engagement is governed. These dynamics will directly inform the design of digital architecture, from CRM and LMS integration to data ethics frameworks and interaction channels. Without alignment, even sophisticated systems can reinforce outdated service delivery modes or restrict platform potential.

This is why business model clarity will have to come first. Map value flows and participation dynamics before committing to major technology investments.

Planning Digital Before Monetising?

Use the Platform-Enhanced Business Model Canvas to map value flows, participation logic, and governance needs before committing to major technology investments.

Boards will have to treat digital as a strategic asset and ethical responsibility, not just a cost centre. Without board-level stewardship, transformation efforts risk becoming fragmented, under-resourced, or misaligned with member expectations.

For many associations, "going digital" has historically meant upgrading systems - launching a new website, rolling out a CRM, or implementing an online learning platform. While these changes are important, they represent only the starting point of a far more strategic journey.

True digital maturity is not defined by the number of systems deployed, it is defined by how deeply digital capability is embedded into the association's culture, value creation, and governance. Mature associations don't just use digital tools. They design around digital as a core capability: to deliver personalisation, anticipate member needs, scale efficiently, and build trust through transparency and responsiveness.

Moving from Tools to Strategic Capability

In a platform-based association, digital is not an "IT project", it is the infrastructure that enables:

- **Real-time member insights**: enabling hyper-relevant engagement, content recommendations, and needs-responsive programming.
- **Personalised experiences at scale**: powered by behavioural data, member profiles, and AI-driven curation.
- **Frictionless interaction**: across membership onboarding, CPD tracking, event participation, and peer collaboration.
- **Governance transparency**: through auditable data practices, responsive service standards, and digital engagement analytics.
- **Ethical use of AI and data**: ensuring all technology decisions are aligned with the association's values and the expectations of its members.

The shift is not just technical, it is conceptual and cultural. Associations will have to move from asking "What system do we need?" to asking "What kind of digital capability will make us more member-centred, trusted, and future-ready?"

Table 9-1 Digital Maturity Milestones for Platform Associations

Maturity Level	Characteristics	Key Capabilities
Foundational	Core systems in place, largely unintegrated	CRM, website, email, event platform
Operational	Basic system integration, digital delivery of services	Online CPD, automated comms, responsive support
Connected	Data flows across systems, member journeys partially unified	Unified profiles, basic analytics, single sign-on
Insight-Driven	Real-time data used to personalise and optimise member experience	Member dashboards, behaviour-triggered automation
Platform-Enabled	Members, partners, and systems interact in a dynamic ecosystem	AI-driven curation, embedded learning, peer-to-peer services
Ethically Intelligent	Governance includes digital ethics, AI accountability, and equity design	Data audits, ethical AI standards, co-designed platform policies

Associations do not need to reach the highest level in every area - but they do need to know where they are and where to invest next to enable sustainable transformation.

As we move into the next section, we introduce a structured digital strategy lifecycle, a model that helps associations plan, build, and evolve their technology capability in line with platform strategy and member expectations.

Digital transformation is an ongoing organisational capability, not a one-off implementation.

Associations that succeed with technology treat it not as a fixed system to be delivered, but as a *dynamic asset* to be governed, evaluated, and evolved over time.

The *Digital Strategy Lifecycle* provides a structured approach for embedding and sustaining digital capability across the association. It moves beyond ad hoc investments or project-based upgrades and supports a long-term digital roadmap aligned to member engagement, revenue generation, and ethical governance.

Strategic Guidance for Boards and Executives

Each stage of the lifecycle has governance and investment implications. Boards should:

- **Review and endorse** the digital strategy roadmap as a core component of annual strategic planning.
- **Monitor** technology-related risks, including cybersecurity, privacy, and vendor dependencies.
- **Set expectations** for measurable outcomes, such as member engagement lift, CPD participation rates, and digital trust scores.
- **Strategic capability-building** frames the digital investment, not just system upgrades.

The digital strategy lifecycle is not just about "doing digital better", it is about ensuring digital *advances the mission*, supports the business model, and strengthens the member experience.

The APSF outlines strategic technology capabilities conceptually, several Australian associations have already demonstrated practical application of these principles. For example, investing in a modular, API-enabled learning platform to support adaptive CPD delivery across global markets., or leveraging AI-driven content personalisation and career pathway tools through a portal platform, enhancing individualised member journeys. Implementing advanced analytics and predictive segmentation to inform member engagement, event targeting, and CPD programming are all examples that underscore that digital maturity should not be aspirational, it should be operationalised within well-led, future-focused Australian associations.

Once associations have a clear digital strategy aligned with APSF, the next step is selecting technologies that drive engagement, operational efficiency, and monetisation. The following table outlines key technologies and their strategic benefits, ensuring associations make informed investment decisions.

Figure 9-1 ***APSF: Technology and Data → Scalable Digital Infrastructure***

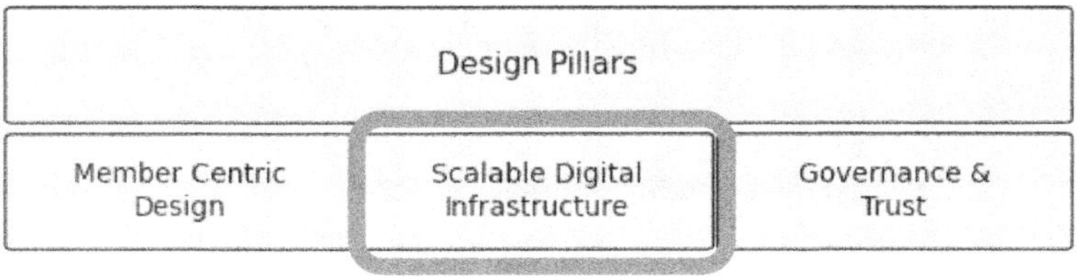

Table 9-2 Strategic Technology Capabilities Map for Associations

Technology Category	Purpose & Benefits	Examples & Aligned APSF Pillars
Member Engagement & Networking Platforms	Fosters real-time interaction, peer collaboration, and sustained member connection.	- AI-powered platforms match members with relevant content and discussions. - Gamification (e.g. leaderboards, badges) enhances engagement. - Virtual spaces support ongoing networking. *Aligned Pillar: Member-Centric Design*
Learning Management Systems (LMS)	Enables on-demand, modular, and stackable learning experiences for continuous professional development.	- Micro-credentials and stackable certificates for career progression. - AI-curated CPD pathways based on role and interest. - Subscription and per-course revenue options. *Aligned Pillar: Scalable Digital Infrastructure*
AI & Automation for Personalisation	Enhances operational efficiency and service quality through tailored member experiences.	- AI content curation and chatbot support for members. - Automated workflows to reduce admin burden. - Predictive analytics for engagement optimisation. *Aligned Pillar: Scalable Digital Infrastructure*
Data Governance & Cybersecurity	Protects privacy, ensures regulatory compliance, and builds trust in digital services.	- Encrypted data storage and secure access systems. - Privacy compliance (e.g. GDPR, Australian Privacy Act, AI ethics). - Cybersecurity automation

Technology Category	Purpose & Benefits	Examples & Aligned APSF Pillars
		and risk flagging. *Aligned Pillar: Governance & Trust*

Table 9-3 **Phased Transformation Pathway**

Transformation Phase	Strategic Focus & Outcomes	Real-World Example
Phase 1: Digital Foundations	Upgrades to core systems (CRM, membership database, basic automation) reduce manual workload and improve data quality.	A professional body replaces spreadsheets with a cloud-based CRM, integrating email marketing and event registration.
Phase 2: Enhancing Member Experience	Personalisation tools (AI, gamification, content curation) drive deeper engagement, retention, and non-dues revenue.	An engineering association launches AI-driven CPD recommendations, resulting in a 40% increase in learning module participation.
Phase 3: Governance & Revenue Integration	Integrating data security, risk automation, and diversified revenue models ensures compliance, trust, and financial growth.	A healthcare association implements blockchain for credential verification, improving auditability and automating CPD compliance.

In the next section, we examine the barriers that frequently stall digital transformation in associations - and provide a framework for identifying and overcoming them.

Example 42. PNA: Phased Technology Rollout

When the Professional Network Association (PNA) began its digital transformation journey, its systems were disjointed, members registered for events via email, CPD records were stored offline, and renewal reminders were sent manually. Recognising this fragmentation was a barrier to engagement and growth, the board approved a phased technology strategy aligned with APSF principles.

Phase 1: Infrastructure Consolidation

PNA began by replacing its outdated CRM with a cloud-based platform that integrated member records, event registrations, and communications. This enabled real-time data visibility and reduced administrative time by 30% in the first six months.

Phase 2: CPD and Learning Management System (LMS)

Next, PNA introduced a modular LMS with CPD tracking. Members could log hours, complete microlearning modules, and receive automated certificate generation. Uptake among early-career professionals increased by 40%, and CPD completion rates improved across all tiers.

Phase 3: Community and Personalisation Layer

Building on the new infrastructure, PNA piloted an AI-powered recommendation engine that curated events, content, and networking suggestions based on members' roles, location, and prior engagement. Member satisfaction scores (NPS) rose from 52 to 71 over one year.

"Rather than buying a stack of tools all at once, we asked: what do our members need us to do better next quarter? That mindset helped us deliver impact early, and build trust in the transformation.": Claire Evans, CEO.

This example shows how a deliberate, sequenced investment in infrastructure not only improves internal efficiency, but also lays the groundwork for deeper engagement, personalisation, and scalable value delivery.

What Gets in the Way: Digital Barriers in Associations

Figure 9-2 ***Digital Transformation Barriers and Mitigators***

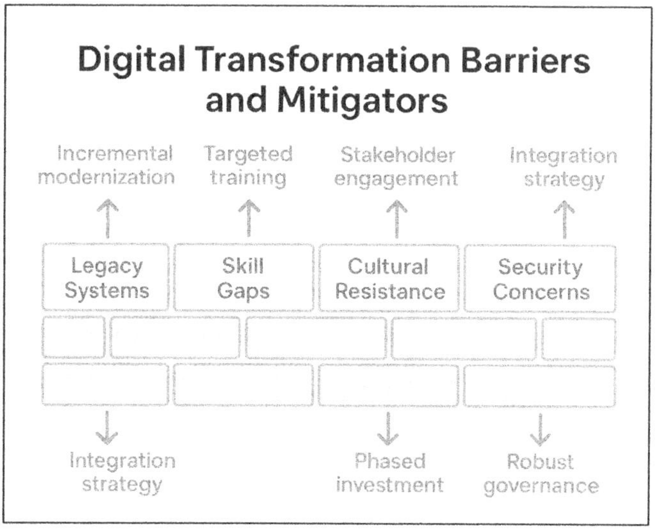

Many associations recognise the need for digital transformation - but few sustain momentum beyond initial projects. Strategic intent often stalls when implementation meets outdated systems, organisational culture, or capacity gaps. These barriers are not just technical; they are structural, cultural, and leadership-related.

This section identifies the most common digital barriers facing associations and offers practical strategies for overcoming them, aligned with the *Digital Strategy Lifecycle*.

Table 9-4 Common Barriers and How to Overcome Them

Barrier	Description	Strategic Response / Mitigation
Legacy Systems	Outdated or unintegrated platforms inhibit responsiveness and scalability	Invest in cloud-based, API-ready infrastructure; prioritise modularity
Digital Skills Gap	Staff and board lack capability to design, govern, or use modern tech	Build internal capacity through upskilling, CPD, and digital champions
Funding Constraints	Limited budgets delay investment in transformation or innovation	Use pilot projects, staged implementation, and platform-aligned business cases
Vendor Lock-In	Proprietary systems create dependency and reduce flexibility	Negotiate open standards; prioritise exit clauses and platform neutrality
Cultural Resistance	Staff or board see digital as a threat to established roles or identity	Frame digital as a member-first enabler; involve staff early in co-design
Governance Bottlenecks	Slow or unclear decision-making slows project approval or iteration	Empower digital advisory groups; set agile decision thresholds
Data Fragmentation	Disconnected systems create inconsistent, incomplete member data	Integrate systems and standardise data fields; build a single member view
Lack of Strategic Ownership	Digital is seen as a project or IT issue, not a board-level responsibility	Embed digital in strategic plans; define board KPIs for digital capability

Reflection for Boards and Executive Teams

These barriers are not failures - they are symptoms of legacy models encountering new expectations. What matters is how proactively associations identify and respond to them. Digital transformation cannot be outsourced to an IT team or external vendor. It requires clear governance oversight, staff and board digital literacy, flexible funding models and a cultural alignment with platform thinking

In a platform-based association, digital is not a department, it is a core strategic capability.

Example 43. PNA: Digital Maturity Milestones

When PNA undertook its first digital audit, it was operating at the foundational level. Core functions like member renewals, event registration, and CPD tracking were manual or hosted on disconnected systems. The board recognised that without integrated digital infrastructure, it would be impossible to deliver personalised member value or support the platform model outlined in APSF.

Level 1: Foundational

The starting point: A basic website, static member database, and legacy email newsletter system. All engagement data was siloed, and there was no unified view of member activity.

Level 2: Functional

PNA implemented a new CRM and launched a single-sign-on portal, consolidating event registrations, payments, and profile management. Member engagement data became accessible and reportable for the first time. This enabled the board to track basic KPIs and plan more informed engagement pilots.

Level 3: Integrated

Next, PNA connected its CRM with a modular LMS, launched behavioural analytics, and introduced automated workflows. This meant members could complete CPD, receive tailored recommendations, and update credentials, all through a seamless experience. Insights from this stage directly shaped content strategy and pricing models.

Level 4: Strategic

By Year 3, PNA added an AI-driven personalisation engine, integrated feedback and evaluation tools, and launched a "digital twin" dashboard for the board to visualise real-time member sentiment and risk indicators. Governance, data, and service strategy were now aligned. The association had become a responsive, insight-driven platform, capable of iterating based on member needs and market signals.

"Moving from foundational to strategic wasn't about buying tech. It was about aligning systems with purpose, and listening more closely to our members at every step.": PNA CIO (Fictional)

This journey illustrates how digital maturity will evolve in tandem with culture, capability, and governance, and how APSF provides the scaffolding to do so systematically.

The next section outlines the evolving role of the board and executive in leading technology governance, ensuring that digital investments are ethical, strategic, and impactful.

For resource constrained associations the following is an example of how to respond.

Example 44. Small Arts Organisations

While there is no direct, named case that matches every detail of the hypothetical Community Arts and Social Enterprise Association (CASEA), there are several well-documented Australian examples that closely parallel its approach, demonstrating how small, under-resourced arts organisations have leveraged open, modular digital tools to drive engagement and operational efficiency.

Key Features in Practice

1. Use of Free and Modular Digital Tools

Many small and medium arts organisations in Australia have adopted free or low-cost digital tools such as Mailchimp (for newsletters), Google Forms (for data capture and basic CRM), WordPress (for websites and event management), and Zapier (for workflow automation).

These tools are often integrated in creative ways to overcome the lack of enterprise-level systems, enabling streamlined event sign-ups, targeted communications, and basic data analytics.

2. Volunteer Led Digital Innovation

Digital transformation in the sector is frequently driven by volunteers or a small core team, with a focus on practical, incremental improvements rather than large-scale IT projects.

Organisations report that mapping member touchpoints and identifying core needs, such as easy event registration, improved communications, and visibility of engagement, are critical first steps.

3. Measurable Impact

Case studies from Creative Australia and the Australia Council for the Arts highlight that even modest digital upgrades can yield significant results: increased event participation, higher newsletter open rates, and new partnership opportunities31.

For example, the adoption of digital event management and email automation has led to doubled event registrations and substantial improvements in communication metrics for several small arts groups1.

Example: Waringarri Aboriginal Arts

- ***Background:*** *Waringarri Aboriginal Arts, a small Indigenous-owned art centre, undertook a digital transformation by updating* *its website, integrating online booking and sales, and training staff in digital content management.*

- ***Tools Used:*** *The centre used a content management system, online forms, and social media integrations, paralleling the CASEA stack.*
- ***Outcomes:*** *The project resulted in increased market reach, improved internal skills, and greater control for artists over their portfolios and sales. The centre reported direct savings and a significant boost in digital engagement4.*

Sector-Wide Support and Strategy

- *National strategies such as the Australia Council's Digital Culture Strategy and Creative Australia's "Think Digital" program provide frameworks and resources for small arts organisations to build digital capability using accessible, interoperable tools.*
- *These programs emphasise that digital progress does not require large budgets or bespoke systems; rather, success comes from strategic use of modular, open platforms and a willingness to adapt.*

Table 9-5 **Digital Tools in Small Arts Organisations**

Tool/Platform	Common Use Case	Example Outcome
Mailchimp	Newsletters, comms	Open rates increased by 20%+
Google Forms	Event sign-up, CRM surrogate	Streamlined registration, data capture
WordPress	Website, event management	Online bookings, embeddable calendar
Zapier	Workflow automation	Automated reminders, data sync
Power BI/ Spreadsheets	Analytics, reporting	Event engagement tracking

Takeaway

The small arts organisations have demonstrated that strategic, interoperable use of free and modular digital tools can deliver platform-like value, even with minimal resources. The CASEA scenario is strongly validated by real-world practice: focus, adaptability, and leveraging open technology are key to driving engagement and operational impact in the community arts sector.

(Australia Council for the Arts, 2021, 2023; Creative Australia, 2024; Waringarri Aboriginal Arts, 2022 Switch Labs, 2024; Creative Australia, 2025)

The Role of the Board and Executive in Tech Strategy

In a platform-based association, technology is no longer just an operational enabler, it is a core driver of member experience, business model execution, and long-term relevance. As such, technology strategy will have to be governed at the highest levels of the organisation.

This means the board and executive team will have to move beyond approving IT budgets or reviewing cybersecurity reports. They will have to develop a shared digital fluency, set the strategic parameters for investment and risk, and steward digital capability as a leadership responsibility.

Table 9-6 Why Digital Governance Belongs at Board Level

Strategic Area	Digital Responsibility
Member Experience	Ensure technology enables personalisation, access, and inclusion
Revenue Strategy	Oversee platform monetisation models (e.g. subscriptions, marketplaces, data)
Risk Management	Review data security, AI governance, and ethical use of automation
Culture and Capability	Support digital literacy across staff, board, and members
Long-Term Sustainability	Align digital investments with strategic goals and measurable outcomes

Digital Governance Questions for the Board

- Are we clear on how digital enables our strategic objectives?
- Is it embedded in our strategy or siloed as a tech function?
- Do we have visibility over our digital assets and risks?
- What systems, data, and external dependencies do we rely on?
- How are we ensuring ethical use of technology?
- Do we have principles for data usage, AI bias, and member consent?
- What metrics are we using to track digital performance?
- Are we monitoring adoption, satisfaction, and ROI - not just uptime?
- Are we investing in digital capabilities - not just digital tools?
- Are we building internal talent, partnerships, and adaptive infrastructure?

Executive Responsibilities

Digital transformation is not solely a boardroom concern, it will have to be operationalised through executive leadership. While the board provides strategic direction and oversight, the executive team is responsible for translating platform thinking into day-to-day capability, culture, and performance. This includes driving integration across functions, embedding digital into service delivery, and stewarding the infrastructure that enables innovation, insight, and engagement.

While the board sets strategy and oversight, the executive team operationalises digital leadership. Key responsibilities include:

- Developing the digital roadmap, aligned to the Association Platform Success Framework and the business model.
- Embedding technology into service design, member journeys, and partner offerings.
- Facilitating collaboration across functions - especially between communications, IT, member services, and education.
- Managing vendor relationships with a focus on interoperability, ethics, and long-term value.

Executives should act as stewards of platform capability, not just service delivery.

Enablers of Strong Digital Governance

Effective digital governance requires more than strategy documents and investment plans, it depends on embedded structures, transparent oversight, and informed decision-making. The following enablers support boards and executive teams to monitor digital maturity, mitigate risk, and ensure technology decisions remain aligned with trust, purpose, and long-term value.

- Board-level dashboards that include digital KPIs (e.g. member engagement rates, digital trust score, system utilisation)
- Digital advisory groups composed of board members, external experts, and member representatives
- Annual digital strategy reviews linked to platform evolution and investment priorities
- Cybersecurity and data ethics briefings to ensure risk visibility and compliance

Integrating APSF Governance

This section links directly to the Governance & Trust pillar of the *Association Platform Success Framework*. Boards will have to oversee not just what is built, but how technology is governed, doing so transparently, ethically, and in service of member value.

The final section of this chapter explores how to embed a continuous mindset of technology evolution - so that digital becomes not just a system or project, but a permanent strategic capability.

Digital Ethics and AI Governance: A Board Imperative

As associations adopt AI tools, behavioural analytics, and automated decision systems, ethical oversight becomes a board-level responsibility, not just a technical function. Members are increasingly concerned with how their data is collected, analysed, and acted upon. Governance structures will have to evolve to anticipate ethical risks related to bias, privacy, algorithmic accountability, and cybersecurity.

Boards should ask:

- Are our algorithms fair, explainable, and inclusive?
- How are members informed, empowered, or protected from automated decisions?
- What protocols are in place for data breaches, system misuse, or third-party vendor failures?

These questions aren't abstract. They're already surfacing in practice.

Example 45. Board Responds to Algorithmic Bias

After launching an AI-powered CPD recommendation engine, the Professional Network Association (PNA) began receiving feedback that some members, particularly those in regional and culturally diverse cohorts, were being overlooked for leadership pathways and advanced learning prompts. A review revealed that the algorithm, while technically functional, had been trained on legacy participation data that unintentionally amplified existing engagement biases. In response, the board convened a digital ethics working group and adopted a Digital Ethics Charter. See Annexure F). The charter included principles for algorithmic transparency, inclusion audits, opt-out controls, and board-level oversight of all automated decision systems. This proactive governance move restored member trust and positioned the board as a capable steward of responsible technology use

Associations that embed ethics into digital transformation, not as an afterthought, but as a design principle, are better equipped to maintain trust, reduce risk, and create lasting value for members. A *Digital Ethics Charter* provides a board-level governance framework for digital ethics, cybersecurity, and AI oversight.

From Digital to Dynamic

Digital maturity is not achieved when an association finishes a system upgrade or launches a new website. It is achieved when technology becomes a dynamic, embedded capability - continuously evolving to support member value, strategic intent, and organisational resilience.

A dynamic association is one where digital technology is embedded seamlessly into every aspect of the member experience, from communications to service delivery. Data is used responsibly and ethically to personalise interactions, anticipate member needs, and improve outcomes over time. Artificial intelligence and automation are introduced not to replace human connection, but to enhance it by increasing capacity and supporting deeper engagement. The board actively governs digital risks, oversees technology investments, and evaluates performance to ensure alignment with strategic objectives. Most importantly, innovation is not treated as a one-off project. It is fostered as both a mindset and a structural capability, providing the foundation for continuous adaptation and long-term relevance.

Table 9-7 Key Shifts for Association Leaders

From...	To...
Technology as a cost centre	Technology as a strategic enabler of engagement and growth
Projects and upgrades	Continuous capability building and ecosystem design
Member access to services	Member participation in a personalised, co-created platform
System integration	Experience integration across all digital touchpoints
IT department ownership	Shared leadership between executive, board, and service teams

Linking Back to the APSF

Technology underpins all three Design Pillars of the *Association Platform Success Framework*:

- **Member-Centric Design** → AI-powered personalisation, CPD tracking, peer engagement
- **Scalable Digital Infrastructure** → Interoperability, security, responsive platforms
- **Governance & Trust** → Ethical AI, digital risk oversight, transparent data usage

To thrive as a platform organisation, associations will have to not only invest in technology but they will have to embed it into their governance, culture, and value creation model.

Snapshot: What a Digitally Mature Association Looks Like

Digitally mature associations don't just use technology, they integrate it into the fabric of governance, member engagement, and value creation. Based on patterns observed across successful platform-based associations, here is what that maturity looks like in practice:

Table 9-8 Digital Maturity

Dimension	Best-Practice Features
Member Experience	Personalised journeys powered by AI; seamless access across CPD, events, and communities.
Technology Stack	Integrated CRM, LMS, and community platforms; real-time analytics; mobile-first design.
Governance	Digital risk oversight; ethical AI charter; agile board subcommittees on innovation.
Revenue Strategy	Diversified income: subscriptions, data services, marketplaces, and tiered offerings.
Data Ethics & Security	Privacy-by-design, member consent protocols, and regular bias audits of algorithms.
Culture & Capability	Digitally fluent staff and leadership; internal innovation labs or cross-functional squads.

These associations treat technology as strategy, not infrastructure. They evolve in partnership with their members, listening, iterating, and building trust through transparency and responsiveness.

Reflection for Boards and Executives

Technology will not replace associations. But associations that fail to embed technology - ethically, strategically, and sustainably - will be replaced by those that do.

Becoming digitally dynamic is not a finish line. It is an ongoing commitment to evolving with your members, your sector, and your purpose.

Example 46. AMI: Digital Transformation

Challenge: *AMI faced member disengagement as younger professionals sought free alternatives for industry updates and CPD.*

Solution: *AMI invested in digital transformation to enhance engagement and create new revenue streams:*

- *AI-Powered Learning Hub: CPD courses tailored to individual career goals.*
- *Freemium Access Model: Free industry updates, but premium access for structured career pathways.*
- *Industry Job Board: Employers pay for featured job postings, creating new revenue.*

- *Event Monetisation: Hybrid event model, with sponsorship tiers for virtual and in-person attendees.*

Impact:

- *Increase in member engagement.*
- *Growth in non-dues revenue streams (CPD subscriptions, sponsorships).*
- *Higher retention of early-career professionals through customisation.*

(Australian Marketing Institute. 2024, 2025)

AMI's example shows how technology-driven engagement supports revenue diversification. Associations should consider a see technology as a monetisation enabler - not just a cost.

Embedding technology is not about systems alone, it is about designing the infrastructure for trust, scale, and sustained engagement in a platform-based world. As this chapter has shown, digital capability underpins every aspect of the modern association: from personalised member journeys and AI-driven services to governance oversight and ethical innovation. But digital infrastructure is only the foundation. What ultimately enables strategic advantage is how associations use this infrastructure to generate insight, not just dashboards, but real-time understanding of member needs, ecosystem dynamics, and future signals. In the next chapter, we explore how to build a data and insight capability that transforms information into foresight, enabling associations to lead with clarity, confidence, and adaptive intelligence.

In the next chapter, we explore how associations can build a data and insight capability that goes beyond dashboards, leveraging the very infrastructure and digital maturity outlined here to enable strategic decision-making, personalised service design, and platform-enabled foresight. The business model defines where value emerges. The digital infrastructure enables it. The next chapter explores how to convert this infrastructure into intelligence, building a strategic data capability that allows associations to sense, respond, and lead with clarity.

Table 9-9 Model–Tech Alignment Checklist

Business Model Area	Aligned Digital Capability
Participation Pathways	CRM, member portals, single sign-on
Value Propositions	LMS, personalisation, job boards
Key Contributions	Content platforms, co-design tools
Risk & Reputational Zones	AI audits, cybersecurity frameworks
Governance & Ethics	Ethics dashboards, data transparency tools

Chapter 10. Agile Governance in a Digital Era

Example 47. The Governance Dilemma

Claire Evans, CEO of the Professional Network Association (PNA), sat in yet another board meeting stalled by risk aversion. The agenda item: implementing an AI-driven member engagement platform. The opportunity was clear - personalised content recommendations, automated CPD tracking, and real-time networking. But as soon as the discussion began, the same objections surfaced.

> *"We need more time to assess the risks," one board member argued.*
>
> *"Our members trust us with their data - what if something goes wrong?" another added.*

Claire had anticipated pushback, but she also knew that indecision was the bigger risk. PNA was already losing members to more dynamic, digital-first competitors. Waiting for a "perfect" solution meant stagnation, while calculated innovation could future-proof the organisation.

Then Sophie, PNA's youngest board member and a former startup founder, leaned in.

> *"We're treating every decision like it's irreversible," she said. "Tech companies iterate. They test small, adjust fast, and scale what works. What if we took that approach?"*

Her words shifted the room's energy. Instead of paralysis by analysis, the conversation turned to pilot programs, risk mitigation, and phased rollouts. Within weeks, PNA launched a limited trial of the AI platform, collecting real-world insights before making a final decision.

By adopting an agile governance approach, PNA overcame its risk aversion, not by ignoring risks, but by testing, learning, and adapting in real time.

Governance at a Turning Point

Most associations are transforming how they engage, deliver value, and generate revenue. Yet in many cases, governance models remain stuck in a legacy paradigm - designed for stable environments, linear decision-making, and known risks.

As associations adopt platform strategies, introduce AI-driven services, and navigate rapid shifts in stakeholder expectations, the limitations of traditional governance become clear. Static committees, quarterly board packs, and slow policy cycles are ill-suited to environments that demand responsiveness, ethical oversight, and real-time risk intelligence.

We have introduced the Design Pillar, Governance and Trust however in this section we look at why and how to increase governance agility to activate the shift to an Association 2.0 model.

In a digital-first association, boards and executives are no longer stewards of static systems, they are custodians of dynamic, data-driven ecosystems. Their responsibilities now extend beyond compliance and fiduciary oversight to include the ethical governance of automated decision-making systems that shape member experience; the development of frameworks for data use, AI, and platform monetisation; and the management of risk across fluid, multi-sided stakeholder environments. Critically, they will have to also enable innovation, not merely regulate it. This demands a shift from control-based governance to a more agile, insight-led model, one grounded in strategic clarity, radical transparency, and the courage to lead amidst uncertainty.

Figure 10-1 APSF: Governance and Trust

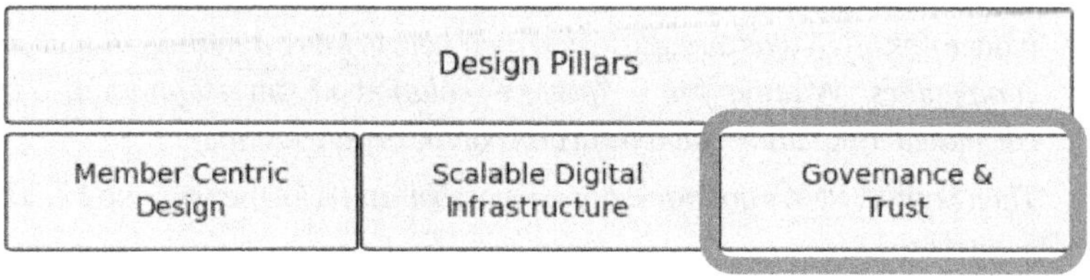

The Role of the Association Platform Success Framework

Agile governance is essential for executing the *Association Platform Success Framework* effectively. It underpins the organisation's ability to adapt, innovate, and lead in a rapidly changing environment. Specifically, it supports the *Member-Centric Design* pillar by enabling rapid service innovation and responsiveness to evolving needs; it strengthens the *Scalable Infrastructure* pillar through flexible oversight of digital investment, risk, and interoperability; and it activates the *Governance & Trust* pillar by embedding ethical decision-making in the use of AI, data, and platform models. This chapter explores how associations can redesign their governance structures and habits to meet these demands, ensuring boards are not only equipped to respond to change, but to lead it with foresight and integrity.

Agile Governance: A Capability for the Platform Era

Agile governance is not about abandoning rigour. It is about enabling speed, adaptability, and ethical stewardship at scale. It ensures decisions are made at the right level, with the right insight, and in alignment with the organisation's underlying business model. This is why model clarity will have to precede agile execution. Use the *Platform-Enhanced Business Model Canvas for Associations* in Chapter 7 to ensure governance mechanisms reflect real value flows, risks, and participant dynamics. It draws from the same principles that underpin successful platform operations: Iteration over rigidity; Insight over hierarchy; Participation over prescription; and Risk awareness over risk aversion.

In the digital era, governance is not just about what decisions are made - but how quickly, ethically, and transparently they are made.

From Traditional to Agile Governance

For over a century, governance models in associations have prioritised stability, compliance, and procedural oversight. These traditional models - grounded in hierarchy, delegation, and static reporting - served their purpose in a slower, more predictable operating environment.

But the digital era demands more. Platform-based associations now operate in dynamic, multi-stakeholder ecosystems where data flows in real time, risks emerge unpredictably, and member expectations shift quickly. In this context, agility is not optional, it is a governance imperative.

Traditional vs Agile Governance Models in Associations

This comparative framework highlights how governance practices are evolving in platform-based associations. It contrasts legacy models, often structured for stability and compliance, with agile governance approaches designed for responsiveness, digital oversight, and member co-creation.

Table 10-1 Traditional vs Agile Governance Models

Traditional Governance		Agile Governance
Fixed hierarchy of board and standing committees	→	Lean governance structures with cross-functional advisory panels
Infrequent, linear cycles (e.g. quarterly meetings)	→	Iterative, frequent decision-making with real-time inputs
Retrospective board reporting	→	Signal-based monitoring using live dashboards
Compliance-driven, risk-averse	→	Risk-aware, innovation-enabled
Technology oversight delegated to IT or operations	→	Board-level stewardship of AI, data, and platform strategy
Periodic consultation via static surveys	→	Embedded feedback via member labs and digital engagement loops
Annual strategy review cycle	→	Continuous, insight-led strategic improvement cycles

Key Differences

1. Authority vs Insight

Traditional boards emphasise control through formal delegation. Agile boards prioritise visibility - ensuring that decisions are based on real-time data, member signals, and system-level trends.

2. Formality vs Flexibility

In a traditional model, every issue is funnelled through a formal agenda and decision gate. Agile governance enables experimentation, pilot testing, and delegation of decision authority to well-informed subgroups.

3. Review vs Responsiveness

Static risk registers, policy reviews, and audit reports are backward-looking. Agile governance embraces *dynamic risk intelligence*, using AI-driven monitoring, scenario modelling, and adaptive risk frameworks.

What Agile Governance Is Not

Agile governance is often misunderstood. It is not about eliminating structure or bypassing accountability, nor does it mean making decisions without due process or embracing constant change for its own sake. Rather,

> *Agile governance is about designing systems that are responsive to change, proactive in managing uncertainty, and grounded in principles while remaining adaptable in application.*

It is not speed that defines an agile board, but its capacity for learning, transparency, and timely, informed action.

Crucially, agility in governance is not achieved through structural tweaks alone, such as dissolving committees or redrawing reporting lines, but through the development of core governance capabilities. These include digital fluency at board level, comfort with ambiguity and iteration, strong internal and external signal sensing, and a shared commitment to experimentation and reflection. As one advisor noted, "The most agile boards are not the fastest - they are the most learning-oriented, transparent, and prepared to act."

In the next section, we examine how this evolution in governance style will be matched by a more mature approach to risk, one that embraces complexity, manages uncertainty, and treats data as both a risk and a strategic asset.

Example 48. Agile Governance

Queensland Public Sector Entities – Cyber Incident Response and Agile Governance

A real and recent example of agile governance and scenario-based delegation in cyber incident response is documented in the Queensland

Audit Office's 2023–24 report, Responding to and Recovering from Cyber Attacks. This report examines how Queensland public sector entities, including local governments, prepare for, respond to, and recover from cyber incidents, with a focus on governance, scenario planning, and delegated authority.

Key Features of the Case

- ***Scenario Planning and Playbooks:*** *Entities are encouraged to develop and regularly test incident response plans, including scenario-based playbooks for a variety of cyber risks. The report highlights that the most effective responses came from entities that had rehearsed and tested their plans through cyber security simulations, which included clear escalation protocols and predefined roles for decision-making.*
- ***Delegated Authority and Agile Response:*** *The report found that entities with clearly documented roles, responsibilities, and thresholds for escalation (such as who has authority to shut down systems or communicate with stakeholders) were able to respond more quickly and effectively. In one audited case, the entity's incident response plan included delegated authority for non-critical incidents, allowing operational teams to act immediately within a defined framework, while reserving board or executive involvement for major incidents.*
- ***Real-Time Briefing and Communication:*** *During simulated cyber incidents, entities used secure dashboards and communication templates to brief executives and boards in real time, enabling rapid ratification of response actions and minimising delays.*
- ***Continuous Improvement:*** *The report emphasises the importance of post-incident reviews, sharing lessons learned, and updating scenario playbooks and delegation protocols based on real-world and simulated events.*

Outcomes and Lessons

- *Entities that continually plan, rehearse, and test their people, processes, and technology are more likely to respond and recover effectively from cyber incidents.*
- *Clear documentation of roles, delegated authority, and escalation thresholds is critical for agile, accountable decision-making during a crisis.*
- *Regular scenario testing and simulations improve both technical and governance responses, ensuring that boards and executives are prepared to act swiftly and appropriately.*

Table 10-2 Key Elements in the Approach

Element	Practice in Queensland Entities
Scenario-based playbooks	Developed and tested for various cyber incident types
Delegated authority	Documented thresholds for operational vs. board-level decisions
Real-time communication	Secure dashboards and templates for rapid executive/board briefing
Post-incident review	Lessons learned inform updates to plans and governance protocols

(Queensland Audit Office. (2024).

This case demonstrates that agile governance, scenario planning, and delegated authority are not just theoretical best practices, they are being implemented and refined in real Australian public sector organisations to improve cyber resilience and crisis response.

Embedding Risk Intelligence in a Platform Context

In a traditional association, risk was largely static and predictable: financial controls, regulatory compliance, reputational oversight, and event-related exposures. Risk was recorded in registers, reviewed annually, and managed through policies and procedures.

But in a platform-based association, risk is fluid, fast-moving, and systemic. Value is co-created with partners, algorithms personalise experiences, and data moves across systems in real time. Risk is no longer simply a matter of control, it is a matter of insight, responsiveness, and ethical judgement.

Table 10-3 The Nature of Risk Has Changed

Traditional Risk Type	Emerging Platform Risk Type
Financial audit risk	Algorithmic bias, AI misjudgement
Policy compliance	Data sovereignty, ethical use of member information
Operational failure	Vendor lock-in, third-party system failures
Governance structure gaps	Speed of reputational risk propagation via digital channels
Strategic uncertainty	Trust erosion through opaque automation or monetisation

From Risk Registers to Risk Intelligence

Traditional risk registers typically list identified risks, assign likelihood and consequence scores, and are reviewed on a quarterly basis, often with a compliance-oriented lens. While this method provides structure, it is increasingly insufficient in the face of complex, fast-evolving environments.

In contrast, *risk intelligence* is a dynamic capability. It involves continuously scanning for signals across digital, stakeholder, and systemic domains, integrating real-time dashboards with strategic foresight tools, and using AI and analytics to detect anomalies, emerging patterns, and latent threats. More importantly, it shifts the mindset from risk as a constraint to risk as a strategic input - a source of learning, adaptation, and even innovation. Agile associations don't just manage risk - they learn from it.

To build genuine agility, associations will have to go beyond reacting to known risks. The following section introduces four categories of strategic risk unique to platform-era associations - risks that demand new capabilities, new mindsets, and new governance responses.

Strategic Risks in Platform Associations

As associations evolve into platform-based organisations, their risk landscape becomes more complex, interconnected, and fast-moving. Traditional compliance-focused risk registers are no longer sufficient. Instead, boards and executives will have to adopt a risk intelligence mindset, one that sees risk not only as something to mitigate, but also as a strategic input into adaptation, innovation, and trust stewardship.

Platform-based associations face a distinctive set of strategic risks. These arise not just from external shocks, but from the very architecture of platforms themselves: their dependencies, their velocity, and their exposure to multi-sided interactions. Risks are no longer linear or isolated, they are amplified through networks, triggered by algorithms, and shaped by partner behaviours. Failure in one part of the ecosystem can rapidly cascade across the whole.

This section outlines four categories of strategic risk most relevant to platform-era associations and introduces tools to help leaders build organisational risk intelligence - a capability that is proactive, participatory, and insight-driven.

- **Digital Concentration Risk:** Over-reliance on a single vendor, system, or platform layer creates systemic fragility.
- **Trust Risk:** Poor transparency in AI decisions, personalisation algorithms, or data use can erode member confidence - even if compliant.
- **Reputational Amplification:** In a multi-sided network, reputational damage spreads faster - triggered by partners, members, or automated systems.
- **Innovation Risk:** Avoiding risk entirely may lead to irrelevance. Strategic risk includes missed opportunities for bold adaptation.

Boards and CEOs will have to ask:

- What early signals are we missing?
- What are we treating as a policy issue that is actually a systemic risk?
- Where are our risk blind spots - especially in digital and reputational domains?

Table 10-4 Building Risk Intelligence Capability

Capability	Example Practice
Signal Monitoring	Real-time analytics dashboards for engagement, sentiment, and digital trust
Scenario Planning	Board workshops modelling AI failure, partner breach, or platform disruption
Cross-Functional Risk Forums	Risk reviewed jointly by IT, member services, ethics, and governance
AI/Automation Registers	Specific tracking of automated processes and their consequences
Ethical Risk Reviews	Evaluation of personalisation, sponsorship, or data monetisation trade-offs

The following case study illustrates how one association has embedded risk intelligence into its platform operations - demonstrating what it looks like to move from static risk registers to dynamic, ethical, and systemic oversight.

Example 49. Evolving Risk Management

The Medical Technology Association of Australia (MTAA) exemplifies how a modern association adapts its risk management approach in response to digital transformation and a more interconnected operating environment. As MTAA and its members increasingly rely on digital platforms for engagement, advocacy, and service delivery, the association's risk landscape has become more dynamic and complex, requiring a shift from traditional, static risk registers to more adaptive and integrated risk management practices[1].

From Static Risk Registers to Dynamic Risk Management

Historically, associations like MTAA managed risk through periodic reviews and compliance-driven policies, focusing on predictable financial, regulatory, or operational exposures. However, the rise of digital health, cyber threats, and data-driven operations has introduced new risks, including:

- *Cybersecurity vulnerabilities and data privacy concerns*
- *Rapidly evolving regulatory requirements for digital health and AI*
- *Reputational risks amplified by digital channels and real-time information flows*

MTAA has responded by advocating for and supporting more continuous, responsive risk management practices. This includes:

- ***Real-Time Monitoring and Threat Sharing:*** *MTAA has welcomed and supported the development of sector-specific cyber threat sharing platforms, recognising the need for real-time monitoring and coordinated responses to digital risks in healthcare*[1].
- ***Scenario Planning and Strategic Foresight:*** *The association participates in scenario-based workshops and consultations, particularly around the regulation and deployment of AI in healthcare. This proactive approach helps prepare for systemic risks and supports strategic decision-making*[3].
- ***Cross-Functional Risk Oversight:*** *MTAA's governance includes working groups and advisory panels (e.g., Cyber Security Working Group, Digital Health Advisory Group) that bring together expertise from IT, member services, ethics, and governance to review risks holistically*[3].
- ***Ethical and Regulatory Focus:*** *MTAA's submissions and advocacy highlight the importance of ethical oversight, especially regarding AI, data use, and cybersecurity. The association supports the development of mandatory guardrails and best practice guidelines for high-risk digital health settings*[32].

Table 10-5 Key Practices in MTAA's Risk Management Approach

Practice Area	MTAA Approach
Cybersecurity	Advocates for real-time threat sharing and sector-specific cyber security investment[12]
Scenario Planning	Engages in scenario-based workshops for AI and digital health risk preparedness[3]
Cross-Functional Governance	Utilises working groups and advisory panels for holistic risk review[3]
Ethical Risk Management	Promotes ethical oversight in AI, data, and digital health practices[3]
Regulatory Engagement	Works with government and regulators to align risk management with evolving standards[23]

Lessons for Platform-Based Associations

MTAA's experience demonstrates that, in a platform context, risk management will have to be:

- **Continuous and Responsive**: Real-time monitoring and early warning systems are essential for identifying and responding to emerging risks.
- **Integrated and Collaborative**: Cross-functional teams and sector-wide coordination improve risk oversight and response.

- **Ethically Grounded**: Ongoing ethical review and alignment with member and public expectations are critical, especially in health and data-driven sectors.
- **Strategically Informed**: Scenario planning and foresight support preparedness for fast-moving, systemic risks.

MTAA's evolving approach to risk management reflects the realities of a platform-based association operating in a digital, interconnected environment. By moving beyond static risk registers to embrace continuous monitoring, scenario planning, and ethical oversight, MTAA is better positioned to manage uncertainty, protect its members, and support innovation in the medical technology sector.

Agile associations don't just manage risk, they learn from it. This case illustrates how risk intelligence in a platform-based association is fundamentally different from traditional risk management: it is dynamic, systemic, and deeply integrated into the digital fabric of the organisation, enabling both resilience and strategic advantage.

This case illustrates how risk intelligence in a platform-based association is fundamentally different from traditional risk management. It is dynamic, systemic, and deeply integrated into the digital fabric of the organisation, enabling both resilience and strategic advantage.

The Role of the Board

The board's role is to embed risk intelligence into strategy. That means ensuring systems are in place to detect and respond, not just review and report, creating space for "difficult" risks - reputational, ethical, and systemic - in board agendas and challenging over-confidence in technology vendors, automation, or compliance alone.

In the next section, we turn to a specific emerging domain of risk, artificial intelligence and digital automation, and the new governance responsibilities they create for boards and leadership teams.

With AI now driving many decisions in member experience, CPD, and service delivery, governance responsibilities will have to extend beyond traditional IT oversight. The next section explores how boards can govern AI systems with the same ethical and strategic scrutiny applied to finances or compliance.

The Board's Role in Governing AI and Digital Trust

As associations integrate artificial intelligence (AI), automation, and algorithmic systems into their platforms, new governance responsibilities emerge - not just for IT teams, but for boards. These technologies can personalise learning, optimise operations, and improve member service. But they also introduce risks: bias, opacity, exclusion, and loss of member trust.

Boards will have to step into a new role: *governing intelligent systems* in the same way they govern finances, strategy, or risk.

Figure 10-2 **Example Risk Dashboard**

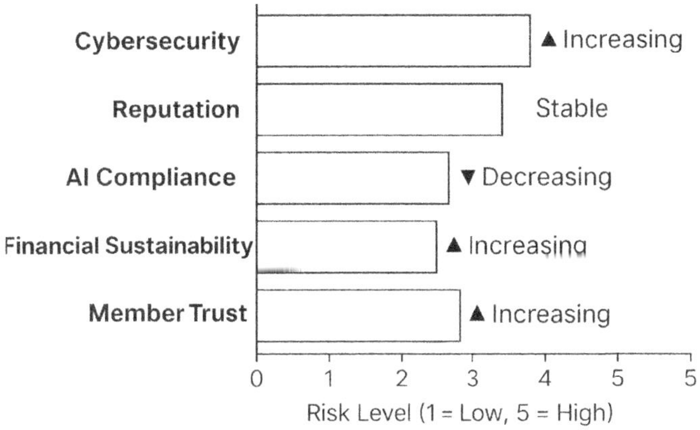

What's Different About Governing AI?

Governing AI is fundamentally different from overseeing traditional information systems. Unlike static tools that store data or automate routine tasks, AI makes decisions, often in real time and with far-reaching implications. These decisions can directly influence member experiences, such as learning pathways, job or mentoring recommendations, CPD compliance status, prioritisation of services, or even risk alerts surfaced to executive teams and boards. As such, AI is not just a technical asset, it is a strategic actor within the association.

Figure 10-3 **The AI Governance Toolbox**

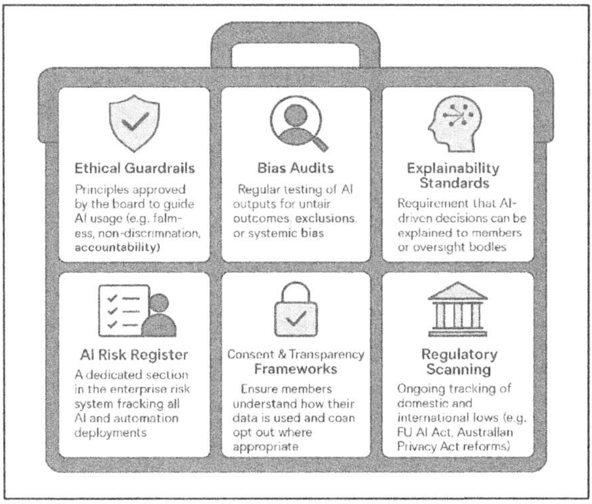

This elevates the board's responsibility to ensure that AI systems are governed with the same rigour and accountability as any other high-stakes decision-making process. Boards will have to consider issues of ethics, transparency, data rights, including privacy, and strategic alignment when deploying or approving the use of AI. If you wouldn't permit an unaccountable individual to make sensitive member-facing decisions, you shouldn't allow an unaccountable algorithm to do so either. Governance in the age of AI demands both technological fluency and moral clarity.

Minimum Oversight Questions for Boards

1. *Do we know where AI is being used across the organisation?*
2. *Have we approved a set of AI principles aligned with our mission and member expectations?*
3. *Is there a mechanism for reviewing harm, bias, or ethical concerns arising from automation?*
4. *Can we explain - in plain language - how our AI tools make decisions?*
5. *Do we have risk ownership for AI embedded in the board or committee structure?*

AI is not simply a technical capability, it is a governance challenge. Trust can be undermined not by malicious intent, but by silent misalignment between technology and member expectations.

Associations that embed ethical oversight early will:

- Build deeper member trust
- Strengthen board legitimacy
- Pre-empt regulatory and reputational risk
- Position themselves as sector leaders in digital responsibility

In the next section, we explore how these principles of agile governance and digital trust translate into new distributed governance models - giving boards more visibility, more flexibility, and stronger member alignment.

Example 50. AI Eligibility Review Controversy

At its June meeting, the board of the Professional Network Association (PNA) was briefed on a proposed upgrade to its CPD platform. The upgrade included a machine learning algorithm that would assess a member's "readiness" for advanced CPD programs, using historic engagement, prior completions, and member profile data to filter applicants automatically.

The vendor framed it as a productivity gain with fewer manual applications, higher match accuracy, and more targeted learning journeys. But the Head of Policy raised a red flag: "Are we creating a digital gatekeeper without oversight?"

The ensuing discussion surfaced deeper questions:

- *The algorithm was trained on past participation data, biasing it toward already engaged members.*
- *There was no transparency mechanism or human appeals process.*

Early testing showed that members from regional and diverse backgrounds were under-represented in the algorithm's "ready now" list.

PNA's board activated its AI Governance Protocol, developed under its Digital Ethics Charter. It mandated:

- *A fairness audit of the training data,*
- *The inclusion of a member appeals process,*
- *Transparent notification to affected members, including why a recommendation was or wasn't made,*
- *An annual algorithm accountability report to be tabled at the AGM.*

"We want to use AI to support access, not to hard-code inequality into our systems.": Board Director, PNA (Fictional).

The incident marked a cultural shift: from seeing AI as a backend tool to recognising it as a governance domain in its own right, with reputational, ethical, and strategic consequences.

Embedding trust and responsiveness into decision-making requires more than agile principles, it demands a structural shift in how authority, oversight, and insight are distributed. The next section explores distributed governance models that maintain board accountability while enhancing agility and participation.

Distributed Governance Models for Associations

Agile governance is not simply about being faster, it's about being closer to where value and risk emerge. In traditional governance models, all strategic authority resides in the board and a set of standing committees. But in a digital, platform-enabled association, this structure can struggle to keep pace with:

- Rapid shifts in technology and regulation
- Multi-sided stakeholder dynamics
- The need for real-time responsiveness and feedback

To bridge this gap, leading associations are adopting distributed governance models - frameworks that preserve accountability while embedding insight, innovation, and member voice deeper into decision-making.

What is Distributed Governance?

Distributed governance is a model in which oversight and decision-making are shared across multiple, specialised structures, rather than concentrated solely within the board or executive. It enables a more agile and informed approach to complex organisational challenges by leveraging targeted expertise, real-time data, and inclusive participation. In practice, this might include board sub-committees, digital ethics panels, AI advisory groups, member forums, or cross-functional risk committees. These structures are designed to respond to emerging risks in specific domains, such as technology, compliance, or member experience, while still feeding into a coherent governance system.

Crucially, distributed governance does not dilute accountability. Instead, it strengthens it by ensuring that decisions are made with the right expertise, at the right time, and with the appropriate level of transparency. In a platform-enabled, data-rich environment, such distributed structures are essential for ensuring strategic responsiveness and trust stewardship across all levels of the association.

Table 10-6 Emerging Models of Distributed Oversight

Structure	Function	Where to Use It
Digital Advisory Group	Oversees digital platform evolution, vendor decisions, member experience	During major tech investment cycles
AI Ethics or Tech Risk Panel	Reviews and guides the ethical use of automation, data, and analytics	In AI-powered member services or personalised CPD
Member Governance Labs	Co-design policies and engagement models with member segments	To strengthen legitimacy and user alignment
Innovation Risk Forums	Reviews pilot projects and "fail fast" experiments to balance agility with risk management	For CPD pilots, engagement tool trials, monetisation testing
Embedded Risk Stewards	Individuals inside teams tasked with raising emerging risks and horizon-scanning	Within tech, policy, or marketing teams using new tools

Benefits of Distributed Governance

In platform-based associations, traditional centralised governance can create bottlenecks and blind spots. Distributed governance provides a more responsive alternative, placing decision-making closer to where insight and impact occur. It enables faster action, broader visibility, and stronger trust by involving the right people at the right levels. Below are four key benefits that make this model essential for modern associations.

1. **Increased agility**: Decisions are made where insight lives

2. **Broader visibility**: Diverse perspectives surface emerging risk and opportunity
3. **Stronger trust**: Members and staff see governance in action, not just in reports
4. **Reduced bottlenecks**: Operational and digital decisions are not trapped at board level

Design Principles for Distributed Models

Effective distributed governance doesn't mean decentralising for its own sake, it requires intentional design. Structures will have to be clear in their remit, connected to strategic oversight, and composed of the right expertise. The following principles help ensure distributed models remain purposeful, agile, and aligned with the organisation's evolving context.

- **Clarity of remit**: Define decision boundaries and escalation pathways
- **Connected reporting**: Feed insights and signals into board risk and strategy oversight
- **Skills-based participation**: Include staff, members, and external experts with relevant knowledge
- **Sunset clauses or rolling reviews**: Ensure governance groups evolve with context and don't become static structures

Questions for Governance Design Teams

- Where in our organisation are the biggest gaps between decision-making and insight?
- How can we involve members meaningfully without slowing responsiveness?
- What mechanisms do we have for surfacing weak signals, not just confirmed problems?
- Which decisions need escalation - and which can be safely distributed?

In the next section, we bring these models to life through a real-world case study - showing how one association successfully shifted to an agile, distributed governance structure without compromising rigour or accountability.

Governance Archetypes

The table below provides a view of governance archetypes commonly used in associations and aligning them with the platform context. This provides directors and CEOs with a comparative view of structures, decision rights, and use cases as associations scale or diversify their ecosystem.

The lifecycle stages align directly with the APSF's Design Pillars, ensuring that digital strategy is not siloed, but part of a coordinated investment in Member-Centric Design, Scalable Infrastructure, and Governance & Trust.

Table 10-7 Governance Archetypes in Platform-Based Associations

Model Type	Key Characteristics & Decision Rights	Platform Alignment & Example Use Cases
Centralised	Top-down governance; board or head office retains most decision rights	Best for single-entity, compliance-heavy platforms. e.g. accreditation bodies, credentialing agencies
Federated	Shared governance between national and regional entities under a common strategy	Balances localisation with consistency. e.g. state-based member orgs, federated peak bodies
Delegated / Networked	Oversight by a central board; operational decision-making delegated to agile teams or panels	Enables responsiveness within ecosystems. e.g. innovation labs, ethics committees, member-led CPD initiatives
Decentralised	Governance distributed through collective, often tech-enabled mechanisms (e.g. token or consensus voting)	Suits transparent, community-driven platforms. e.g. DAOs, Web3 orgs, open-source policy labs

Strategic Consideration for Boards:

- Centralised models enable control but risk slow adaptation.
- Federated models support growth but require strong integration and clarity of delegation.
- Delegated/networked models enable agile response and inclusion.
- Decentralised models can build trust and innovation, but require new governance skills.

The following case study shows how one association redesigned its governance model from the ground up - aligning structure, capability, and culture to meet the demands of digital transformation.

Example 51. Agile Governance in Practice

To understand how agile and distributed governance can work in practice, consider the experience of a hypothetical national professional association that undertook a full governance redesign in response to digital transformation, declining engagement, and reputational risk following a data breach.

The Challenge: *The association had:*

- *A traditional governance structure: board, finance committee, and a risk & audit committee*
- *Quarterly meetings with long board packs and slow decision cycles*
- *Limited oversight of major digital investments*
- *No formal role for member feedback in strategic planning*
- *A growing sense that governance was "out of step" with its digital-first strategy*

Leadership recognised that as the association digitised services, diversified revenue, and adopted AI-enabled platforms, the governance model also needed to evolve.

The Response: A Governance Reset

- *The board initiated a six-month governance redesign process with the following goals:*
- *Increase responsiveness to digital, reputational, and ecosystem risks*
- *Embed ethical oversight into AI and automation decisions*
- *Improve data flow from frontline insights to board-level strategy*
- *Create meaningful spaces for member input and cross-functional collaboration.*

Table 10-8 The New Governance Model

Feature	***Description***
Digital Oversight Group	*Subcommittee of the board monitoring digital transformation, platform strategy, and technology investment risks*
AI Ethics Advisory Panel	*Cross-functional group reviewing personalisation, algorithmic bias, and data usage policies*
Member Experience Lab	*Member-led group co-designing engagement models and giving structured feedback on new services*
Innovation Risk Forum	*Quarterly open forum for piloting and debriefing experiments before scale-up*
Live Risk Dashboard	*Replaced static risk register with dynamic, real-time monitoring integrated into board portal*

Outcomes required

- *Faster decision cycles: Time to approve digital pilots reduced*
- *Improved trust: Post-implementation survey showed higher confidence in board oversight*
- *Better alignment: Strategic plans now include member signals and platform performance data*
- *Regulatory preparedness: The board is now proactively scanning and scenario-testing AI and data regulation changes.*

This case illustrates how modern governance can maintain board accountability while improving responsiveness, stakeholder alignment, and insight flow.

Table 10-9 Lessons for Other Associations

Insight	Application Tip
Structure follows capability	Build governance around insight sources and decision velocity needs
Boards don't need to know AI - but will have to govern it	Use advisory panels and briefings to bring relevant expertise to the table
Agility doesn't mean informality	Distributed governance still needs charters, clarity, and reporting lines
Experimentation requires visibility	Pilot innovation with guardrails, but integrate learnings into strategy

By rethinking governance as a capability - not just a structure - we were able to match the speed of digital without sacrificing oversight or integrity.

In the final section of this chapter, we synthesise the key shifts and principles of agile governance, offering a pathway for boards ready to lead through complexity - not just manage it.

From Oversight to Orchestration

The governance models of the past were designed to enforce compliance, control risk, and maintain order. These functions still matter - but they are no longer enough.

In the digital era, associations operate within multi-sided ecosystems, powered by intelligent platforms, real-time data, and stakeholder co-creation. In this context, boards will have to evolve from controllers of information to orchestrators of trust, agility, and strategic direction.

This chapter has shown that agile governance is not simply a structural choice, it is a strategic enabler that underpins all Design Pillars of the *Association Platform Success Framework*. It activates Member-Centric Design by supporting real-time responsiveness to member needs and co-creating policy through participatory governance models. It enhances Scalable Infrastructure by enabling adaptive oversight of digital systems, AI, and vendor ecosystems. And it fortifies Governance & Trust by embedding ethical scrutiny, transparency, and distributed decision-making into the platform's operating model.

Boards that align agile governance with the APSF are not just modernising processes they are building the institutional muscle to navigate risk, foster innovation, and steward trust in complex, dynamic environments.

Agile governance is not a management trend, it is a response to the complexity, speed, and ethical demands of the platform age.

Table 10-10 Key Shifts for Modern Governance

From...	To...
Static committees	Dynamic oversight and advisory panels
Annual risk reviews	Real-time risk intelligence and scenario-based governance
Retrospective reporting	Insight dashboards and forward-looking metrics
Policy compliance	Ethical decision-making and adaptive governance
Top-down engagement	Participatory co-design and member feedback loops
Technology as operations	Technology as a board-level strategic asset

Boards that embrace agile governance are better positioned to:

- Navigate regulatory complexity and AI disruption
- Build and retain member trust through ethical technology use
- Enable faster, more informed decisions
- Steward culture, innovation, and purpose - not just compliance

Agility is not the absence of rigour. It's rigour in motion - adaptive, insight-driven, and accountable.

Table 10-11 Governance Maturity Model Attributes

Governance Maturity Level	Cultural & Strategic Attributes	Data & Trust Characteristics
Compliance-Oriented	Risk-averse; avoids innovation; minimal tolerance for deviation	Manual reporting; reactive compliance; basic controls in place
Structured	Process-focused; escalates within defined hierarchies; steady operational rhythm	Periodic dashboards; formal policies; responsibilities are defined and enforced
Adaptive	Innovation encouraged in pilots; decision rights	Real-time data informs decisions; transparency

	delegated within clear frameworks	embedded in operational controls
Strategic	Innovation embedded; courage to act on insight; embraces calculated risk	Predictive insights support foresight; ethical leadership and trust are design features

Table 10-12 Governance Maturity Behaviours

Behaviour	Lower Maturity (Compliance / Structured)	Higher Maturity (Adaptive / Strategic)
Innovation	Risk-averse; innovation limited or procedural	Actively encouraged; integrated into strategy and culture
Courage	Avoids decision-making risk; escalates cautiously	Embraces uncertainty; makes timely, informed decisions with clarity of mandate
Use of Data & Insight	Relies on backward-looking reports; limited analytical capability	Uses real-time and predictive data; insight embedded in governance and foresight

How to Use This Matrix

- Review with the board during strategic planning or governance reviews.
- Link to capability-building actions in technology, data, and decision-making.

Table 10-13 Governance Maturity Snapshot for Platform Associations

Maturity Level	Governance Posture	Defining Behaviours	Data & Insight Use
Compliance-Oriented	Risk-averse, reactive	Follows policy; avoids innovation	Manual reports; limited analytics
Structured	Process-focused, steady-state	Escalates issues; governs via committee cycles	Periodic dashboards; defined roles
Adaptive	Innovation-tolerant, insight-led	Delegates within frameworks; learns from experimentation	Real-time signals; integrated decision support
Strategic	Foresight-driven, mission-aligned	Anticipates risk; acts with clarity; embeds ethical oversight	Predictive analytics; member-centric transparency

Use This Matrix To:

- Reflect on your current board governance behaviours
- Identify priority capabilities to build agility and trust

- Align with the APSF and your digital maturity strategy

Insight: Governance is not a structure, it's a system of behaviours. Boards that govern with learning, speed, and transparency are best placed to lead in the platform era.

Reflection Questions for Boards:

- Where does our current governance model fall on this matrix?
- What decisions are currently delayed due to structure, not substance?
- How are we ensuring ethical oversight of AI and automation?

The Path Forward for Boards

1. Assess your governance model against platform-era demands
2. Map key risks and decisions to the right structures and capabilities
3. Invest in digital fluency at board and executive levels
4. Create space for participation - from staff, members, and subject matter experts
5. Lead with courage and clarity - not just caution

The next frontier in agile governance is data: how associations collect, analyse, and act on the insights that power member personalisation, revenue growth, and risk management. In the next chapter, we explore how to build a strategic data and insight capability that is ethical, actionable, and board-visible - enabling governance that learns, adapts, and leads from the front.

Part V. Implementation and Capability

No platform-enabled association can thrive without the right enabling infrastructure. Part III focuses on the foundations: data capability, digital insight, AI governance, and agile oversight. It examines how associations can build systems that support innovation, trust, and responsiveness. These chapters help leaders integrate technology with strategy, embed ethical use of data and automation, and redesign governance structures to match the complexity of the digital era.

Chapter 11. Strategy, Culture and Capability

Example 52. The Culture Gap

Claire Evans closed her laptop and looked around the room. It had been a difficult executive meeting. The agenda was packed with urgent initiatives: a new digital onboarding system, a member-led CPD pilot, and a proposal to partner with an EdTech startup. Yet the energy in the room was flat.

"I feel like we're dragging strategy up a hill," she said quietly.

Heads nodded. The CIO mentioned that staff were confused about the difference between projects and pilots. The membership lead admitted that frontline teams were still measured on old KPIs. "We're saying we want innovation, but people are scared of breaking something. Or being blamed if they do."

It wasn't resistance. Everyone supported the vision of a modern, member-centric PNA. But the structures, incentives, and habits in the organisation still reflected an older model, one optimised for stability, not agility.

After the meeting, Claire walked back to her office thinking about the gap. It was no longer a strategy problem. The roadmap was sound, the board was aligned, and funding had been approved. What they lacked was strategic fitness, the internal capability and culture needed to execute in a fast-moving, platform-based environment.

She scribbled a question in her notebook.

What do we need to unlearn in order to change for real?

The Engine of Organisational Evolution

External change may spark the need for transformation, but it is internal capability that determines whether associations survive or thrive. A compelling strategy without the culture to support it is inert. The most sophisticated platform technology is wasted without teams capable of iterating, collaborating, and adapting in real time.

This chapter explores how associations can align *strategy, culture, and capability* to deliver on the promise of Association 2.0. It reframes transformation as a systems challenge that requires intentional design across leadership behaviour, team structure, learning systems, and organisational mindset.

From Strategic Plans to Strategic Fitness

Traditional strategic planning, often framed in three to five-year cycles, is increasingly unfit for purpose. In an environment shaped by uncertainty, speed, and complexity, what matters most is *strategic fitness*, the ability to sense, adapt, and respond in real time while staying anchored in purpose.

High strategic-fitness associations:

1. Use **short-cycle planning** (e.g. 12 to 18-month adaptive roadmaps)
2. Embrace h**ypothesis-driven strategy** and continuous learning
3. Treat member insight and **ecosystem feedback** as strategic assets
4. **Empower cross-functional teams** to test and iterate ideas

Short Cycles Outperform Long Cycles

Long planning cycles often assume a stable operating environment where risks, opportunities, and member needs evolve slowly. This assumption no longer holds true. When plans are locked in for three to five years, they can quickly become obsolete, leaving boards managing yesterday's priorities with tomorrow's resources.

Short planning cycles provide three critical advantages:

- **Responsiveness**: Associations can pivot as member expectations, technologies, or policy environments shift, without waiting for the next "big plan" refresh.
- **Learning Orientation**: Short cycles encourage experimentation, where assumptions can be tested and adjusted before they calcify into sunk costs.
- **Strategic Relevance**: By embedding regular recalibration points, associations ensure their strategy reflects the real conditions of their ecosystem, not an outdated snapshot.

From Documents to Rhythms

The platform model demands responsiveness at scale. Instead of producing static documents, associations should establish *strategic rhythms*: recurring cycles of sensing, framing, acting, and adjusting. This moves strategy from a periodic exercise into an organisational practice.

In this model, the "north star" is not a five-year plan but a set of enduring goals (purpose, value creation, impact) that guide continuous adaptation. Short-cycle planning keeps the organisation agile while ensuring coherence with those longer-term aims.

Situating Short Cycles in an Extended Vision

An extended vision, say, a ten-year vision, provides the long-term direction of travel, the "why" and "where" the association intends to be. But the pathway to achieving that vision should be navigated through short-cycle planning, which translates aspiration into adaptive, testable steps.

The Relationship Between Long Horizon and Short Cycles

- **Vision as Anchor**: The ten-year vision articulates enduring goals of legitimacy, impact, systemic value, that remain stable even as conditions shift.
- **Cycles as Navigation**: Twelve to eighteen-month cycles act like course corrections, allowing the association to adapt its route while keeping sight of the destination.
- **Learning as Compass**: Each cycle generates insights that refine not only the immediate roadmap but also the broader understanding of how to achieve the vision.

Practical Model

1. **Ten-Year Vision**. Broad, aspirational outcomes (e.g. "By 2035, we will be the primary ecosystem hub for [profession/sector], enabling trust, innovation, and public impact.").
2. **Three-Year Strategic Horizons**: Medium-term priorities that frame major thrusts (e.g. digital transformation, advocacy capacity, global partnerships). These horizons may evolve but keep the organisation aligned with the vision.
3. **12–18 Month Adaptive Roadmaps**: Concrete, testable initiatives that operationalise strategy in the current environment. At the end of each cycle, roadmaps are reviewed against both the three-year horizon and the ten-year vision.

Governance Implications

Boards play a critical role in holding the tension between durability and agility:

- Ensuring the ten-year vision remains relevant and legitimate.
- Monitoring progress through short-cycle metrics and learning loops.
- Encouraging management to adapt tactics without losing sight of strategic intent.

Metaphor

Think of the ten-year vision as a destination port. The three-year horizons are the charted routes, and the 12–18 month cycles are the adjustments to sails and course in response to shifting winds and currents. Without the destination, short cycles risk drifting; without short cycles, the vessel risks running aground in unpredictable seas.

Capability-Building for Platform Success

To implement platform thinking, associations will have to build capabilities across several key dimensions:

Table 11-1 Capability-Building

Capability Domain	What It Enables
Member Insight	Understanding needs, preferences, behaviours for personalisation
Agile Execution	Rapid development, testing, and delivery of services
Digital Fluency	Confident, ethical use of tools, platforms, and automation
Collaborative Design	Co-creation with members and partners
Strategic Foresight	Anticipating trends and aligning strategy to future drivers
Governance Agility	Delegation, transparency, and oversight aligned to transformation pace

Leadership teams should assess their current capability profile using a maturity model (such as the Governance Capability Heatmap) and identify priority gaps to close.

Culture as Strategy's Enabler

Peter Drucker's maxim that "culture eats strategy for breakfast" holds particularly true in times of transformation. Associations with risk-averse, compliance-centric cultures will struggle to implement platform strategies.

Three cultural traits are essential, *Curiosity*, the hunger to learn from members, partners, and data; *Courage*, the willingness to challenge legacy norms and test new models; and *Collaboration*, a mindset that values shared ownership, experimentation, and feedback.

These traits will have to be modelled at the board and executive levels. A learning culture is not created by training sessions. It emerges from how leaders act in meetings, frame decisions, and respond to failure.

Practical Levers for Cultural and Capability Change

Transformation relies on concrete levers that shift behaviour and align systems. Associations can initiate change by acting across five domains:

Structure

- Shift from function-based silos to cross-functional teams
- Create agile pods or project squads for key initiatives

Incentives

- Recognise and reward collaboration, experimentation, and member-centricity
- Introduce transformation KPIs for teams and leaders

Learning

- Invest in internal upskilling for platform tools, data fluency, and service design

- Establish peer-to-peer learning labs or communities of practice

Leadership

- Coach executives and board members in systems thinking and adaptive governance
- Use quarterly strategy pulses to model agility and responsiveness

Rituals and Rhythms

- Replace static monthly reporting with fortnightly sprint reviews
- Hold retrospectives and reflection sessions as part of normal operations

Each of these signals a shift from hierarchy to learning, from control to enablement.

Example 53. PNA: Building Adaptive Capacity

As part of its shift to a platform model, PNA recognised that digital infrastructure alone was insufficient. Member engagement would stall unless the organisation could work differently.

PNA implemented:

- *A monthly "capability lab" for staff to explore data tools and member journey mapping*
- *A cross-departmental agile squad tasked with redesigning onboarding*
- *Quarterly CEO-led retrospectives to reflect on strategic experiments and their outcomes*

Results required were faster delivery of member-centric services, improved staff engagement, and the emergence of peer mentors across the team.

***The lesson**: culture and capability are not side projects. They are core infrastructure for platform transformation.*

Reflection Questions for Boards and Executives

- Are we learning faster than our environment is changing?
- Do our incentives reward adaptation, collaboration, and insight use?
- What signals do our board practices send about agility, trust, and curiosity?
- Have we allocated real resources (time, people, budget) to capability development?

Leading from Within

Strategy is not just a plan. It is a practice. Capability is not just a checklist. It is a posture. Culture is not just about morale. It is the fuel that enables strategy to fly.

Associations that modernise their internal systems will be positioned not just to survive disruption but to orchestrate value, lead ecosystems, and model the governance standards of the future.

Platform success begins on the inside.

Example 54. Capability Self-Assessment Worksheet

Strategy, Culture, and Capability Purpose

Use this worksheet to evaluate your association's current strengths and areas for improvement across the six core capability domains required for platform-based success. Complete individually or in teams, then compare and discuss results.

Instructions

For each capability domain, rate your current state using the scale below: 1 = Not yet developed; 2 = Early progress; 3 = Functional but limited; 4 = Developing well; 5 = Strong and embedded

Table 11-2 Capability Self-Assessment

Capability Domain	Description	Your Rating (1–5)	Evidence or Comments
Member Insight	We understand member needs through data, feedback, and behaviour analysis.		
Agile Execution	We can quickly develop, test, and adjust new programs or services.		
Digital Fluency	Our staff and leaders are confident using digital tools and systems effectively.		
Collaborative Design	We involve members, staff, and partners in co-designing services and strategy.		
Strategic Foresight	We scan for future trends and integrate them into planning and decision-making.		
Governance Agility	Our board and leadership structures enable timely, responsive decisions.		

Interpretation Guide

- 24–30: Strong capability foundation. Focus on continuous improvement and leadership development.
- 18–23: Moderate capability. Consider targeted development in weaker areas.
- 12–17: Gaps likely to affect strategy execution. Prioritise improvement projects.
- Below 12: Foundational challenges. Recommend facilitated workshop or organisational reset.

Next Steps

- What is our strongest domain?

- Where is the biggest gap between aspiration and reality?
- What two capability areas should we prioritise in the next 90 days?
- How can the board and executive team model the behaviours we want to see?

Example 55. Engineers Australia

Engineers Australia (EA), the nation's peak body for engineering professionals, provides a compelling real-world example of how an association can bridge the gap between strategy, culture, and capability to deliver on a platform-based vision. Facing rapid technological change, evolving member expectations, and the need for greater agility, EA embarked on a multi-year transformation to modernise its internal systems, leadership behaviours, and organisational mindset.

The Challenge: The Culture and Capability Gap

Despite a clear strategic roadmap and board alignment, EA's leadership recognised that legacy structures and habits were impeding progress. Staff were still measured on traditional KPIs, and risk-averse mindsets limited experimentation. There was broad support for innovation, but the culture remained optimised for stability rather than agility. This "culture gap" manifested as slow project delivery, confusion over new digital initiatives, and hesitancy to challenge established norms.

The Transformation: Building Strategic Fitness

EA's transformation focused on intentionally aligning strategy, culture, and capability:

Short-Cycle Planning: *EA shifted from static, multi-year plans to adaptive 12–18 month roadmaps, enabling faster response to member and market feedback.*

Agile Execution: *Cross-functional "agile squads" were established to deliver key projects, such as the digital member platform and new CPD offerings. These teams were empowered to test, iterate, and learn rapidly.*

Capability Labs and Peer Learning: *Monthly "capability labs" were introduced, where staff explored new digital tools, data analytics, and member journey mapping. Peer mentors emerged, fostering a culture of shared learning and experimentation.*

Leadership and Governance Agility: *The executive team modelled adaptive leadership through quarterly retrospectives, openly reflecting on strategic experiments and failures. The board revised its governance rhythms, replacing static reporting with sprint reviews and real-time feedback loops.*

Incentives and Recognition: *New KPIs and recognition systems rewarded collaboration, experimentation, and member-centricity, rather than just compliance and process adherence.*

Outcomes

- ***Faster Delivery:*** *Member-centric services were delivered more quickly, with agile squads reducing project lead times and increasing satisfaction.*
- ***Improved Staff Engagement:*** *Staff reported higher engagement and confidence in using digital tools, with a notable increase in cross-team collaboration.*
- ***Cultural Shift:*** *The organisation moved from a compliance-centric to a learning-oriented culture, where curiosity, courage, and collaboration were actively modelled by leaders.*
- ***Strategic Fitness:*** *EA became more responsive to external change, using member insight and ecosystem feedback as strategic assets.*

Lessons for Associations

- *Culture and capability are not side projects, they are core infrastructure for transformation.*
- *Strategic fitness requires ongoing investment in learning, adaptive leadership, and systems that reward agility and collaboration.*
- *Platform success begins on the inside: Modernising internal culture and capability is essential for delivering value in a fast-moving, platform-based environment.*

Table 11-3 Capability Self-Assessment Example

Capability Domain	Description	EA's Progress (1–5)	Evidence/Comments
Member Insight	Understanding needs through data, feedback, behaviour analysis	4	Member analytics, journey mapping, feedback loops
Agile Execution	Rapid development, testing, and delivery of services	4	Agile squads, short-cycle planning
Digital Fluency	Confident, ethical use of digital tools and platforms	4	Capability labs, digital upskilling
Collaborative Design	Co-creation with members and partners	3	Member co-design workshops, cross-functional teams

Strategic Foresight	Anticipating trends, integrating into planning	4	Scenario planning, regular strategy pulses
Governance Agility	Delegation, transparency, oversight aligned to transformation pace	4	Board sprint reviews, adaptive governance frameworks

Interpretation: EA demonstrates a strong capability foundation, with continuous improvement in collaborative design and member co-creation.

Part VI. Implementation and Measuring Success

Even the best-designed strategy fails without disciplined execution. Part IV equips associations with practical tools to track progress, align governance, and adapt in real time. It introduces diagnostic scorecards, capability assessments, and implementation frameworks that support continuous improvement. Boards and executives will find guidance on how to structure transformation efforts, prioritise investment, and embed accountability for impact across the organisation.

Chapter 12. Measuring What Matters

Example 56. Are we measuring the right things?

Claire Evans, CEO of the Professional Network Association (PNA), reviewed the latest performance dashboard. Membership numbers had increased by 6%, Continuing Professional Development (CPD) attendance was stable, and sponsorship income remained steady. Yet, something felt amiss.

Despite these positive indicators, platform usage was stagnant. Member-generated content was minimal, new discussion forums were inactive, and the AI-powered career hub was underutilised. The metrics indicated success, but Claire's instincts suggested otherwise.

At the subsequent board meeting, she posed a critical question:

> *"What if we're focusing on the wrong metrics?"*

This inquiry initiated a comprehensive reassessment of how PNA defined and measured success. It became evident that traditional metrics were insufficient. To lead effectively in a platform-centric era, they needed to evaluate member engagement, network effects, governance capability, and sustainable value creation.

This chapter builds on that insight.

Introduction: What You Measure Is What You Mobilise

Metrics are not neutral; they shape organisational behaviour and priorities. The indicators associations choose to monitor influence resource allocation, staff actions, and board perceptions of success. In the context of platform-based associations, traditional metrics like membership counts or event attendance fail to capture the dynamic nature of engagement and impact.

This chapter repositions measurement as a strategic capability. Associations will have to develop systems that assess not only inputs and outputs but also engagement patterns, relationship quality, governance trustworthiness, and impact sustainability.

The objective is not to accumulate more data but to derive meaningful, actionable insights that inform decisions across all organisational levels.

From Retrospective Reporting to Navigation

Too often, performance data is gathered for compliance or retrospective reporting. Strategic associations treat measurement as a *navigation system,* not a scorecard. They ask:

- Are we measuring what drives relevance and member value?
- Do our KPIs reflect outcomes, not just activity?
- Are insights shared regularly and in a way that supports decisions?

Boards will have to shift their posture from reviewing lag indicators to demanding forward-looking metrics and real-time visibility.

From Legacy Indicators to Impact Metrics

The transition to platform-based operations demands new performance lenses.

Table 12-1 Legacy Indicators to Impact Metrics

Traditional Metric	Limitations	Platform-Era Equivalent
Total membership	Doesn't reflect member activity or value exchange	Active users and peer-to-peer engagement
Event attendance	Point-in-time, not continuous engagement	Ongoing participation in digital and learning ecosystems
Revenue growth	May mask risk or over-dependence	Revenue diversification and recurring income streams
Survey satisfaction	Lagging, not predictive	Real-time sentiment tracking and behavioural analytics

This dashboard illustrates how real-time data integration enhances visibility and decision velocity across the association. Boards can use this view to monitor digital performance, engagement health, and risk signals on a rolling basis.

Static indicators fail to capture the dynamism of platform ecosystems. Platform metrics should be continuous, behavioural, and predictive, offering governance teams real insight into future risks and opportunities.

Rethinking KPIs for Modern Associations

In the platform era, traditional metrics such as event attendance or membership counts are insufficient to capture the dynamic nature of member engagement, financial health, governance agility, and innovation capacity. Modern associations require a more nuanced set of Key Performance Indicators (KPIs) that reflect these multifaceted dimensions.

These KPIs serve as vital tools for strategic alignment, informed decision-making, and continuous improvement. They encompass areas like:

- Engagement and Network Activation
- Financial Sustainability
- Governance Agility and Integrity
- Platform Operations and Innovation

Four Dimensions of Platform Performance

In a platform-based association, performance will have to be measured across four interconnected dimensions:

Table 12-2 Four Dimensions of Platform Performance

Dimension		What to Measure
1.	Engagement & Network Activation	Peer connections, member contributions, retention, referral behaviours
2.	Financial Sustainability	Non-dues revenue, recurring income, revenue diversity, cost-to-serve
3.	Governance Agility & Integrity	Decision speed, delegation effectiveness, trust score, AI and tech oversight
4.	Platform Operations & Innovation	Service velocity, platform uptime, user satisfaction, idea-to-delivery timeframe

Each dimension supports the others. For example, improved platform operations may lead to better engagement, which supports higher retention and financial sustainability.

1. Engagement and Network Activation

This dimension evaluates how effectively the platform fosters active participation and connection among members. Key metrics include:

- **Active User Ratio**: Percentage of members who log in and engage with the platform regularly.
- **Peer-to-Peer Connections**: Number of direct interactions between members, indicating community building.
- **Content Contribution Rate**: Frequency and volume of member-generated content, reflecting engagement levels.
- **Referral Rate**: Proportion of new members joining through existing member referrals, showcasing network growth.

2. Financial Sustainability

Assessing the financial health and resilience of the association involves tracking:

- **Non-Dues Revenue Percentage**: Share of income derived from sources other than membership fees, indicating diversification.
- **Recurring Revenue Ratio**: Proportion of income that is predictable and consistent over time.
- **Cost-to-Serve**: Average expense incurred to deliver services to each member.
- **Lifetime Value (LTV) to Customer Acquisition Cost (CAC) Ratio**: Comparison of the total value a member brings over time to the cost of acquiring them.

3. Governance Agility and Integrity

Effective governance in a dynamic environment requires monitoring:

- **Decision-Making Velocity**: Time taken from issue identification to resolution at the board or executive level.
- **Delegation Effectiveness**: Extent to which decision-making authority is appropriately distributed within the organisation.
- **Transparency Measures**: Availability and clarity of information regarding decisions and policies to stakeholders.
- **Compliance and Ethical Standards**: Adherence to legal requirements and ethical norms, including data protection and equity considerations.

4. Platform Operations and Innovation

This dimension focuses on the operational efficiency and innovative capacity of the platform:

- **System Uptime**: Reliability of the platform, measured by the percentage of time it is fully operational.
- **Innovation Cycle Time**: Duration from idea conception to implementation of new features or services.
- **User Satisfaction Scores**: Feedback from members regarding their experience with the platform.
- **Adoption Rates of New Features**: Speed and extent to which new functionalities are embraced by users.

By systematically tracking these dimensions, associations can gain a comprehensive understanding of their performance, identify areas for improvement, and align their strategies with the evolving needs of their members and stakeholders.

Platform Ecosystem Impact Scorecard

As associations evolve into orchestrators of platform ecosystems, traditional performance metrics, such as financial return, membership numbers, or operational KPIs, will not be sufficient. Boards and executives will need to assess how effectively the association's platform enables external actors, strengthens the ecosystem's health, and creates shared value across boundaries.

The *Platform Ecosystem Impact Scorecard* is designed to complement internal metrics by focusing on ecosystem-scale effectiveness. These indicators help boards understand whether the association is truly functioning as a convener, enabler, and orchestrator of its wider system.

Table 12-3 Platform Ecosystem Impact Scorecard

Dimension	Example Indicator	Strategic Relevance
Stakeholder Reach	Percentage of identified stakeholder segments engaged in platform activities	Measures ecosystem breadth and inclusivity
Value Exchange	Average interactions per stakeholder per month (e.g. CPD, mentoring, job boards)	Captures how actively the platform enables value co-creation
Diversity of Contribution	Percentage of contributions (content, feedback, ideas) from members vs partners vs staff	Gauges health of co-creation and participatory engagement
Partnership Activation	Number of ecosystem partners contributing to shared initiatives	Assesses collaboration depth and activation of external capabilities
Trust and Governance	Stakeholder trust index: perceptions of fairness, data use, platform integrity	Indicates legitimacy and trust in platform governance
Ecosystem Innovation	Number of new offers enabled through ecosystem partnerships	Reflects external innovation enabled by the platform
Impact Beyond Membership	Number of cross-sector initiatives influenced (e.g. policy co-design, etc.)	Demonstrates systemic impact beyond traditional member services

Using the Scorecard

Boards and executive teams can use this scorecard to:

- Set annual targets for ecosystem engagement and impact
- Track progress toward orchestrator maturity
- Inform ecosystem partnership strategies
- Balance internal optimisation with external enablement

Orchestrators measure success not just by internal metrics, but by the health, trust, and innovation of the ecosystem they convene.

Platform Operations & Innovation

In a platform-based association, operational excellence is not a back-office function, it is core to the member experience, innovation lifecycle, and value delivery. Platforms succeed not by building everything, but by enabling seamless, scalable interactions between members, systems, and partners.

This requires a shift from traditional service performance metrics to indicators that capture

- **Technical resilience**: How reliably systems function in real time.
- **Innovation throughput**: How quickly new services or features are developed, tested, and deployed.
- **Service intelligence**: How friction, usage, and automation interact to influence member satisfaction and operational efficiency.

Boards and executives will need visibility into these metrics not just for IT assurance, but to inform prioritisation, resourcing, and risk.

Why These Metrics Matter

- **Platform uptime** is the foundation of trust. Downtime doesn't just affect experience, it disrupts value creation across the ecosystem.
- **Innovation velocity** reflects whether the association is learning, testing, and evolving fast enough to stay relevant. This should include both member-facing tools and backend enhancements.
- **Member experience score** should be grounded in continuous user feedback and behavioural data (e.g. NPS + abandonment + issue resolution time) - not just annual surveys.
- **Automation index** helps assess how scalable and cost-effective operations are. A rising index suggests better use of infrastructure and staff focus on high-value work.

These metrics are especially powerful when tracked in real time or reported quarterly to boards through performance dashboards. They ensure the leadership team can spot platform bottlenecks, identify low-friction opportunities for innovation, and reduce manual load that constrains scalability.

Table 12-4 Operations and Innovation Metrics

Metric	Description	Use
Platform uptime	Percentage of time digital services are operational	Maintain ≥99.9% for core CPD, CRM, and payment systems
Innovation velocity	Rate at which new platform features or services are deployed	Target 4–6 new releases or improvements per year
Member experience score	Composite of usability, support responsiveness, and satisfaction	Informs design decisions and friction reduction
Automation index	Ratio of automated to manual processes in core operations	Benchmark for digital maturity and efficiency

Data Without Context Is Not Insight

In the platform era, data is abundant, but insight is scarce. Associations collect vast amounts of information, yet without proper context, this data fails to inform strategic decisions effectively. To transform data into actionable insight, associations will have to embed a culture of measurement that aligns with their strategic objectives.

This involves:

- **Data Governance Policies and Ethical Use Standards**: Establishing clear guidelines ensures data is handled responsibly, maintaining member trust and compliance with regulations.
- **Regular Member and Stakeholder Feedback Cycles**: Continuous engagement with members and stakeholders provides real-time insights into their needs and experiences.
- **Agile Experimentation Supported by Shared Learning**: Encouraging a culture of experimentation allows associations to test new ideas and learn from outcomes rapidly.
- **Internal Dashboards and Team Reflection Sessions**: Utilising dashboards for real-time data visualisation and facilitating team discussions promotes collective understanding and swift action.

The *Association Platform Success Framework* provides a structured foundation for transforming raw data into strategic insight, guided by four Core Pillars. These pillars ensure that data is embedded meaningfully within the association's operations, culture, and governance.

Drawing this back to the APSF the Core Pillars provide the scaffold.

Core Pillar 1: Courage

Courage reflects a culture of bold, values-led leadership. In a data context, this means being willing to ask difficult questions, confront unexpected findings, and use evidence to challenge assumptions and drive change, even when it's uncomfortable.

Example: Encouraging experimentation and using data to test new initiatives, even if outcomes are uncertain.

Core Pillar 2: Trust & Security

This pillar emphasises ethical data governance, transparency, and robust security. Associations will have to manage member data responsibly, communicate clearly about its use, and ensure systems are secure, building the trust necessary for members to engage openly.

Example: Implementing clear data governance policies and regular audits to ensure compliance and accountability.

Core Pillar 3: Innovation

Innovation is about using data to spark new ideas, services, and ways of working. Embedding real-time feedback loops, dashboards, and shared learning mechanisms supports a responsive and adaptive culture.

Example: Using member behaviour data to co-design new educational offerings or digital services.

Core Pillar 4: Data Driven Insight

This pillar captures the ultimate goal: using data not just to observe activity, but to generate meaningful, actionable insights. Data becomes a strategic asset when interpreted in context and aligned with core goals.

Example: Leveraging member segmentation data to tailor value propositions and improve retention.

From Data to Insight

When associations map their data practices, including scorecards, dashboards, and stakeholder feedback, to these Core Pillars, they move beyond reporting and *towards learning and transformation*. This alignment supports informed strategic planning, targeted member engagement and improved resource allocation decisions.

Figure 12-1 APSF – Core Pillars

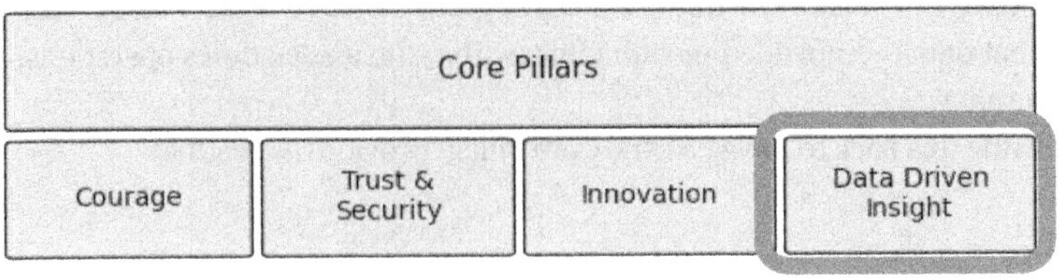

The Role of the Board

Boards are central to activating this framework. By asking insightful, open-ended questions, they ensure that data is interpreted, not just collected:

- What are we seeing that we didn't expect?
- What member behaviours are shifting?
- Where are we losing energy or momentum?

These inquiries drive deeper reflection, enabling data to serve as a strategic compass that keeps the association aligned with its mission and member needs.

From Data to Insight: Governance Dashboards

Metrics only matter if they inform decisions.

Associations should consider building real-time governance dashboards across the four domains. These dashboards enable boards and executives to:

- Spot declining engagement before churn
- Assess which revenue streams are underperforming
- Track risk signals in real time
- Align innovation efforts with member needs

Measurement is not an add-on; it is the diagnostic engine of platform success. When designed with intention, KPIs drive alignment between purpose, performance, and decision-making. They allow boards and executives to:

- Detect weak signals before they become systemic risks
- Course-correct strategy using timely insight
- Embed accountability without sacrificing agility

Boards should regularly review whether their KPIs are reinforcing the value logic of their platform or merely tracking the past. The *Association Platform Success Framework* provides the scaffolding. The scorecard and dashboard systems in this chapter bring it to life.

In modern associations, data is not just a by-product of service; it is the compass of leadership.

Performance Reviews as Governance Tools

In a platform-based association, performance data is not merely an operational checkpoint; it serves as a strategic governance tool. Boards should utilise dashboards, scorecards, and trend reports to assess progress, but also to interrogate alignment, uncover blind spots, and adapt decision pathways. Performance reviews become forums for learning, recalibration, and strategic stewardship.

Well-designed metrics empower boards to assess:

- **Strategy alignment**: Are outcomes consistent with the organisation's evolving purpose and the *Association Platform Success Framework* roadmap?
- **Business model sustainability**: Is value being monetised ethically, at scale, and with long-term resilience?
- **Executive and committee accountability**: Are delegated roles driving value, or creating bottlenecks that hinder agility?
- **Risk preparedness**: Are early signals, such as churn, trust issues, sentiment shifts, or vendor problems, being identified and addressed promptly?

These reviews shift board engagement from static oversight to dynamic orchestration.

To operationalise this approach, boards should embed the following elements into their annual review cycle.

Table 12-5 Annual Strategy and Performance Review

Element	Purpose
Dashboard briefing	Real-time trend review with board-level narrative interpretation
Scorecard updates	Performance against APSF-aligned metrics and previous-year priorities
Emerging risk reports	Insight-driven analysis of environmental, digital, or ethical threats
Forecast models	Forward-looking member behaviour scenarios and revenue trajectory mapping

Insight-led governance does not begin and end with compliance. It requires asking the harder questions:

- What are we learning?
- Where are we drifting?
- What will define success 18 months from now?

In this model, performance reviews are not about validating past choices, they are about equipping boards to navigate complexity, uncertainty, and rapid change.

Conclusion: Measurement as Strategic Infrastructure

In the platform era, measurement transcends traditional reporting; it becomes the navigational compass guiding associations through complexity and change. Effective measurement systems are not merely about tracking activities but about understanding and enhancing the association's capacity to deliver value, adapt to emerging challenges, and sustain trust among stakeholders.

To lead effectively, associations will have to measure:

- Not just how many people they reach, but how they participate

- Not just what revenue they earn, but how resilient it is
- Not just whether governance is in place, but whether it enables adaptation

Boards will have to demand, and be equipped to interpret, metrics that reflect the realities of a networked, AI-enhanced, digitally mediated membership organisation.

Strategic performance systems, aligned with the APSF, empower boards to govern more intelligently, executives to lead more proactively, and members to witness an organisation that is continuously learning and adapting. What you measure is not just a reflection of your priorities; it becomes the story you tell and the future you build.

The next chapter explores how these insights translate into practical dashboards, measurement routines, and governance integration, ensuring that platform performance is not just measured, but continuously improved.

Chapter 13. Partnering for Ecosystem Impact

Example 57. Partnering for Ecosystem Impact

Claire Evans, CEO of the Professional Network Association (PNA), had spent the past year reshaping the association into a digital-first platform. Member engagement was up, the AI-driven CPD platform was delivering strong usage metrics, and internal operations had become markedly more efficient. Yet something was missing.

At the strategic board retreat, she posed a new kind of question:

"If we're serious about member outcomes, industry impact, and future relevance, who do we need to partner with that we haven't yet?"

That question reframed the conversation from internal performance to external coordination. PNA's next frontier was becoming an enabler of shared value across its ecosystem.

This chapter explores how associations move from inward-facing organisations to ecosystem orchestrators. It introduces partnership models, examines governance implications, and presents a framework for designing impact-driven alliances that enhance value creation and societal relevance.

Why Ecosystem Thinking Matters

Platform-based associations sit within broader systems of members and professionals, industry players and regulators, technology partners and educators, communities and governments

Ecosystem thinking reframes the association's role from service provider to orchestrator of connections, knowledge, and value across stakeholders.

Table 13-1 Traditional vs Ecosystem-Oriented Associations

Attribute	Traditional Association	Ecosystem-Oriented Platform
Purpose	Serve members	Create shared value across stakeholders
Focus	Member benefits	Systemic impact
Collaboration Approach	Transactional sponsors	Strategic partnerships
Value Exchange	One-directional	Multi-directional
Role in Sector	Representative body	Convenor and orchestrator

The Association as Ecosystem Orchestrator

In a platform environment, associations can play one of three roles: *platformisers*, who build infrastructure; *guardians*, who enforce standards; or *orchestrators*, who enable value creation through partnerships, trust, and structured interaction.

It is the orchestrator role that holds the greatest strategic potential. Associations are uniquely positioned to coordinate stakeholder relationships across sectors, design the governance rules and shared protocols that enable participation and facilitate multi-directional value exchange, from skills and jobs to data and innovation.

What makes associations especially suited to this role is their embedded legitimacy. Unlike commercial platforms, they operate with sectoral trust, ethical expectations, and the authority to convene diverse actors.

Orchestration is more than a strategic pivot, it is a governance-intensive model that requires setting boundaries, aligning incentives, and enabling co-creation at scale.

There are core capabilities associations need to govern ecosystems effectively and orchestration is a distinctive capability. It is not about controlling every outcome, but about enabling interaction, coordination, and trust across a complex network of actors.

Associations will have to shift from managing bilateral relationships to curating the architecture of collaboration.

Table 13-2 outlines the four core orchestration capabilities.

Table 13-2 Orchestration Capabilities

Orchestration Capability	Description
Boundary Setting	Define who participates in the platform and under what terms.
Incentive Alignment	Create clear, mutual value propositions for all ecosystem actors.
Interaction Design	Structure engagement pathways that foster high-value exchanges.
Governance Layering	Blend centralised and distributed decision-making to enable scale with flexibility.

Associations bring a distinctive strength to the orchestration role, which is the *embedded legitimacy* they carry. Unlike commercial platforms that often struggle with trust and credibility, associations can draw on their normative authority, setting professional standards, stewarding ethics, and convening policy dialogues. This enables them to orchestrate ecosystems with a level of credibility and neutrality that commercial actors often cannot match.

Yet, orchestration also carries significant governance demands. It involves navigating competing interests, balancing openness with quality assurance, and governing without full control. As Ritala and Jovanovic note, "orchestrators face inherently higher governance complexity as they manage interactions across ecosystem participants, often without direct control over all processes."

This echoes Adner's (2017) argument that strategy in an ecosystem will have to move beyond internal assets and competition. It will have to instead focus on *alignment* across interdependent actors, many of whom the association neither owns nor commands.

Orchestration, then, is not simply a new strategic role. It is a new governance paradigm, one that requires boards and executives to expand their conception of oversight, accountability, and value stewardship across complex, collaborative systems. Associations that step confidently into this role will not only increase their relevance, but they will also redefine how trust, impact, and innovation are coordinated in the sectors they serve.

Designing Strategic Partnerships

In an ecosystem model, partnerships are not bolt-on sponsors, they are essential embedded contributors to shared outcomes.

Table 13-3 **Four Strategic Partnership Models for Associations**

Model	Partner Type	Value Exchange	Association Role
Knowledge Co-Creation	Universities, think tanks	Joint research, policy development	Convenor
Platform Integration	EdTech, CRM, analytics	Technology infrastructure and member personalisation	Integrator
Market Enablement	Employers, consultancies	Talent development, CPD, job placement	Enabler of interaction
Collective Impact	Government, NGOs	Sector-wide social, economic, or environmental change	System orchestrator

Cases of Sector-Specific Orchestration Models

Ecosystem orchestration is not confined to any one sector or structure. While the principles remain consistent, alignment, trust, governance, and shared infrastructure, the way orchestration is enacted depends heavily on the dynamics of the sector. These live cases illustrate how associations across different domains have moved beyond traditional partnerships to play a central orchestrating role in their ecosystems.

Example 58. Pharmaceutical Society of Australia

Press Release: 5 December 2024

"The Pharmaceutical Society of Australia (PSA) and Audirie are celebrating the first anniversary of partnership, empowering thousands of learners through immersive AI-powered simulations and enhancing their patient counselling and clinical communication skills.

In the first year of partnership, PSA and Audirie have:

- *Empowered thousands of pharmacists, interns, and pharmacy assistants through immersive AI-powered simulations.*
- *Enhanced patient counselling and clinical communication skills with cutting-edge technology tailored to the unique needs of pharmacy professionals.*
- *Strengthened our shared commitment to excellence in education and improved health outcomes for communities across Australia.*

PSA is expanding use of AI-powered pharmacist prescriber simulations in 2025, giving more learners access to nation-leading technology.

... Audirie Co-founder and CEO, Michael Alexander, also highlighted the utilisation of AI as a powerful tool in improving learning outcomes. ... "Our partnership with PSA has been a transformative journey. Over the past year, we've empowered pharmacists, pharmacy assistants and pharmacy interns with cutting-edge AI simulations that enhance their skills and confidence. Together, we are shaping the future of pharmacy education and professional development in Australia."" (PSA 2024)

Example 59. Orchestrating a Workforce Capability

Australia's aged care sector faces persistent workforce shortages and increasing complexity in care delivery. In response, leading associations have shifted from traditional roles as training providers or policy advocates to become system orchestrators, aligning diverse stakeholders to build sector-wide workforce capability. This case examines how such an association-led platform approach is being realised in practice.

Strategic Focus: Sector-Wide Workforce Enablement

Rather than owning every element of workforce development, the association's strategy is to:

- ***Align contributions*** *from universities, technology vendors, employers, and government.*
- ***Enable sector-wide capability*** *through a digital platform that integrates learning, placement, and funding.*

- ***Govern and coordinate*** *the network, ensuring standards, interoperability, and shared outcomes.*

Table 13-4 Key Partnerships and Platform Components

Partner Type	Role in the Platform Ecosystem
University	Co-designs micro-credentials and supports clinical placements
Software Partner	Digitises learning, compliance, and credentialing pathways
Employers	Offer job guarantees, structured placements, and on-the-job learning
Government	Co-funds pilot programs and aligns platform with policy objectives

Real-World Parallels in Australia

1. ***Aged Care Workforce Industry Council (ACWIC) – Workforce Planning Tool***
   - ***Platform Function:*** *ACWIC launched a free online Workforce Planning Tool, co-designed with providers, to help aged care organisations map workforce needs, identify gaps, and plan for the future. The tool is designed for practical use by HR and workforce planners, supporting both learning and compliance.*
   - ***Collaborative Approach:*** *The tool's development involved input from sector stakeholders, including providers, government, and technology partners, reflecting a system orchestration model.*
2. ***Micro-Credentialing and Digital Credentials Initiatives***
   - ***Sector Example:*** *Providers such as Five Good Friends have partnered with universities and technology vendors to deliver micro-credential programs, rapidly upskilling hundreds of workers through short, targeted courses aligned with sector needs.*
   - ***National Strategy:*** *Reports and recommendations from the Aged Care Workforce Strategy Taskforce and the Royal Commission have called for digital credentialing, sector-wide learning pathways, and recognition of prior learning to support workforce mobility and capability.*
3. ***University and Employer Partnerships***
   - ***Clinical Placement Models:*** *Universities Australia and sector submissions highlight the value of university-aged care partnerships for co-designing learning, expanding clinical placements, and embedding career pathways in aged care.*

- ***Employer Involvement:*** *Employers are increasingly offering structured placements and job guarantees as part of workforce development platforms, often in partnership with education providers and supported by government funding.*

4. ***Government Co-Funding and Policy Alignment***

- ***Pilot Programs:*** *Government departments have co-funded pilot programs to test new models of workforce development, including digital learning platforms and micro-credentialing, ensuring alignment with national policy goals and regulatory requirements.*

Platform Outcome

The result is a ***national workforce capability platform*** *that:*

- *Links learning, placement, and funding into a single, member-facing hub.*
- *Enables real-time workforce planning, skills recognition, and career progression.*
- *Supports sector-wide standards, compliance, and continuous improvement.*
- *Positions the association as a trusted orchestrator and network governor, rather than a direct provider of every service.*

Lessons for Associations

- ***System orchestration****, not ownership, enables scale, flexibility, and innovation.*
- ***Cross-sector partnerships*** *are essential for building sustainable workforce capability.*
- ***Digital platforms*** *can integrate learning, compliance, and employment pathways, supporting both individual and sector needs.*
- ***Governance and alignment*** *are critical: the association's role is to set standards, ensure interoperability, and coordinate contributions for collective impact.*

(Aged Care Workforce Strategy Taskforce, 2018; Aged Care Workforce Industry Council, 2022; Portable, 2023; Australian Ageing Agenda, 2023; Inside Ageing, 2023; Universities Australia, 2020; Australian Government Department of Health and Aged Care, 2024)

These case models reinforce that ecosystem orchestration is a sector-agnostic capability. What changes is the actors, the infrastructure, and the mechanisms of value coordination. Associations that embrace this role do not need to build everything, they need to build the scaffolding that allows others to collaborate, co-create, and amplify shared outcomes.

Governance for High-Impact Partnerships

As associations evolve from service providers to ecosystem orchestrators, partnerships are no longer peripheral, they are central to strategy execution. However, ecosystem partnerships introduce new forms of complexity: risk is shared, value is co-created, and outcomes often emerge over time rather than being pre-defined.

This demands a governance approach that moves beyond bilateral contracts or informal MOUs. Associations will have to build fit-for-purpose partnership governance capabilities, particularly in five critical domains:

- **Strategic clarity**: ensuring each partnership directly advances the platform mission.
- **Risk governance**: managing brand, compliance, and reputational exposure across multi-party value chains.
- **Data and IP management**: establishing ownership, access, and ethical use rights for shared resources.
- **Representation and legitimacy**: ensuring the right people are at the table, with appropriate delegations and engagement channels.
- **Review and exit protocols**: enabling flexible, timely course corrections or disengagement when value or alignment diminishes.

The following questions support boards and executives in assessing partnership maturity and readiness, particularly where value is co-created and governance is distributed.

Table 13-5 Partnership Governance Considerations

Area	Questions for Boards and Executives
Strategic alignment	Does this partnership advance our platform strategy, member value proposition, or ecosystem role?
Risk appetite	What risks (e.g. brand, compliance, innovation failure) are we prepared to absorb, mitigate, or transfer?
IP and data governance	Who owns and controls the content, data, or algorithms developed through this partnership? How are they governed?
Representation	Do we have the right voices at the table, internally (across functions) and externally (across stakeholders)?
Exit and review mechanisms	Is there a clear mechanism for reassessment, exit, or redesign if the partnership no longer delivers shared value?

Effective ecosystem partnerships require dynamic governance structures, those capable of stewarding collaboration, not just compliance. Boards will have to be willing to shift from traditional oversight to *stewardship of co-created value*, ensuring that partnerships enhance trust, distribute accountability fairly, and remain aligned to mission through life-cycle reviews.

In a platform world, partnership is not a transaction. It is a governance domain in its own right. Associations operating as platforms will have to move beyond ad hoc collaborations. They will have to establish shared accountability structures, mutual value frameworks, and transparent oversight. Strategic partnerships influence not just program delivery, but identity, trust, and systemic impact.

High-impact partnerships benefit from alignment with ISO 37000's principles on stakeholder responsiveness and ISO 37005's indicators of distributed decision integrity.

Barriers and Enablers to Ecosystem Success

As associations expand their impact through partnerships, with universities, startups, vendors, government agencies, and cross-sector networks, success depends not just on shared goals, but on shared ways of working. These collaborative ecosystems offer immense potential for innovation and member value, but they also introduce new complexity.

Time and again, we see partnerships that are strategically sound on paper struggle in practice. The cause is rarely a lack of ambition or resources. Instead, it often stems from cultural drag, governance misalignment, or unspoken assumptions that create friction as the work unfolds.

The common barriers that can derail even high-potential collaborations, whereas the key enablers help ecosystem partnerships thrive over time. The following examples highlight how performance breakdowns can emerge not from flawed strategy, but from misaligned pace, processes, or priorities, and what governance responses are available when partnerships lose momentum.

Common Barriers:

- Legacy mindsets: Seeing partnerships as funding, not value creation
- Misaligned incentives: Competing agendas between stakeholders
- Rigid governance: Limited ability to share control or iterate

Key Enablers:

- Clear shared purpose
- Adaptive governance frameworks
- Real-time feedback loops
- Trust-based leadership and accountability

These enablers are not just theoretical. Without shared purpose, adaptive structures, and trust-based working norms, even well-funded partnerships can unravel. The following vignette illustrates how cultural misalignment - not strategic error - stalled a high-potential collaboration.

Example 60. When Good Strategy Meets Cultural Drag

The fictitious National Health Technology Association (NHTA) had struck what looked like a breakthrough partnership with a well-regarded analytics startup. The goal was bold: co-develop a national dashboard that would allow members to benchmark digital maturity across hospitals and clinics.

The business case was sound, the technology was proven, and both parties were aligned on paper.

But within six months, the partnership stalled.

What went wrong?

Cultural disconnects emerged quickly: The startup embraced rapid iteration, open feedback, and lean documentation. However, the association's internal teams were risk-averse, preferred formal review cycles, and required multiple signoffs for each data source and report.

Misaligned incentives surfaced later: The startup wanted visibility and case studies to support its investor roadmap. NHTA, cautious about perceived vendor bias, restricted joint branding and limited member access to test pilots.

Trust eroded through silence: Confusion over IP ownership and communication protocols led to a breakdown in collaboration. Neither party exited - but neither advanced.

"We had a shared goal - but not a shared rhythm. We didn't ask early enough how we work, not just what we want.": Project Lead, NHTA.

Example 61. Governance Insight: Exit or Endure?

Boardroom Scenario:

The board of the PNA convened an unscheduled strategy session. Their flagship co-creation partnership with a major university, aimed at developing an AI-powered CPD recommendation engine, was in trouble.

The issue wasn't contractual breach. It was performance. After two years:

- *Pilot results were inconclusive*
- *Member engagement with the new tool was low*
- *Project costs were escalating with no revenue offset*

Yet the university was a prestigious partner. The collaboration had generated goodwill, political visibility, and substantial media exposure.

Some directors felt strongly: "If we withdraw now, it could signal failure and damage relationships in the education sector."

Others were more pragmatic: "Our members don't care about prestige. They want functionality. This is tying up capital we could use for a more responsive solution."

The CEO proposed a compromise: an independent project review with agreed sunset criteria. If the project didn't meet these by the next board cycle, the exit clause would be triggered.

"We need a governance model that lets us pivot without burning bridges."

Governance Insight

Boards will have to balance reputational risk, resource stewardship, and strategic accountability. Co-creation partnerships require pre-agreed review mechanisms and neutral evaluation processes to avoid paralysis when political or relational stakes are high.

Figure 13-1 maps how different partnership types vary in governance complexity based on two critical variables: trust and shared risk. Low-trust, high-risk partnerships require tight governance, while high-trust, low-risk collaborations can operate with more agility. This visual helps boards assess where greater oversight, clearer delegations, or adaptive protocols are required.

Figure 13-1 **Partnership Governance Complexity**

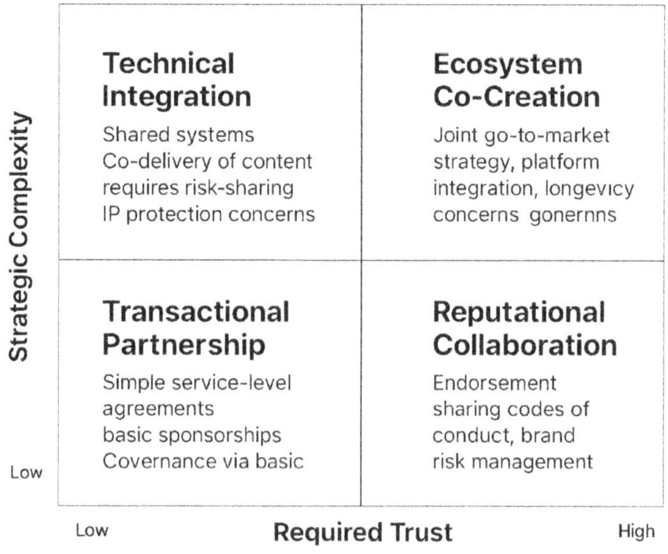

From Service Provider to Ecosystem Enabler

In a platform world, associations that act alone risk irrelevance. Ecosystem orchestration is not about scaling the association, it is about scaling its impact.

Key Takeaways:

1. Ecosystem partnerships unlock value beyond what associations can deliver alone.
2. Orchestration requires governance innovation, shared metrics, and cultural agility.
3. Associations that lead ecosystems shape not just member experiences, but the future of their entire sector.

The next chapter explores how to embed these ecosystem strategies into innovation systems that support continuous experimentation, feedback, and evolution - ensuring the association remains future-ready and impact-driven.

Figure 13-2 synthesises the association's evolving role as an ecosystem orchestrator, showing the shift from internal service delivery to multi-actor value enablement. It highlights the platform mechanisms, stakeholder interfaces, and governance enablers that underpin orchestration in practice.

Figure 13-2 Eco Systems Orchestration

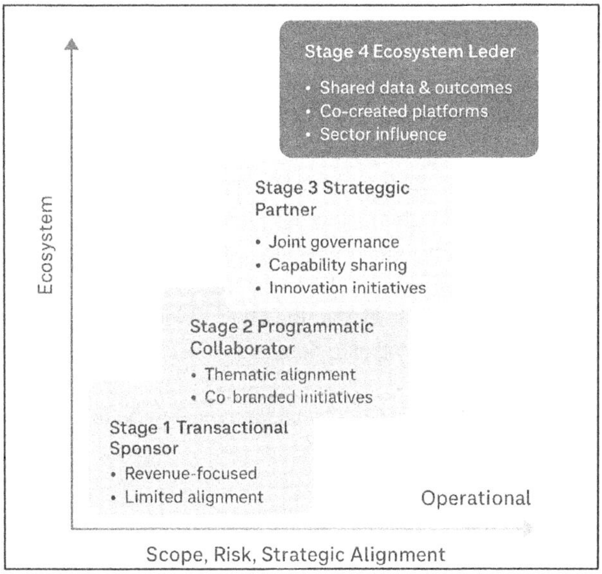

Example 62. Governance - ISO37000, ISO37005

The shift to ecosystem partnerships challenges associations to move beyond transactional oversight and adopt fit-for-purpose governance that supports co-creation, agility, and shared value. International standards such as ISO37000: Governance of Organisations and ISO37005: Governance Maturity Indicators provide a useful scaffolding for assessing partnership governance maturity.

Table 13-6 Key ISO Principles and Their Relevance to Partnerships

ISO Principle	Partnership Application
Purpose	Clarify how each partnership advances the association's strategic role as orchestrator.
Value Generation	Define mutual value creation across all parties, not just revenue or service delivery.
Responsiveness to Stakeholders	Ensure inclusive representation in design, oversight, and review mechanisms.
Ethical Behaviour	Align with standards for fairness, transparency, and integrity in joint IP, data use, and branding.
Stewardship and Sustainability	Design exit protocols and lifecycle reviews that protect long-term impact and shared resources.

ISO 37005 Maturity Lens

ISO 37005 introduces a cultural and behavioural maturity model. For partnerships, this means boards should look beyond structural compliance and assess:

- How trust is built and maintained between parties
- Whether decision rights and escalation paths are clear
- If feedback and adaptation mechanisms are embedded
- How the partnership balances agility with rigour over time

Rather than applying these standards rigidly, associations should use them as a design framework, a way to test whether their governance systems are enabling trusted, adaptive, and mission-aligned collaboration across the ecosystem.

Tip: Include periodic reviews of key partnerships in board governance calendars using ISO-aligned reflection prompts.

Table 13-7 Partnership Strategy Matrix

Partnership Type	Strategic Purpose	Governance Role	Examples
Sponsor	Revenue generation	Compliance, brand control	Industry event sponsor
Co-Creator	Joint content, services, R&D	IP agreements, project oversight	CPD platform with EdTech startup
Policy Partner	Advocacy or standards development	Shared representation, joint panels	Sector-wide taskforce with government
Platform Integrator	Enhance member services and analytics	Data governance, system interoperability	API-based partnership with HR tech firm

Governance Maturity for Ecosystem-Centric Boards

Governance Maturity Ladder supports boards in evaluating their governance posture in a platform context. It builds on the adaptive and strategic capability models in earlier chapters, expanding the lens to include foresight, orchestration, and network governance.

In platform-based associations, governance maturity is not just about compliance or operational control, it is about adaptive foresight and system stewardship. This ladder provides a clear progression for boards to assess their governance posture and identify the next frontier of leadership.

Table 13-8 Governance Maturity Ladder

Level	Label	Core Characteristics
1	Foundational (Compliance-Focused)	Governance limited to statutory duties; reporting focused; minimal strategic role.
2	Tactical Governance	Board receives operational updates; planning input is occasional; risk and budget compliance dominate.
3	Strategic Governance	Board shapes and monitors strategy; KPI frameworks defined; alignment with purpose.
4	Performance Governance	Focus on outcomes, value creation, and investment logic; governance tracks ROPI, friction, and value delivery.
5	Ecosystem Governance	Board governs as stewards of a network, not just an organisation; emphasis on platforms, partnerships, and co-creation.
6	Foresight Governance	Future-literate governance using simulation, horizon scanning, and design to inform long-range decision-making.

Boards that aim to lead ecosystems, not just manage organisations, will have to cultivate maturity at Levels 5 and 6. These levels reflect not only strategic intent but cultural capacity, adaptive learning, and system stewardship. The journey to foresight governance is not linear, but it is essential for platform-era associations committed to relevance, trust, and impact.

Example 63. Building a Digital Health Ecosystem

Australia's digital health transformation offers a compelling case of ecosystem strategy in action. Through national collaboration between government, research, industry, and professional bodies, digital innovation is being embedded not just as technology, but as infrastructure for care, coordination, and capability. Two initiatives in particular, the Digital Health Cooperative Research Centre (DHCRC) and the Australian Digital Health Agency (ADHA), demonstrate how platform logic, co-design, and national alignment can accelerate system-wide change.

The Challenge: *Australia's health system faces enduring pressures: ageing populations, chronic disease, workforce shortages, and care fragmentation. Digital health holds promise, but unlocking it requires shared investment, co-designed tools, and interoperable infrastructure that empowers frontline providers, particularly in under-supported fields like allied health.*

The Partnership Model in Action:

Digital Health Cooperative Research Centre (DHCRC)

- ***Form****: A national consortium of over 60 partners including universities, providers, vendors, and policy bodies.*
- ***Mission****: To connect care, enable workforce innovation, and accelerate commercialisation of digital health solutions.*
- *Ecosystem Impact Examples:*
- *Aged Care Tool: With Telstra Health and RMIT, DHCRC co-developed a predictive analytics tool now embedded in software across 350+ aged care facilities, supporting early intervention for 60,000+ residents.*
- *Academic Leadership Network: Established a national council of senior academics to align education, research, and practice in digital health disciplines.*

Australian Digital Health Agency (ADHA)

Role*: National steward of Australia's digital health infrastructure, strategy, and sector engagement.*

Allied Health Initiative:

- *Tripled investment in 2024–25 to fund digital integration for allied health via partnerships with 16 software vendors.*
- *Grounded in a sector-wide survey (with AHPA) highlighting gaps in fit-for-purpose clinical systems.*
- *Delivered via structured co-design, solution architecture support, stakeholder workshops, and integration with national infrastructure such as My Health Record and e-prescribing.*

Outcomes and Lessons

- ***Care Integration****: Allied health professionals now access shared care records and digital prescribing tools, improving decisions and continuity of care.*
- ***Scalability****: Successful pilots (e.g. aged care deterioration detection) now deployed at scale.*
- ***Workforce Uplift****: Leadership networks and microlearning pilots are building digital fluency across disciplines.*
- ***Cultural Shift****: The co-design approach has seeded a broader culture of shared governance and innovation across the sector.*

Strategic Takeaways for Associations

- ***Design with, not for****: Co-design builds adoption, trust, and contextual fit.*
- ***Leverage diversity****: Industry, academia, government, and professions each bring unique value, alignment unlocks it.*
- ***Build platforms, not silos****: Digital strategy will have to focus on integration and capability, not just tools.*
- ***Coordinate nationally, act locally****: Central stewardship enables scalable, interoperable solutions with local flexibility.*

(Australian Digital Health Agency, 2025); Digital Health Cooperative Research Centre, 2024))

Conclusion: Ecosystem Orchestrator

In the evolving landscape of associations, the shift from traditional service provision to ecosystem orchestration marks a pivotal transformation. Associations are no longer confined to delivering member services; they are now positioned to convene diverse stakeholders, fostering collaborative environments that drive systemic impact.

Ecosystem orchestration involves more than forming partnerships; it requires a strategic approach to governance, aligning incentives, and facilitating co-creation among members, industry players, educators, and regulators. This role leverages the association's inherent legitimacy and trust to coordinate complex networks, enabling innovation and adaptability across the sector.

Effective orchestration demands dynamic governance structures that balance control with flexibility, ensuring that partnerships are purpose-driven and resilient. Associations will have to cultivate shared visions, establish clear value propositions, and implement mechanisms for continuous feedback and iteration.

By embracing this orchestrator role, associations can amplify their influence, drive meaningful change, and remain relevant in a rapidly transforming environment. The journey from service provider to ecosystem enabler is not merely a strategic choice but a necessary evolution to meet the complex challenges and opportunities of today's interconnected world.

Part VII. Tools for Change

Strategy is only as valuable as its execution. Part V brings together the practical tools, diagnostics, and frameworks that help associations turn platform thinking into sustained transformation. These tools are designed to support strategic planning, boardroom reflection, and operational decision-making. From readiness assessments to governance scorecards and business model stress tests, this section enables leaders to diagnose capability, track progress, and embed adaptive learning across their organisation. Whether used as part of a major transformation effort or for ongoing strategic alignment, these tools are built to scale and evolve with your association.

Part V shifts the focus from ideas to implementation. It introduces practical tools, scorecards, and diagnostic frameworks that support boards, executives, and change leaders in turning insight into action.

These tools are not checklists. They are designed as conversation starters, alignment frameworks, and decision-support systems that reflect the complexity and opportunity of the platform era. Whether used in a boardroom strategy session, an executive offsite, or a cross-functional workshop, they help organisations take the next step, from concept to capability.

Chapter 14. Diagnostic Tools for Transformation

Example 64. Where to Start

Claire Evans, CEO of the Professional Network Association (PNA), stared at the whiteboard covered in sticky notes from their recent strategy retreat. The board had agreed: the future was platform-based, member-led, and digitally enabled. But one nagging question kept surfacing: Are we ready?

Some parts of PNA had made real progress - a new CPD platform, stronger analytics, a growing member community. Others lagged behind. Legacy systems, cultural resistance, and unclear capabilities stood in the way. As one director put it bluntly: "We know where we're going, but we don't know how far we've come."

Claire knew what they needed wasn't just a plan, it was a diagnostic tool. Something that could help the board assess where they stood across key domains, set priorities, and track progress. Not another report, but a framework for transformation.

This chapter introduces a set of diagnostic tools designed to help association boards and executives assess their platform readiness, governance agility, and strategic capabilities. It gives boards the ability to ask - and answer - the right questions.

Why Associations Need a Diagnostic Approach

Transformation within associations rarely unfolds in a straight line. While strategic ambition is widespread, many boards struggle to execute because they lack a shared, evidence-based understanding of their starting point. Legacy infrastructure, inflexible funding models, and patchy digital literacy often hold back change. Moreover, associations face increasing demands from members, funders, and partners to demonstrate agility, responsiveness, and impact.

In this context, diagnostic tools provide a practical and strategic advantage. They allow boards to assess readiness across critical domains - from digital infrastructure and engagement models to decision-making structures and commercial resilience. The result is not just insight, but actionable clarity.

Diagnostics also support prioritisation. Associations can't fix everything at once. A well-designed diagnostic helps boards distinguish between urgent gaps - such as outdated systems or risky revenue concentration - and longer-term capabilities that can evolve over time. This enables a staged, confident approach to transformation.

Crucially, diagnostics create alignment. One of the most common causes of reform failure is the disconnect between board direction, executive delivery, and operational capability. A shared diagnostic framework allows all levels of governance to work from the same map, strengthening cohesion and shared accountability.

For directors, diagnostics provide ongoing insight. They shift governance from passive oversight to active, data-informed stewardship. Boards can track progress, adjust direction, and intervene where needed - without relying solely on anecdote or lagging indicators.

Table 14-1 The Strategic Value of Diagnostic Tools

Purpose	What It Supports	Platform-Based Assoc.
Strategic Clarity	Identifies current state across systems, culture, and capability	Avoids overestimating readiness based on ambition alone
Prioritisation	Differentiates urgent issues from longer-term opportunities	Enables phased, focused investment
Governance Alignment	Creates a shared evidence base across governance layers	Strengthens cohesion and decision discipline
Board Engagement	Tracks change through structured indicators	Enables more strategic, data-informed board oversight
Transformation Compass	Provides a method for real-time orientation and course correction	Supports agile leadership in complex, fast-moving environments
Ecosystem Enablement	Assesses capability to support multi-sided interactions	Core to platform design and orchestration effectiveness

Multi-sided ecosystems introduce complexity: value is co-created, risks are distributed, and change is non-linear. Diagnostic tools provide the compass that allows associations to orient, reorient, and lead transformation with confidence.

If strategy is the map, diagnostics are the compass. They tell you where you are, and how to steer forward with purpose.

Business Model Innovation and Governance Readiness

In platform-era associations, business model innovation is no longer a periodic strategy exercise. It is an ongoing governance capability. From new pricing logics and data monetisation to spin-out ventures and participatory services, innovative models reshape how value is created, distributed, and governed.

The *Business Model Health Check* helps boards diagnose whether current monetisation and value pathways are resilient, ethical, and scalable. It highlights alignment risks and unlocks opportunities to adapt the revenue architecture without undermining trust or mission. When used in conjunction with the *ROPI Readiness Checklist* and *Monetisation Governance Charter*, the Business Model Health Check becomes part of an integrated oversight system, giving boards a line of sight from commercial innovation to strategic integrity.

Association 2.0 Transformation Compass

To support platform-era transformation, associations need more than strategic ambition, they need a structured way to assess readiness, prioritise investments, and govern change. The *Association 2.0 Transformation Compass* brings together three core diagnostic tools into a single strategic framework.

This compass is designed for boards and executive teams who want to lead with clarity. It enables a unified view across operations, governance, and business model health. Each tool assesses a key dimension of transformation:

Table 14-2 Association 2.0 Transformation Compass

Diagnostic Tool	Core Focus	Strategic Purpose
Platform Readiness Diagnostic	Member experience, digital infrastructure, culture	Identifies foundational capabilities and transformation barriers
Governance Agility Scorecard	Decision-making, oversight, board responsiveness	Assesses governance maturity and strategic adaptability
Business Model Health Check	Revenue mix, cost structure, innovation funding	Tests financial resilience, alignment, and commercial strategy

Together, these tools form a coherent governance system for strategic leadership in the platform age. Used regularly, they give boards a clear line of sight into where the organisation stands, and what it needs to do next.

Figure 14-1 The Association 2.0 Transformation Compass

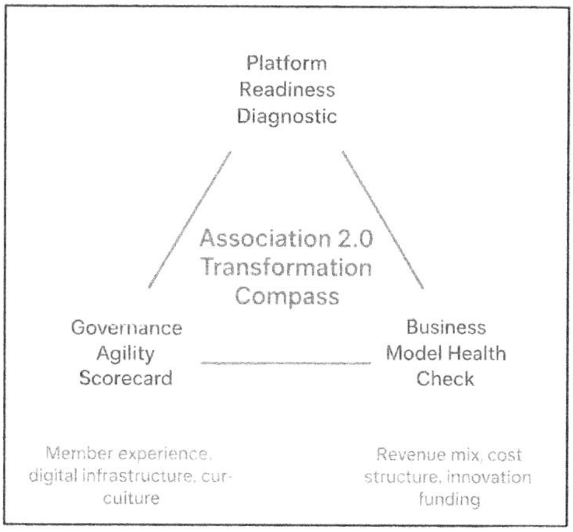

Mapping Diagnostic Insights to APSF Pillars

Diagnostic tools are most valuable when embedded in a clear strategic framework.

To support interpretation and action, each domain within the Association 2.0 Transformation Compass can be mapped back to the layers of the *Association Platform Success Framework*. This allows boards to view diagnostic results not just as standalone assessments, but as signals of platform design strength, organisational coherence, and transformation readiness.

The following table provides an extended mapping across the full diagnostic suite.

Table 14-3 Extended Diagnostic–APSF Alignment

Diagnostic Tool or Domain	Aligned APSF Design Pillar(s)	Strategic Focus
Platform Readiness Diagnostic	Scalable Digital Infrastructure	Modular systems, digital readiness, secure architecture, platform logic
	Member-Centric Design	Personalisation, member journey optimisation, participation triggers
Governance Agility Scorecard	Governance & Trust	Risk oversight, decision agility, board responsiveness, ethical governance
Business Model Health Check	Member-Centric Design	Value proposition, service design, co-creation pathways
	Scalable Digital Infrastructure	Monetisation mechanics, tiering models, platform scalability
Insight Ecosystem Diagnostic	Governance & Trust	Data ethics, AI oversight, evidence-based governance
	Scalable Digital Infrastructure	Cross-functional data use, analytics, dashboard integration
Engagement Loop Designer	Member-Centric Design	Member contribution, trust cues, personalised feedback loops
Monetisation Governance Charter	Governance & Trust	Ethical revenue, shared value, reputational alignment
Digital Trust Dashboard	Governance & Trust	Consent, automation, safety, platform transparency

Diagnostic Tool or Domain	Aligned APSF Design Pillar(s)	Strategic Focus
Ecosystem Metrics Dashboard	Governance & Trust	Accountability to sector outcomes, multi-sided legitimacy
Technology Alignment Framework	Scalable Digital Infrastructure	Procurement, integration, scalability, future-proofing
Member Co-Creation Canvas	Member-Centric Design	Designing programs with members, participatory models
Exit Strategy Design Canvas	Governance & Trust	Sunset planning, decision rights, mission alignment
ROPI Readiness Checklist	Scalable Digital Infrastructure	Investment preparedness, platform viability
	Governance & Trust	Oversight, decision thresholds, ethical readiness

Integration Tip:

In board briefings or transformation sprints, consider using pillar-colour coding across your diagnostics dashboard to identify:

- **Underperforming design areas** (e.g. weak member co-creation or poor infrastructure alignment)
- **Overstressed governance elements** (e.g. repeated friction in platform monetisation or decision bottlenecks)
- **Gaps in pillar activation** (e.g. solid infrastructure, but low trust or shallow engagement)
- **Use colour-coding or icon overlays in board reports** to highlight underperforming or overstressed design areas. This enables board members to quickly identify which APSF pillars need attention and how that links to diagnostic outcomes.

This encourages strategic discussion not just on what is wrong, but which pillar of design needs intervention, making it easier to assign board ownership, allocate resources, or time reform initiatives.

Mapping Diagnostic Domains to APSF Design Pillars

Table 14-4 Core Compass Diagnostics Mapped to APSF Layers

Diagnostic Domain	Mapped APSF Layer(s)	Strategic Focus
Platform Readiness Diagnostic	Design Pillar: Scalable Infrastructure Integration Pathway: Personalisation Core Pillar: Trust & Security	Scalable infrastructure, digital enablement, secure member experience, personalised journeys

Governance Agility Scorecard	Design Pillar: Governance & Trust Core Pillars: Courage, Trust & Security	Ethical oversight, risk agility, decision speed, responsive governance
Business Model Health Check	Design Pillar: Scalable Infrastructure Integration Pathway: Collaboration Core Goal: Efficient Resource Allocation	Revenue resilience, innovation funding, cost-to-value alignment, service co-creation

Integration Tip:

Note: The same integration technique applies here. As noted above, colour-coded visualisation of APSF design pillars can help boards interpret scorecard results and link insights directly to governance or investment responses.

Aggregated of Composite Score Cards

Aggregated score cards provide an insightful means of visualising the overall performance.

Figure 14-2 Visualising Capability Maturity Across Strategic Domains

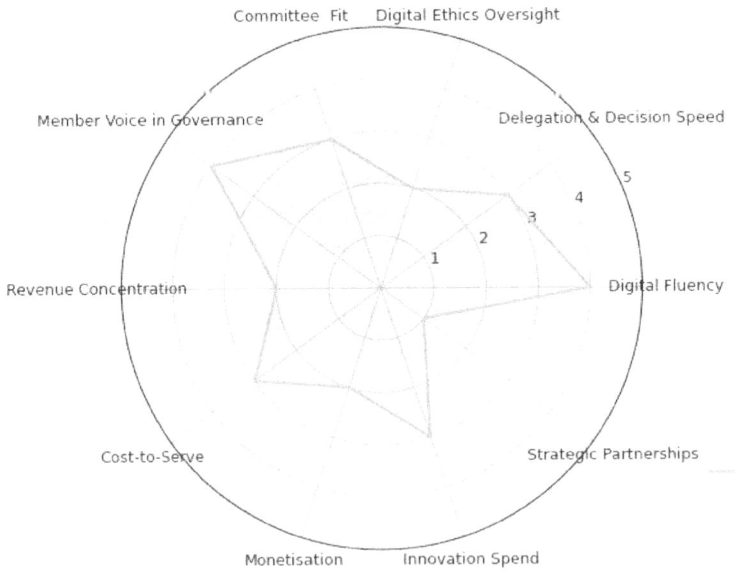

Embedding Diagnostics into Board Practice

Aggregated scorecards provide a powerful visual mechanism for identifying strengths and vulnerabilities across governance, platform readiness, and business model dimensions. Each axis reflects a key performance or risk area. Lower scores indicate greater exposure to transformation barriers, while higher scores signal maturity, agility, or strategic advantage.

Boards can use this tool to benchmark overall organisational health, prioritise investment and reform, track progress over time across domains, align board, executive, and operational perspectives. A composite view supports strategy execution by offering an integrated snapshot of capability and resilience.

While few associations use all three tools in a formal, integrated way, the underlying practices are well established. Digital maturity models, governance self-assessments, and revenue risk diagnostics are increasingly embedded in strategic reviews, accreditation audits, and funding due diligence. What this playbook offers is a coherent suite - designed specifically for platform-era associations - that connects these diagnostics to transformation readiness, agile governance, and business model evolution.

In this sense, the Association 2.0 Diagnostic Suite does not invent a new language, it organises and elevates existing practices into a board-ready, strategy-aligned framework that can be applied consistently across time and governance levels.

An integrated radar chart could combine all 17 indicators from the Governance Agility Scorecard, Platform Readiness Diagnostic, and Business Model Stress Test. It presents a unified visual of organisational transformation readiness, highlighting maturity levels, performance gaps, and systemic vulnerabilities across governance, operational, and financial dimensions. This diagnostic tool enables boards and executives to engage in structured strategic discussions, prioritise investment, and align on transformation pathways.

Figure 14-3 Aggregated Scorecard View

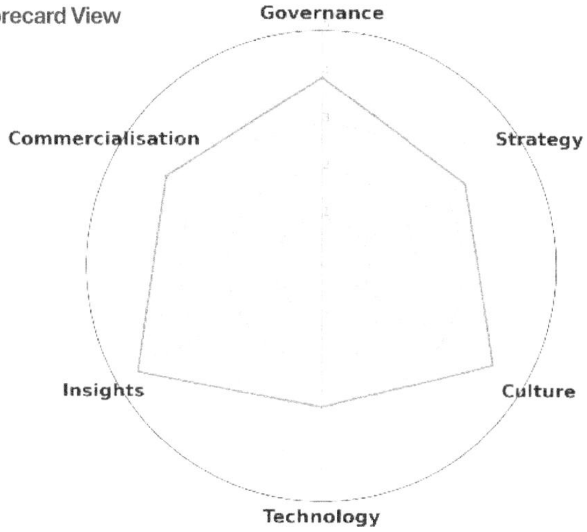

This figure brings together three core diagnostic perspectives, *Governance Agility*, *Platform Readiness*, and *Business Model Health*, into a unified visual. The spider graph illustrates an organisation's relative maturity across 17 key transformation domains. Each axis represents a distinct capability or strategic risk area.

The Composite Diagnostic serves as a powerful tool to identify cross-domain capability gaps or bottlenecks, reveal potential interdependencies between governance, operational capacity, and financial resilience, enable boards and executive teams to align priorities and track transformation progress over time, and facilitate rich strategic dialogue in workshops, planning sessions, or board reviews.

The shaded area reflects a sample diagnostic score, highlighting both strengths and vulnerabilities. Boards are encouraged to revisit this tool periodically to support iterative, evidence-based transformation.

Integration Options:

- Use as agenda items at strategy and finance meetings
- Conduct an annual diagnostic review to refresh strategy
- Include diagnostic trends in board reporting packs
- Run a facilitated board workshop to interpret insights and set targets

Foresight as a Governance Capability

In complex, fast-moving environments, governance will have to evolve beyond insight and be skilled in adaptiveness. The most advanced boards develop foresight with the ability to anticipate emerging risks, sense weak signals, and shape strategic options before threats or opportunities fully materialise.

> *This capability combines scenario thinking, horizon scanning, and design based approaches to enable governance that is pre-emptive, not reactive.*

High-foresight boards:

- Integrate predictive analytics and member signal data into decision cycles.
- Run "what if" exercises to simulate future states and map option spaces.
- Use structured scenario planning to test strategic resilience under different futures.
- Engage in regular future-focused briefings that include emerging trends, technology, policy shifts, and sector evolution.

Foresight is not just about vision, it is a form of discipline and governance preparedness. It requires systems, tools, and board habits that continually refresh understanding of what might change, why it matters, and how the association could lead through uncertainty.

The final level of the Governance Maturity Ladder, Level 6: Foresight Governance, signals this shift. It is where boards govern not only the organisation but the trajectory of the ecosystem it enables.

Table 14-5 Characteristics of Foresight-Driven Boards

Dimension	Foresight-Governance Practice
Strategic Planning	Scenario-based strategy with multiple futures tested
Board Decision Cycles	Use of early signals and option mapping alongside KPI reviews
Insight Integration	Predictive dashboards embedded in board reporting
Meeting Structures	Future-focused retreats; briefings on emerging tech, demographics, AI
Risk Framing	Opportunity-seeking, not just defensive posture

Putting Diagnostics into Practice

Diagnostic tools only create value when they are embedded in governance practice. Rather than treating diagnostics as one-off exercises, boards should integrate them into the rhythm of strategic oversight and resource allocation.

Boards can use diagnostic tools to:

- Benchmark organisational health across key transformation domains
- Prioritise capability investments based on data, not instinct
- Track transformation progress year-on-year using repeatable measures
- Guide risk-based resource allocation and reform agendas
- Foster evidence-informed conversations in the boardroom

Each diagnostic tool should be assigned a primary governance sponsor, such as the Digital and Risk Committee, the Strategy and Finance Committee, or a Transformation Working Group. Ownership ensures diagnostic insights are not only reviewed but acted upon.

The three tools can be implemented in various ways:

- As an annual board workshop ahead of strategic planning
- As a standing item in governance reporting frameworks
- As part of new board induction and director education
- As a signal to funders and stakeholders of commitment to adaptive governance

Over time, associations that use diagnostics consistently will develop a more mature capability to assess, interpret, and act on change. The tools themselves may evolve, but their governance value endures: clarity, accountability, and adaptation.

Governance Tip: *Each diagnostic should be assigned a primary committee sponsor (e.g. Digital & Risk, Finance & Strategy).*

Conclusion: Start Where You Are

Diagnostics do not tell you where you *should be,* they tell you where you *are*. That is their power.

Associations that treat transformation as a destination without a compass will lose momentum. Those that assess, adapt, and act iteratively are more likely to build resilience, earn trust, and create long-term value.

A diagnostic is not a judgement, it's a mirror. What matters is what you do once you've looked. Associations that act on this insight are not just managing change - they are leading it.

Chapter 15. The Playbook in Action: Applying the Framework

The *Association Platform Success Framework*, introduced in Chapter 1, defines what platform transformation looks like. This chapter answers the next question: how do we get there? The Six-Step Playbook provides a structured, board-ready approach to applying platform logic in real-world association settings

Use this chapter if you are...

- A CEO initiating a transformation program
- A board assessing strategic alignment
- A committee chair leading governance reform
- A program manager planning platform pilots

Why Associations Need a Playbook

Associations today are not lacking in ideas, they are often overwhelmed by them. What's missing is a structured, strategic way to translate platform thinking into action. This chapter provides that bridge, offering a clear, staged approach for leaders to apply the *Association Platform Success Framework* to their unique context.

This is not about checklist compliance. It is about empowering boards and executives to lead transformation that is strategically aligned, culturally feasible, and financially sustainable.

Case Studies in Action

To illustrate how associations are applying this framework in practice, the following case studies demonstrate the six-step Playbook in action, one real-world example and one fictionalised but plausible scenario.

Overview: The Six-Step Playbook

Each step builds progressively from awareness to sustained change. This is not a linear path, it is a cycle of capability development, experimentation, and refinement.

Table 15-1 Six-Step Playbook

Step	Strategic Focus	Primary Outcome
1. Diagnose	Understand your current model	Clarity on where you are and why
2. Align	Set shared direction across board, staff, and stakeholders	Unified strategic vision
3. Design	Choose the right platform model and features	A realistic and adaptive strategy
4. Pilot	Test key initiatives at low risk	Evidence for what works
5. Scale	Expand and embed successful models	Organisational capability uplift
6. Review	Measure, learn, and iterate	A cycle of continuous improvement

Step 1: Diagnose: Where Are You Now?

Many associations begin with ambition but lack a clear picture of their starting point. The Association 2.0 Transformation Compass provides a structured baseline. By combining the Platform Readiness Diagnostic, Governance Agility Scorecard, and Business Model Health Check, boards can diagnose capability gaps and transformation readiness with precision.

Recommended Tools:

- Business Model Canvas (adapted for associations)
- APSF Readiness Assessment
- Member Engagement Heatmaps
- Digital Maturity Self-Assessment

Key Questions:

- What is our current value proposition, and is it still relevant?
- Where are we over-invested in legacy systems?
- What signals from members are we ignoring?

* *For full tool details, see Chapter 15– Chapter 18.*

Step 2: Align: Build a Shared Understanding

Platform transitions fail when strategy is siloed or lacks legitimacy. Alignment between the board, CEO, staff, and key stakeholders is essential to avoid friction and ambiguity.

Recommended Tools:

- Strategy Alignment Workshops; Engagement Pulse Surveys; APSF Governance Diagnostic

Key Actions:

- Frame transformation as an organisational commitment, not a project
- Use governance as a unifier, embed change into board processes and risk frameworks
- Establish a transformation oversight mechanism (e.g. Change Committee or Steering Panel)

Step 3: Design: Choose Your Platform Model

No two associations will follow the same path. This step is about making strategic design decisions grounded in your diagnosis and stakeholder insights.

Design Variables:

- Will you adopt a freemium, subscription, or marketplace model?
- How will CPD, peer connection, and content be integrated?
- What role will AI, automation, and digital credentials play?

Tools:

- Platform Business Model Matrix; Value Proposition Refinement; Member Journey Mapping

"Design for participation, not just consumption."

Step 4: Pilot: Test Before You Scale

Avoid the trap of large-scale transformation driven by assumptions. Instead, pilot with purpose. Choose one or two initiatives that align with your platform vision and test them in the field.

Pilot Domains:

- A new member engagement platform with AI-driven content
- Tiered CPD subscriptions
- Peer-to-peer mentorship networks

Governance Tip:

- Predefine what success looks like
- Empower staff within risk-based Delegations of Authority
- Use member signals and data, not just staff feedback, as evidence

Step 5: Scale: From Initiatives to Institutional Change

Successful pilots should evolve into strategic programs. At this stage, the focus shifts to resourcing, culture, and integration.

Scaling Success Requires:

- Budget allocation with ROI discipline
- Workforce capability uplift (digital, data, platform stewardship)
- Change leadership, not just change management

Platform Integration Priorities:

- CRM and analytics infrastructure
- Member experience design
- Governance frameworks for AI, cybersecurity, and co-design

Step 6: Review: Institutionalise Learning and Accountability

Review is not a post-mortem, it is a strategic asset. Boards should oversee a continuous improvement loop that ties platform strategy to real-world results.

Measurement Anchors:

- Use the Association Platform Success Scorecard
- Integrate digital risk and trust signals into board reporting
- Track engagement and contribution, not just consumption

Governance Actions:

- Annual review of APSF implementation progress
- Board and CEO performance aligned to platform success metrics
- Member insight formally integrated into strategic planning

Example 65. PNA: Governance Transformation Pilot

The Professional Network Association (PNA), recognised its traditional governance structure was hindering its ability to respond to emerging issues such as AI regulation and data privacy reform.

Application of the Playbook:

Diagnose: *PNA used the APSF diagnostic tool to map its governance structures against strategic imperatives. It identified bottlenecks in decision-making and limited stakeholder representation on its national board.*

Align: *A facilitated retreat involving board and key committee members built shared commitment to a new governance model centred on agility, inclusivity, and transparency.*

Design: *A hybrid governance approach was proposed, including a standing Innovation Committee, refreshed delegations of authority, and a new digital engagement policy.*

Pilot: *The Innovation Committee was piloted for six months to test decision agility on emerging policy matters. A digital voting platform was also introduced for key member resolutions.*

Scale: *Based on strong results, including a quicker response to a federal AI consultation, elements of the pilot were embedded into PNA's constitution and board charter.*

Review: *PNA now runs an annual governance effectiveness review aligned with its strategy cycle and uses an agile decision register to track outcomes.*

Impact: *The pilot led to improved member trust scores and increased media presence for PNA on complex issues. The board now sees itself as an ecosystem orchestrator, better positioned to shape the future of the profession*

These two examples demonstrate how associations, regardless of size or sector, can translate the APSF and six-step model into measurable transformation outcomes.

Common Pitfalls and How to Avoid Them

Platform transformation is rarely linear. Associations that attempt to implement the Playbook without sufficient depth of planning, alignment, or iteration often fall into common traps. The table below outlines frequent pitfalls observed in association strategy execution, with recommended mitigation strategies drawn from practical experience and platform literature.

Table 15-2 Traps

Pitfall	Avoidance Strategy
Relying on legacy metrics	Many associations continue to evaluate success using only historical benchmarks, event attendance, member renewals, or surplus margin. These metrics may miss emerging indicators of member trust, influence, and digital engagement. *What to do*: Redefine success using broader value creation metrics, such as Net Promoter Score (NPS), platform participation rates, ecosystem influence, and contribution to member outcomes. Tie KPIs directly to the APSF pillars.
Thinking technology is the strategy	A common misstep is conflating digital tools (a CRM, LMS, or app) with strategic transformation. Without clarity on member value and organisational capability, technology becomes a cost centre rather than a growth enabler. *What to do*: Start with member pain points, value drivers, and growth opportunities. Ensure every technology investment is linked to a business capability in the APSF. Use capability mapping and journey design to shape technology needs, not the other way around.
Underinvesting in governance change	Associations often attempt platform strategies without adjusting board and committee structures, delegation frameworks, or decision rights. This creates bottlenecks and dilutes accountability. *What to do*: Revisit governance frameworks in parallel with platform design. Ensure Delegations of Authority are responsive to digital initiatives. Create an innovation subcommittee or working group with mandate clarity and reporting pathways. Consider agile decision registers to support timely, transparent oversight.
Moving too fast (or too slow)	Either extreme, paralysis by analysis or rushing to scale without evidence, undermines transformation. Moving too fast can expose the organisation to reputational, financial, and member trust risks. Moving too slow allows irrelevance to creep in. *What to do*: Use pilot initiatives to test assumptions and validate value propositions. Create a "safe-to-fail" space within the strategy cycle. Invest in learning loops, with short review sprints and adaptive governance. Deploy MVPs (minimum viable products) and scale only when member feedback and performance data support it.

Additional Considerations

- **Cultural resistance**: Staff and volunteer leaders may resist shifts in identity, control, or ways of working. Address this through transparent communication, training, and reinforcing new norms.
- **Overextension**: Trying to implement too many platform features or services simultaneously often results in diluted impact. Prioritise initiatives aligned with core strategic intent and member readiness.

- **Insufficient data infrastructure**: Without clean, integrated data, insight-driven decisions become guesswork. Invest early in data governance and analytics capability.

Example 66. Scaling Without Alignment

The Australian Knowledge Alliance (AKA), a mid-sized professional association focused on industry certification, launched a new Continuing Professional Development (CPD) platform with high expectations. It promised on-demand microlearning, AI-personalised pathways, and digital badges for professional recognition.

The rollout was rapid and resource-intensive, but within six months, it became clear the initiative was faltering. Member uptake was far below projections. Feedback was mixed. Many users found the experience confusing. Staff were inundated with troubleshooting requests, and senior leaders began questioning the return on investment.

An internal review revealed the root cause: the platform had been built without a clear value proposition or member journey map. The association had skipped the Diagnose and Align stages of the Playbook, assuming that advanced technology alone would drive engagement. The platform's features were not matched to member needs, and governance structures had not been updated to support platform-based decision-making.

In response, AKA paused the project and returned to fundamentals. Through a series of member listening labs, stakeholder alignment workshops, and governance diagnostics, they reshaped their approach. A new platform strategy was developed - with segmented learning pathways, simpler user interfaces, and co-designed content validation panels. The project was relaunched in phases, and this time, adoption exceeded expectations.

Lesson: *Transformation is not a race to scale. It's a rhythm of alignment, design, and iteration. When strategy is decoupled from member experience and governance readiness, even the most promising platforms can stall.*

Example 67. CPA's Digital Transformation Challenge

CPA Australia, one of the country's largest professional associations, provides a real and recent example of the risks and challenges that can arise when digital transformation and platform initiatives are not fully aligned with member needs, organisational culture, and internal capability.

The Scenario

In 2023, CPA Australia undertook a major internal revamp, including a costly technology project known as the Member Management and Finance (MMF) project. This involved migrating to a new Microsoft Dynamics 365 platform, managed by Deloitte, to replace outdated systems that were "not capable of supporting member and employee needs." The transformation was intended to modernise operations and improve member engagement through enhanced digital services and a new operating model.

However, the scale and pace of the project led to significant disruption:

- ***Staff Reductions and Restructuring:*** *CPA Australia cut 121 jobs, nearly one-fifth of its workforce, double the original target. The layoffs and role changes were justified as "efficiencies" gained from the tech project and new ways of working, but insiders described the atmosphere as "despondent" and "grim," with trust breaking down between executives and staff.*
- ***Service Disruption and Member Impact:*** *The MMF project and new operating model caused disruption to normal business activities, including a halt to member communications and changes in service delivery. This was observable to members and affected their experience.*
- ***Decline in Staff and Member Satisfaction:*** *An employee engagement survey showed only 28% of staff were "strong advocates" for working at CPA Australia, and around 40% did not feel "psychologically safe" at work, an 8% increase from the previous year. Member satisfaction also declined across all key performance indicators in 2023, with overall satisfaction dropping from 7.08/10 in 2022 to 6.87. KPIs for CPD, brand trustworthiness, thought leadership, and advocacy also fell short of targets.*
- ***Financial and Reputational Consequences:*** *Despite a price increase for membership and program fees, and a financial turnaround from a $33.8 million loss in 2022 to a $1.9 million loss in 2023, the disruption and dissatisfaction among members and staff persisted. The organisation's leadership acknowledged that all survey results fell short of targets, and the changes caused "disruption for our current employees as roles changed".*

Lessons for Associations

Alignment Is Critical: *Even with a clear strategy and investment in technology, transformation can falter if not matched by internal capability, cultural readiness, and member-focused design.*

Change Management and Communication: *Large-scale digital projects require careful change management, transparent communication, and support for both staff and members to maintain trust and engagement.*

Member Experience Will have to Remain Central: *Disruption to member services and a decline in satisfaction can undermine the intended benefits of digital transformation, regardless of operational efficiencies or financial improvements.*

Table 15-3 **CPA Australia's Digital Transformation Experience**

Area	*Intended Outcome*	*Challenge /Outcome*
Technology Upgrade	*Modernise member services*	*Disruption, halted communications*
Workforce Changes	*Efficiency, new ways of working*	*Job cuts, low morale, trust breakdown*
Member Engagement	*Improved satisfaction*	*Decline in satisfaction and KPIs*
Financials	*Cost savings, revenue growth*	*Short-term loss, then modest improvement*

(Accounting Times (2024, April) CPA Australia axed 121 staff, services for internal revamp: report).

Reflection: Strategy in Motion

The playbook is not a prescription, it is a framework to support adaptive strategy in a world where members are more connected, informed, and mobile than ever before.

The associations that thrive in the next decade will not be the biggest, but the most adaptive, the most trusted, and the most purpose-aligned.

Boards that treat platform strategy as a living system, not a project, will lead associations that shape their sectors, not just serve them.

Boardroom Reflection

- Are our governance structures aligned with platform strategy?
- Have we tested our model with real member behaviour, not assumptions?
- What capabilities are needed to move from pilot to scale?

Chapter 16. The Path to Association 3.0

Example 68. The Future Is Already Emerging

Claire Evans, CEO of the Professional Network Association (PNA), stood at the close of their annual strategy retreat. The association had made enormous strides: it had transitioned from a traditional membership body to a dynamic platform, diversified revenue, introduced AI-driven member services, and restructured governance for speed and integrity.

But now, a new challenge loomed.

"Are we ready for what comes next?" she asked the board. "Because transformation isn't a destination. It's a capability. And our environment won't stop evolving."

This is the pivot point many associations now face. Association 2.0 was the essential reset, reimagining business models, engagement, and governance for a platform economy. But the pace of change is accelerating, and new questions are surfacing.

- How will associations navigate Web3, decentralised identities, and AI ethics?
- How will they maintain trust in a post-truth world?
- And how do they ensure long-term impact when member expectations shift from content consumption to purpose-driven contribution?

The answer lies in building the conditions for the impending Association 3.0.

What is Association 3.0?

Association 3.0 is not a new technology stack. It's a paradigm shift: a move from digital transformation to digital embodiment, where the association becomes an adaptive, ethical, and decentralised node in its ecosystem. It redefines success as *collective value creation*, not just organisational survival.

Table 16-1 Association 3.0 Model

Dimension	Association 2.0	Association 3.0
Core Model	Platform-based, member-centric	Ecosystem-enabled, member-empowered
Technology Use	AI-driven, personalised, scalable	AI-integrated, ethical, distributed
Governance	Agile, risk-intelligent, insight-led	Participatory, decentralised, trust-enhancing

Dimension	Association 2.0	Association 3.0
Value Creation	Engagement, revenue diversification	Co-creation, shared impact
Metrics	KPIs across engagement, finance, governance	Value-to-network, equity, inclusion, social proof
Leadership Focus	Strategy, digital capability, culture	Systems stewardship, purpose alignment, foresight

Why the Path Matters

The transition to Association 3.0 is not inevitable. It will have to be designed. Associations that fail to evolve will be overtaken, not by other associations, but by new ecosystems: social networks, DAOs (decentralised autonomous organisations), tech-enabled alliances, and movements that mobilise communities without legacy structures.

Association 3.0 is not about copying these models. It is about learning from them and building trusted institutions that can thrive in this fluid, fast-paced environment.

Returning to the Framework

The *Association Platform Success Framework*, first introduced in Chapter 2 as a design model and detailed in Chapter 16 as a structured implementation roadmap, provides the foundation for this next evolution. It supports associations not only in modernising operations but in building the strategic and cultural capacity to adapt continuously. The pillars of Member Centric Design, Scalable Digital Infrastructure, and Governance & Trust are as essential in Association 3.0 as they were in 2.0 - but they will have to now stretch further.

While the APSF was operationalised through a six-step roadmap in Chapter 16, this chapter explores how each core pillar can evolve to support the deeper ambitions of Association 3.0.

Table 16-2 Evolving the APSF for Association 3.0

APSF Pillar	Association 2.0 Focus	Association 3.0 Evolution
Member-Centric Design	Designed for members' needs and preferences	Member-Led Co-Design: Members actively shape governance, data standards, and program priorities
Scalable Infrastructure	Integrated and efficient digital systems	Interoperable & Distributed Architecture: Supports portable identities, tokenised credentials, and decentralised services

APSF Pillar	Association 2.0 Focus	Association 3.0 Evolution
Governance & Trust	Insight-led, risk-intelligent, and agile	Participatory & Transparent Governance: Uses explainable AI, public audit trails, and real-time feedback mechanisms
Legal & Institutional Design	Traditional incorporated association model	Composable & Adaptive Structures: Enables hybrid legal models, DAOs, community tokens, and stewardship governance frameworks

In this way, the APSF becomes more than a model for transformation, it becomes an evolving architecture. Leaders are asked to reimagine its boundaries for greater openness, inclusion, and future readiness.

From Modernisation to Reimagination: A Maturity Spectrum

The journey from Association 2.0 to Association 3.0 is not a single leap but a spectrum of organisational maturity. Each phase represents a progressive evolution in how associations create value, engage their stakeholders, and structure their governance. Rather than viewing transformation as a binary between legacy and future models, boards and executives should understand this transition as a staged pathway, from *modernisation* to *reimagination*.

This maturity spectrum offers a strategic lens through which leaders can assess their current positioning and readiness for what comes next.

Figure 16-1 **Capability Development Radar for Association 3.0**

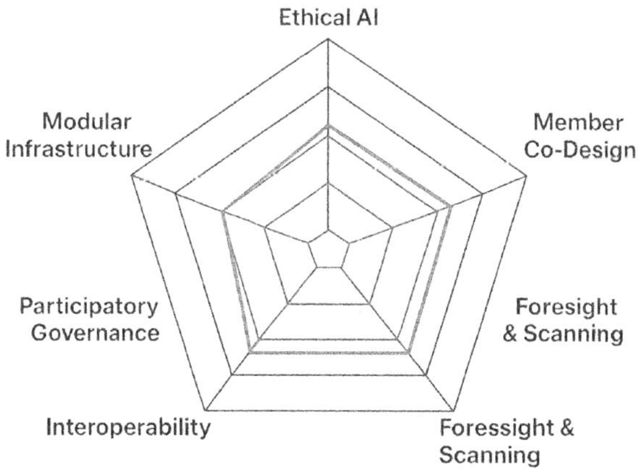

Table 16-3 Maturity Spectrum: From Association 1.0 to 3.0

Domain	Association 1.0 Legacy Model	Association 2.0 Modernisation	Association 3.0 Reimagination
Governance	Representative board structures; slow consensus cycles	Agile, risk-informed governance; digital oversight and adaptive delegations	Distributed, participatory or trustless governance (e.g. DAO-inspired or hybrid models)
Member Value	Static benefits, access to events or journals	Personalised digital experiences, learning, and support	Network-enabled co-creation, peer recognition, and reciprocal value flows
Business Model	Annual dues, event fees, sponsorship	Diversified revenue (freemium, digital offerings, partnerships)	Ecosystem monetisation (e.g. tokenisation, shared IP, data collaborations)
Technology Use	Back-office systems (CRM, email, CMS)	Integrated platforms, AI-enhanced tools, automation	Intelligent infrastructure: decentralised ID, embedded AI, interoperable protocols
Stakeholder Role	Passive members, governed by elected reps	Active contributors, segmented and digitally engaged	Platform actors: co-governance, co-design, co-delivery
Decision-Making	Scheduled, formalised cycles	Responsive, data-informed, with pilot-first mentality	Continuous, real-time, and sometimes autonomous

From Tools to Transformation

In Association 2.0, the emphasis is on modernising core operations, investing in digital infrastructure, diversifying income, and embedding agile governance. It is where most associations begin their transformation journey. However, Association 3.0 signals a more radical shift, one that reimagines the association not as a single organisation, but as an orchestrator, convener, or steward of a broader ecosystem of contributors.

In this reimagined model:

- Power is shared, not centralised.
- Innovation emerges from the edge, not just from the executive team.
- Governance is adaptive, decentralised, and inclusive of new voices.

This shift is not inevitable, nor is it suitable for every association. But for those operating in rapidly disrupted or innovation-driven sectors, the 3.0 model may offer a more sustainable and resilient form of strategic alignment.

Implications for Leaders

Board members and executives should use this spectrum to:

- **Diagnose** their current stage of maturity.
- **Debate** their strategic appetite for reimagination versus incremental reform.
- **Design** governance, member engagement, and technology investments aligned to where they are, and where they want to be.

Understanding that modernisation is a phase, not an endpoint, equips leadership teams to avoid premature complacency and prepare for the strategic design choices that Association 3.0 will demand.

Figure 16-2 From Association 1.0 to Association 3.0

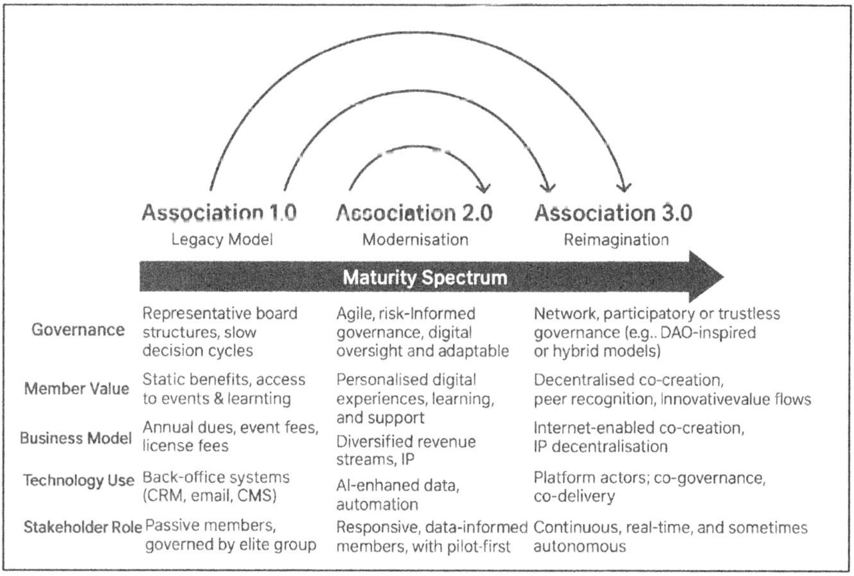

This spectrum illustrates the evolution of associations across five key dimensions as they transition from legacy structures (1.0) to modernised operations (2.0) and onward toward platform-enabled reimagination.

Signals of the Future

As signals of platform maturity continue to emerge, it is helpful to view the transition from Association 2.0 to Association 3.0 not as a binary shift, but as a *maturity spectrum*. This model allows boards to self-assess where they sit on the journey from operational modernisation (2.0) to strategic reimagination and ecosystem orchestration (3.0). The figure below outlines this transition as a staged evolution across five dimensions: governance, business model, technology, value creation, and member participation.

Associations can begin preparing for 3.0 by spotting emerging signals and investing in enabling capabilities.

Signals to Watch:

- Web3-enabled credentialing (blockchain-based CPD records)
- Decentralised voting on policy positions or funding allocations
- Open data collaboratives across sector participants
- Ethical AI committees with member and public oversight
- Reputation-based economies where trust metrics drive engagement

Capabilities to Build:

- Ethical foresight and technology scanning
- Member governance labs and participatory decision-making tools
- Modularity in platforms for future integrations
- AI and data governance policies with adaptive feedback loops
- Purpose-driven culture aligned to systemic impact

Figure 16-3 Signals of the Future

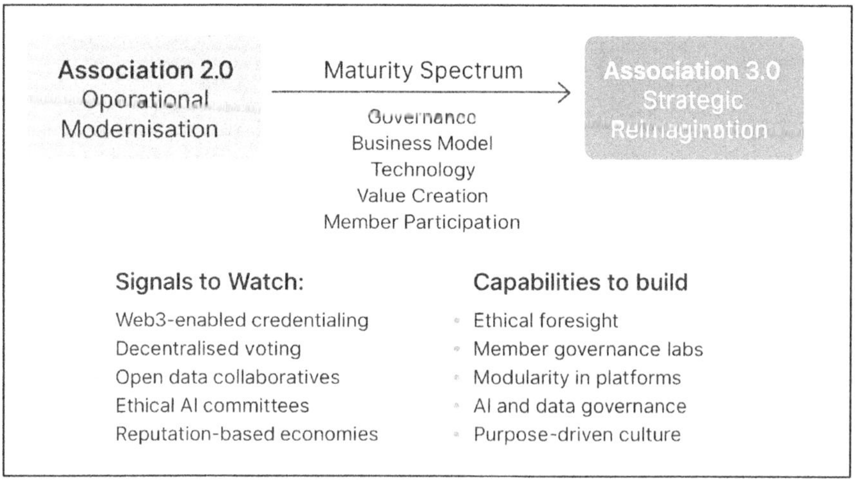

Guiding Questions for Boards and Leaders

1. How to shift from delivering value *to* members, to enabling value *by* and *through* members?
2. What are the minimum ethical and transparency thresholds we want all AI and data systems to meet?
3. How do we share power to ensure inclusion and legitimacy in doing so?

4. What platform architecture or legal model might allow for more decentralised participation?
5. How can we measure success in terms of ecosystem impact - not just organisational outputs?

Designing for Association 3.0: Five Starting Moves

Use this checklist to initiate your boardroom conversation and signal practical action in the shift from Association 2.0 to Association 3.0. Each move represents a foundational step that builds momentum for deeper transformation.

Table 16-4 Five Starting Moves

Starting Move	Description	Board Prompt
1. Establish a Member Governance Lab	Create a space for co-design and participatory experimentation with policy, programs, and data use.	How can we invite members into meaningful governance decisions without compromising integrity or speed?
2. Map Ecosystem Participation	Identify partners, platforms, and adjacent actors you can enable, convene, or co-create with.	Where are we positioned in the ecosystem, and who's missing from the table?
3. Pilot Modular Digital Capabilities	Trial token-based recognition, interoperable identity, or portable credentials to test value-sharing mechanisms.	What modular tool or standard could we introduce that gives members greater control or visibility?
4. Define Ethical AI and Data Guardrails	Establish minimum ethical thresholds for algorithms, automation, and data exchange, before they scale.	Have we set ethical boundaries and transparency standards that build trust into our tech use?
5. Reframe Value Creation Metrics	Begin shifting success indicators from internal outputs to network-wide impact and equity measures.	How will we know if we've created value beyond the organisation itself?

From Framework to Foresight

The journey to Association 3.0 is not mapped in a single strategic plan, nor delivered through a single digital upgrade. It is a continuous and deliberate evolution, anchored in purpose, enabled by governance, and fuelled by the collective imagination of members, boards, and leadership teams.

The *Association Platform Success Framework* was not designed merely to digitise the past. It was developed to build capacity for the future, capacity for adaptive leadership, networked engagement, strategic experimentation, and long-term resilience. It provides a structured yet flexible approach to navigating complexity, unlocking new forms of value, and responding to the shifting expectations of members and stakeholders in an increasingly platform-shaped world.

But frameworks are not enough.

What matters now is how leaders act, how they reframe risk, embrace uncertainty, and create the space for co-creation, participation, and innovation. The real work of transformation lies not just in what associations do differently, but in how they think differently, how they govern with agility, partner with integrity, and evolve their role from service providers to ecosystem stewards.

This book has offered a roadmap from Association 1.0 to 2.0, and signalled the possibilities of Association 3.0. The maturity spectrum presented in this chapter is both a reflection and a provocation. It challenges boards to ask not *when* change will come, but *how ready they are to lead it.*

To thrive in the decades ahead, associations will have to embrace a mindset of continuous evolution, grounded in principles of trust, transparency, equity, and shared value. They will have to design for emergence, not control. And they will have to measure success not only by outputs delivered, but by the quality of relationships sustained and the ecosystems they help enable.

Not as gatekeepers. But as convenors. As platforms. As catalysts of transformation.

The future of associations is not a question of relevance. It is a question of courage.

- Who will step forward?
- Who will design beyond the legacy?
- Who will lead not for certainty, but for significance?

Association 3.0 is not a forecast, it's an invitation. It asks boards not to predict the future, but to shape it.

The Modern Association Toolbox

Chapter 17. Toolbox for Diagnosis and Strategic Readiness

Tool 1: Mini Survey –Member Preferences

Purpose – To gather input from members on what they value most, their engagement preferences, and their appetite for pricing and service flexibility. You can distribute this as a short online form or during member renewal cycles.

Section A – Member Profile

1. What best describes your current career stage?
   ☐ Student
   ☐ Early career
   ☐ Mid-career
   ☐ Senior/Executive
   ☐ Retired
2. How long have you been a member of this association?
   ☐ Less than 1 year
   ☐ 1–3 years
   ☐ 4–7 years
   ☐ More than 7 years

Section B – Value and Engagement Preferences

3. Which of the following do you currently use or value most? *(Select up to 3)*
   ☐ CPD and learning modules
   ☐ Events and conferences
   ☐ Advocacy and representation
   ☐ Networking and peer forums
   ☐ Job board or career services
   ☐ Research or industry insights
   ☐ Member discounts or insurance
4. How would you describe your ideal membership experience?
   ☐ All-inclusive annual package
   ☐ Basic access with the option to pay for extras
   ☐ Monthly subscription model
   ☐ Free basic access with premium upgrades

Section C – Pricing and Flexibility

5. Would you prefer:

☐ One annual payment
☐ Quarterly or monthly payments
☐ Pay-per-use access for specific services

6. How likely are you to stay a member if more flexible options were introduced?
   ☐ Very likely
   ☐ Somewhat likely
   ☐ Neutral
   ☐ Unlikely
   ☐ Very unlikely

Section D – Open Feedback

7. Is there anything missing from your current membership that you'd like to see included?

[Open comment box]

8. What would make you more likely to recommend this association to a colleague or friend?

[Open comment box]

Tip for Implementation

Responses should be analysed by segment (e.g. age, career stage, tenure) to identify patterns that inform modular design, pricing tiers, or benefit bundles.

Tool 2: Governance Readiness Assessment

Purpose

This tool enables boards and executives to assess whether their governance frameworks are sufficiently prepared to support major transformation, particularly platform-based change and digital innovation. It integrates strategy alignment, risk oversight, delegation frameworks, and digital governance.

Sections to Include in the Toolbox Format

Board Decision Matrix

A diagnostic matrix to assess governance readiness before change.

Factor	High Readiness	Moderate	Low Readiness	Board Actions
Strategic Alignment	Aligned with mission and long-term goals	Needs refinement	Misaligned	Conduct strategic review
Committee Oversight	Clear roles and reporting lines	Some ambiguity	No clear oversight	Define roles and reporting
Stakeholder Engagement	Broad support	Partial buy-in	Resistance	Consult and adjust strategy
Risk Appetite & Mitigation	Defined and embedded	Partial frameworks	Reactive risk posture	Define and embed frameworks
Delegations of Authority	Enables agile decisions	Bottlenecks exist	Lacks clarity	Review and update delegations
Financial & Operational Capacity	Fully resourced	Partial gaps	Unfunded or weak capability	Conduct impact analysis
Digital & AI Governance	Policies in place	Basic coverage	No policy foundation	Establish digital governance

Change Governance Checklist

Governance Stage	Actions for Boards
Pre-Change	Define rationale and alignment, assess stakeholders, establish digital oversight, confirm risk appetite, clarify delegations, assess funding.
During Change	Monitor risks, review progress, use dashboards, ensure compliance, pilot before scaling.
Post-Change	Conduct review, evaluate governance structure, assess impact, document lessons.

Risk Readiness Scorecard

Area	Score (1–5)
Strategic alignment	
Board governance capability	
Stakeholder engagement	
Risk mitigation & compliance	
Delegations of Authority	
Financial sustainability	
Digital/AI governance	
Real-time monitoring ability	
Total Score	/40

Scoring Guide:
• 35–40 – Strong readiness
• 25–34 – Moderate readiness
• Below 25 – Address critical governance gaps before change

Use Case and Strategic Application

This tool should be used by:

- Boards prior to endorsing major change programs
- Governance or audit committees reviewing organisational readiness
- CEOs to brief the board and ensure support structures are in place

Tool 3: Board Capability Matrix – Modernising the Traditional Skills Matrix

Purpose

This tool helps boards move beyond the traditional compliance-based skills matrix toward a dynamic, strategic view of governance capability. It integrates reflection on board composition, behavioural attributes, and emerging skills needed to govern digital ecosystems, data, and member value in the platform era.

Table 17-1 Strategic Governance Review

Governance Capability	Current Capability (1–5)	Desired Capability (1–5)	Notes / Gaps
Strategic Risk Oversight			E.g. High comfort with operational risk, low with strategic foresight
Data & Insight Governance			
Platform & Technology Literacy			
Ethical AI & Automation Oversight			
Stakeholder & Ecosystem Engagement			

Supplementary Reflection Checklist

Use the following prompts to guide discussion about board composition and future needs:

☐ Do we have directors with real-world experience in digital transformation?

☐ Is data literacy, cybersecurity, or AI governance represented on the board?

☐ Are we over-represented by traditional industry backgrounds at the expense of emerging voices?

☐ Do we regularly review and update our board capability map?

☐ Are we equipping the board to govern platforms, networks, and ecosystems, not just institutions?

How to Use This Tool

Incorporate into annual **board skills matrix reviews**.

Use during board evaluations, composition planning, or succession discussions.

Revisit after strategy reviews to check alignment with capability needs.

Pair with the *Governance Heatmap Visual* or present in a workshop format.

Board Capability Evaluation Rubric

(Supporting Tool for the Board Capability Matrix – Toolbox Item 10)

Level	Capability Maturity Description
1 – Absent	No director currently holds this capability. It has not been discussed or prioritised by the board.
2 – Emerging	One or two directors have limited experience in this area. Capability is recognised but underutilised.
3 – Developing	Capability is present in some members and occasionally influences board discussions or decisions.
4 – Embedded	Capability is regularly applied, with clear board routines, active use in strategy, and visible leadership.
5 – Strategic	Capability is distributed across the board, used to anticipate risk and guide decisions. It shapes board culture, foresight, and continuous improvement.

Capability Domain Definitions (for use with rubric)

Domain	What It Evaluates
Strategic Risk Oversight	Board's ability to anticipate, monitor, and respond to emerging risks, including platform disruption.
Data & Insight Governance	Confidence in governing data quality, privacy, insight use, and ethical analytics.
Platform & Technology Literacy	Understanding of digital platforms, interoperability, and their impact on membership and revenue models.
Ethical AI & Automation Oversight	Oversight of fairness, explainability, and bias in algorithmic systems used by the association.
Stakeholder & Ecosystem Engagement	Ability to govern through partnerships, networks, and multistakeholder collaboration.

How to Use the Rubric

Apply individually and then discuss as a board for calibration.

Track change over time by using the rubric annually.

Use scores to:

- Prioritise director development,
- Inform board recruitment,
- Link governance capability to APSF implementation progress.

Example Scoring Output

"In our last review, we were Level 2 (Emerging) in Platform & Technology Literacy. We now have two directors with fintech and digital product experience, and we're using that capability to challenge our member platform design. We self-assessed at Level 3 and targeted a move to Level 4 by next year."

Tool 4: Governance Capability Heatmap

Purpose

This tool helps boards assess their current capability against the strategic needs of a modern, platform-based association. It is designed to prompt conversation, identify development priorities, and support structured board evaluations.

Table 17-2 Board Self-Assessment

Governance Capability	Current Capability (1–5)	Desired Capability (1–5)	Notes / Gaps
Strategic Risk Oversight			E.g. Focus has been reactive; need to assess foresight use
Data & Insight Governance			
Platform & Technology Literacy			
Ethical AI & Automation Oversight			
Stakeholder & Ecosystem Engagement			

Scoring Guide

1 = **Absent** – No observable capability or conversation

2 = **Emerging** – Initial awareness or sporadic practice

3 = **Developing** – Capability is present but inconsistently applied

4 = **Embedded** – Consistently demonstrated and aligned to strategy

5 = **Strategic** – Used proactively to guide governance decisions

How to Use This Tool

- Complete individually or collectively as a board.
- Use in board effectiveness reviews, induction planning, or skills matrix updates.
- Reassess annually to track cultural and structural shifts.

Insightful governance isn't just about structure, it's about growing the right capabilities for the future.

Tool 5: Insight Ecosystem Diagnostic – Board & Executive Self-Assessment Tool

Purpose

This tool helps association leaders assess the maturity and integration of insight capability across strategic and operational domains. It supports evidence-based governance by identifying where insight is driving decisions, and where it isn't.

Table 17-3 Insight Integration Scorecard

Domain	Key Questions	Current Rating (1–5)	Comments / Gaps
Board & Governance	Are board papers and strategy sessions informed by forward-looking insight and member trend data?		
Strategic Planning	Is predictive data used to test assumptions, prioritise goals, and guide investment?		
Executive Decision-Making	Do executives use insight to adjust programs, pricing, and engagement tactics in real time?		
Member Engagement	Is behavioural data used to personalise journeys and prevent churn?		
Risk & Compliance	Are AI, digital, and reputational risks monitored through dashboards and early warning systems?		
Finance & Forecasting	Are budgeting and revenue strategies guided by dynamic modelling and scenario testing?		
Operations & Delivery	Is data used to optimise CPD uptake, event delivery, or service design?		
Insight & Analytics Hub	Is there a central, trusted source of insight that serves all functions and enables continuous learning?		

Scoring Guide

1 = **Not evident** – No use of insight in this domain

2 = **Emerging** – Some isolated examples or pilot use

3 = **Developing** – Insight is present but not routine or reliable

4 = **Embedded** – Insight regularly informs decisions in this area

5 = **Strategic** – Insight is critical, proactive, and continuously improved

How to Use

Complete as a board or executive team exercise.

Discuss gaps and score variation across domains.

Use to prioritise investment, training, or integration work.

Re-assess annually to track improvement and culture shift.

Tool 6: Platform Maturity Spectrum

Purpose

To help associations assess their current state, identify transformation gaps, and plan strategic moves toward a platform-enabled, ecosystem-oriented model aligned with the ***Association Platform Success Framework***.

Spectrum Overview

Stage	Association 1.0	Association 2.0	Association 3.0
Value Logic	Deliverer of member services	Enabler of engagement and contribution	Orchestrator of ecosystem-wide value
Engagement	Passive membership, events, newsletters	Interactive, multi-channel, co-designed offerings	Deep participation, member-led programs, peer exchange
Revenue Model	Membership dues + event fees	Hybrid monetisation (direct + indirect)	Outcome-based, value exchange across actors
Technology	Functional tools (CRM, email, LMS)	Integrated digital stack with analytics	Scalable, adaptive infrastructure with AI and automation
Governance	Compliance-focused board	Agile, insight-driven, strategic governance	Co-governance, ecosystem accountability, trust stewardship
Data & Insight	Minimal data use	Performance tracking, member segmentation	Predictive analytics, real-time intelligence, AI oversight
Innovation	Incremental, committee-led	Pilot-based, responsive to insight	Distributed, member-driven, ecosystem-integrated
Partnerships	Transactional sponsorships	Strategic alliances	Shared-value, multi-stakeholder coalitions
Member Role	Service recipient	Active participant	Co-creator, network node
Platform Characteristics	None	Multisided logic emerging	Fully embedded platform mindset and design

Assessment Guide

Score your association against each dimension on a scale of 1 (legacy mode) to 5 (ecosystem orchestration).

Dimension	Score (1–5)	Notes / Gaps / Next Step
Value Logic		
Engagement		
Revenue Model		
Technology		
Governance		
Data & Insight		
Innovation		
Partnerships		
Member Role		
Platform Logic		

Interpreting Results

Score Range	Interpretation
10–25	Association 1.0 (Foundational) – High risk of obsolescence; begin with diagnostic and strategic education
26–40	Association 2.0 (Transitional) – Core elements in place, but integration and member value need maturing
41–50	Association 3.0 (Ecosystem Ready) – Operates as a dynamic platform; prioritise scaling, co-governance, and sector leadership

Suggested Use

- As a board retreat tool or transformation workshop artefact
- To prioritise APSF-aligned investments and pilot opportunities
- For executive performance review and roadmap alignment
- As part of a maturity model portfolio with:
    - Governance Agility Scorecard
    - Insight Ecosystem Diagnostic
    - Monetisation Readiness Matrix
    - Exit Strategy Design Canvas

Tool 7: APSF Alignment Diagnostic

Purpose

To assess the organisation's current level of alignment with the **Design Pillars** of the *Association Platform Success Framework*:

Design Pillar	Prompt	Rating (1–5)
Member-Centric Design	Are members actively involved in shaping content, services, and governance?	
Scalable Digital Infrastructure	Are our digital systems modular, integrated, and aligned with future needs?	
Governance & Trust	Do our governance processes build trust, accountability, and adaptive capacity?	

How to Use

- Invite board or executive team members to complete individually
- Compare responses and discuss blind spots
- Use low-scoring areas as **priority zones** for transformation pilots
- Repeat quarterly or annually to track cultural and strategic shifts

Why Use the Design Pillars

- They **link directly to implementation** (especially for technology, co-creation, and oversight)
- They are the **foundation for platform transformation** (e.g. used in readiness checks, digital audits)
- They are **reflected in multiple other tools**, including the Tech Alignment Tool, Full Implementation Checklist, and Digital Trust Dashboard

Best Used During:

Strategy retreats, readiness assessments, prioritisation workshops.

Tool 8: Monetisation Decision Matrix

Purpose

To evaluate potential monetisation strategies against five critical dimensions that determine strategic fit, ethical viability, and scalability in a platform-based association.

This matrix can be used during board strategy sessions, product reviews, or innovation sprints to support monetisation planning and decision-making.

Instructions

For each proposed revenue model (e.g. tiered CPD subscriptions, paid mentoring, member marketplace), score the model on each of the five dimensions using a 1–5 scale:

- 1 = Major concern or misalignment
- 3 = Neutral or uncertain impact
- 5 = Strong alignment and strategic value

Then total the score and reflect on any red flags or areas requiring mitigation.

Evaluation Lens	Guiding Question	Score (1–5)	Comments / Mitigations Needed
1. Strategic Alignment	Does the model reinforce our long-term goals, purpose, and platform logic?		
2. Member Value	Will members perceive this as fair, valuable, and aligned with their participation?		Consider optics, effort vs value, recognition models
3. Scalability	Can this model scale sustainably across segments and over time?		Think about effort-to-reward ratio, tech readiness
4. Tech & Data Readiness	Do we have the systems, integration, and data governance to support this?		Includes digital infrastructure and data ethics
5. Ethical & Reputational Fit	Could this model damage trust, introduce bias, or trigger backlash?		Consider risks around overreach, member exploitation

Total Score (out of 25):

21–25: Strong candidate; minimal friction; likely strategic fit

16–20: Promising, but address gaps before rollout

10–15: High-risk; redesign or reconsider

Below 10: Do not proceed without major rework

Optional Use Cases:

- Evaluate up to **three revenue models** side-by-side in a board workshop.
- Use in conjunction with the **Platform Revenue Model Matrix** to visualise where value is created vs monetised.

- Integrate with the **ROPI** diagnostic to assess alignment with investment strategy.

Tool 9: Platform Revenue Model Matrix

Purpose:

To help associations map, evaluate, and diversify their revenue strategy using platform economics principles. This tool is designed to illuminate not only *how* income is generated, but *where* value originates in a multi-actor system, and *whether* the monetisation logic supports long-term sustainability, trust, and scalability.

It builds on the foundational concepts from *Ecosystem Economics for Modern Associations*, particularly Chapter 6 (Revenue by Design) and Chapter 7 (Pricing, Packaging, and Member-Centred Strategy), where platform monetisation is reframed as a function of interaction design, participation logic, and value orchestration.

To help association leaders map, evaluate, and diversify their revenue strategies based on where value is generated (by the association, members, or ecosystem partners), and how value is monetised (directly through access or usage, or indirectly via data, trust, or facilitation).

This matrix encourages associations to shift from transactional thinking (e.g. fees-for-service) to a multi-sided, platform-based view of value creation and revenue.

Table 17-4 Platform Revenue Model Matrix

	Monetisation is Direct (payment is tied to usage, access, or rights)	**Monetisation is Indirect (revenue flows from adjacent services, data, or trust)**
Value Created by Association	Traditional products, publications, paid CPD courses Example: Webinar fees, journal subscriptions	Brand leverage, white-labelling, trust-based licensing Example: Reputation licensing, certification revenue
Value Created by Members	Marketplace models, peer coaching, content royalties Example: Member-led training sessions, paid mentoring	Data-sharing, community co-creation, indirect value from vibrant participation Example: Sponsored forums, learning analytics
Value Created by Partners / Ecosystem	Commercial partnerships, co-developed programs Example: Paid industry briefings, co-branded CPD	Outcomes-based payments, grants, API monetisation, network effect value Example: Commissioned policy impact, platform infrastructure funding

Instructions for Use

1. **Map all current revenue streams** into the relevant cell. Ask:
    - Who creates the value?
    - Is the revenue direct or indirect?
2. **Identify gaps or overreliance.** For example:

- Too much dependence on top-left = fragile, labour-intensive revenue.
- Bottom-right may be underdeveloped but offers high scalability and systems-level impact.

3. **Use to design diversified monetisation models**, ensuring balance across all four quadrants.

Strategic Insights:

- Associations overly reliant on the top-left (direct monetisation of internally-produced content) often experience scalability ceilings and burnout.
- The bottom-right (indirect monetisation of ecosystem value) offers the most sustainable, mission-aligned growth but requires investment in trust, interoperability, and governance.
- Middle-right (indirect value from member participation) is ideal for associations with vibrant communities, sponsorship, grant funding, or data-cooperative models thrive here.

Integration with Other Tools:

- Use alongside the **Monetisation Decision Matrix** to assess feasibility and trust alignment.
- Pair with the **ROPI framework** to calculate long-term return on monetisation strategies.
- Integrate into **strategy offsites**, board evaluation sessions, and commercialisation sprints.

Figure 17-1 Platform Revenue Model Matrix

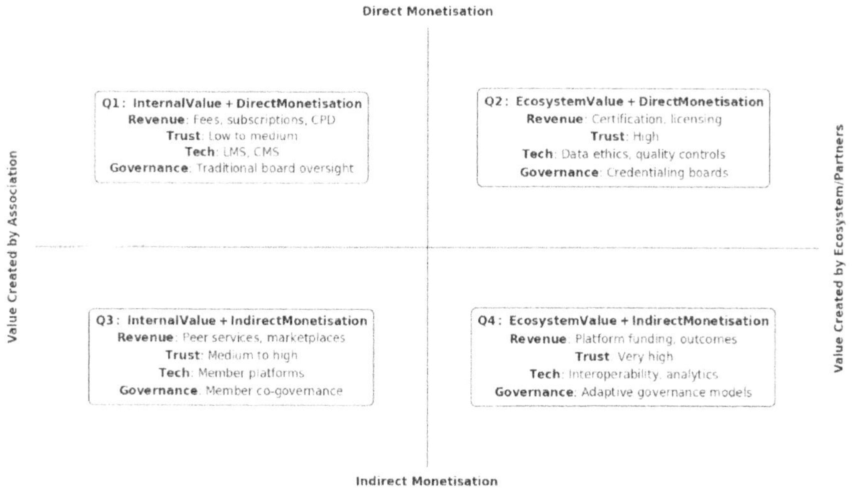

Figure 17-2 Governance and Monetisation Modes

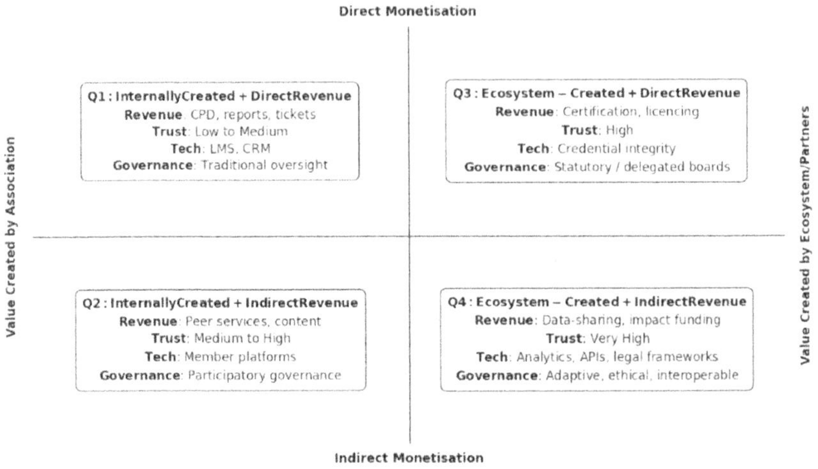

Tool 10: Return on Platform Investment (ROPI) Diagnostic

This diagnostic builds on the strategic design principles introduced in the book, **Ecosystem Economics for Modern Associations,** *where platform investment logic, monetisation design, and ecosystem readiness are discussed in depth.*

Purpose

To assess the *strategic, economic, and governance return* of platform-aligned investments across five dimensions. *Return on Platform Investment* helps associations evaluate:

- How well a proposed initiative fits the platform model
- Whether the investment enables *scalable, multi-sided value*
- What alignment risks or opportunity costs may be introduced

Table 17-5 Five Evaluation Dimensions

Dimension	Key Question	Rating (1–5)	Comment / Evidence
1. Value Creation Leverage	Will this investment enable others to create value (not just us)?		
2. Participation Multipliers	Does it increase peer, partner, or member engagement in ways that compound over time?		
3. Alignment Fit	Is this well-aligned with our platform logic, capabilities, and ecosystem strategy?		
4. Interoperability & Reuse	Can this initiative integrate with other systems, data, or value flows?		
5. Trust & Governance Enablement	Will this investment increase transparency, equity, or member confidence?		

Scoring Guidance:

21–25: High ROPI, strongly aligned, ecosystem-enabling, and scalable.

16–20: Moderate ROPI, some adjustments or risk mitigation needed.

10–15: Low ROPI, may be incompatible with long-term platform logic.

Below 10: Likely misaligned, re-scope or reconsider.

Suggested Format Options:

1. **Printable 1-page PDF worksheet** (for board and exec sessions)
2. **Table format in Chapter 5 or Toolbox**
3. **Interactive slide template** (for facilitated workshops)

Figure 17-3 ROPI by monetisation strategy

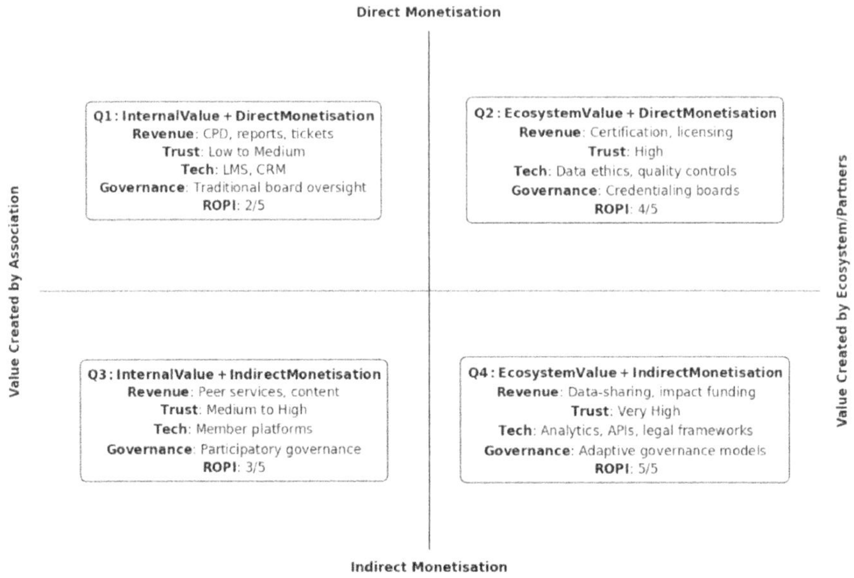

This figure visualises strategic return across four monetisation quadrants, highlighting where high-ROPI investments typically reside based on value orchestration and trust infrastructure alignment.

ROPI Score Calculation Method

Each investment is scored across **five key platform-aligned dimensions**, using a 1 to 5 scale:

Score	Description
1	Very weak alignment or significant risk; little to no platform leverage
2	Weak alignment; may add limited value or duplicate existing functions
3	Neutral or mixed alignment; some value but limited scalability or reuse
4	Strong alignment; supports platform participation and trust infrastructure
5	Very strong alignment; enables multi-sided value creation, trust, and reuse at scale

Each dimension is scored independently, and the *overall ROPI score* for a quadrant or investment is either:

- An average of the five scores, or
- A strategic weighting (if some dimensions are prioritised, e.g. Trust Enablement in sensitive sectors)

Example Breakdown (for a Q4 initiative):

Dimension	Score (1–5)	Reasoning
Value Creation Leverage	5	Enables member-generated learning content
Participation Multipliers	4	Designed for peer interaction and feedback
Alignment Fit	5	Fully aligned with platform strategy and APSF
Interoperability & Reuse	4	Built using open standards and APIs
Trust & Governance Enablement	5	Includes reputation system and audit trails

Total Score: 23 / 25 → ROPI Rating = 5/5

Chapter 18. Toolbox - Designing the Platform Business Model

These tools are suitable for assisting in the design stage of the platform development process.

Tool 11: Member Co-Creation Canvas

Purpose

To help associations identify **where members can co-create value**, not just consume services, reinforcing the platform logic of interaction, contribution, and shared purpose.

Canvas Structure

Area	How Members Could Contribute
Program Design	Co-design learning programs, lead webinars
Policy Development	Participate in working groups, review draft positions
Content	Submit articles, host podcasts, run peer forums
Data Insight	Share real-world experience, contribute feedback loops
Governance	Serve on innovation panels or advisory circles

How to Use It

- **Workshop Setting**: Bring this into a leadership or cross-functional team session.
- **Audit Existing Participation**: Map where members already contribute across these areas.
- **Identify Gaps**: Spot where contribution is low or absent, ask why.
- **Design Experiments**: Set 1–2 co-creation initiatives (e.g. a peer-led CPD sprint or member-led insight forum).
- **Track and Acknowledge**: Recognise contributors and build feedback channels to close the loop.

Why It Matters

This tool operationalises the shift from a service provider model to a platform host model, as illustrated in the *PNA case study*. Member co-creation was central to PNA's transformation and delivered improved relevance, engagement, and trust.

Integration Tips

- Pair it with the **Engagement Heatmap** to assess current activity by segment.
- Use as input to **Boardroom Retreats** on value strategy or renewal design.
- Include in **Member Experience Labs** or product design sprints.

Tool 12: Engagement Loop Designer

Purpose
The Engagement Loop Designer helps associations deliberately craft and evaluate the feedback loops that sustain member and stakeholder participation. Engagement is not a one-off transaction; it is an iterative cycle of value exchange where trust, recognition, and reciprocity accumulate over time. This tool guides boards and executives to identify, map, and refine these loops so that engagement becomes self-reinforcing rather than episodic.

Core Insight
Engagement loops are the "flywheels" of modern associations. When well designed, they generate momentum: a member contributes, receives visible value or recognition, which motivates further participation, which in turn strengthens the association's ecosystem. Conversely, weak or broken loops lead to disengagement, churn, and a fragile sense of belonging.

How It Works
The Engagement Loop Designer is structured around three steps:

1. **Map the Loop**
    - Identify the starting point (e.g., a new member joining, an existing member engaging in CPD, a volunteer leading a project).
    - Track the sequence of interactions, value flows, and recognition mechanisms that follow.
    - Visualise the loop as a cycle rather than a linear process.
2. **Test the Reinforcement**
    - Ask: what motivates a member to return for the next cycle of engagement?
    - Identify friction points (delays, unclear value, lack of recognition).
    - Evaluate alignment with the association's broader platform strategy (e.g., does the loop cross into learning, networking, advocacy?).
3. **Design for Acceleration**
    - Introduce design levers such as reciprocity (peer-to-peer exchange), gamification (milestones, recognition), and convening power (exclusive forums, policy input).
    - Ensure feedback mechanisms are timely and transparent—members should clearly see the outcomes of their contributions.
    - Build in pathways for scaling: small wins that encourage members to step into deeper or adjacent forms of engagement.

Applications

- **Board Level**: Use to test whether engagement strategies are creating sustainable value loops or just one-off campaigns.
- **Operational Level**: Map engagement loops across different pillars (learning, advocacy, networking) to find gaps or overlaps.
- **Strategic Transformation**: Apply the tool when shifting from Association 2.0 to 3.0, ensuring member engagement becomes ecosystem-based rather than transactional.

Example Loops

- **Learning Loop**: Member completes CPD → gains recognition/points → shared credential in professional profile → encouraged to enrol in next program.
- **Advocacy Loop**: Member submits policy input → sees position reflected in advocacy campaign → receives update on outcome → motivated to contribute again.
- **Network Loop**: Member joins an event → connects with peers → receives follow-up opportunity → builds habit of attending and sharing knowledge.

Diagnostic Questions

- What are our strongest current engagement loops?
- Where are loops breaking down (low repeat participation, declining trust)?
- Do we have loops that cut across different member value propositions (e.g., learning leading into advocacy)?
- How do we measure the velocity and strength of these loops?

Core Loop Concept

Engagement loops are **cyclical pathways** where a member:

- Engages (joins, attends, contributes)
- Receives value (learning, recognition, access)
- Is prompted to act again (renew, contribute, share)
- Feeds insight or value back into the system (feedback, content, mentoring)

Well-designed loops increase retention, deepen trust, and drive scalable co-creation.

Canvas Structure

Loop Stage	Design Questions	Examples
1. Trigger	What motivates the first action or visit?	Email, referral, campaign, career need
2. Action	What specific behaviour do we want to encourage?	Join, sign up for CPD, ask a question
3. Value Moment	What is the immediate and longer-term value they receive?	Downloaded resource, CPD points, peer recognition
4. Re-engagement Cue	What prompt encourages return or next step?	Personalised follow-up, invite to contribute
5. System Feedback	What do we learn from the interaction, and how does the system adapt or improve?	CRM update, AI tuning, program improvement
6. Loop Extension	How does the member's action create value for others?	Forum reply, mentoring offer, event referral

Loop Typologies to Consider

Loop Type	Target Behaviour	Example Context
Learning Loop	Return to CPD, courses, micro-credentials	CPD dashboard + dynamic content recommendations
Contribution Loop	Submit content, lead webinars, mentor	Member hub + badge recognition + share feature
Network Loop	Engage in forums or small groups	Discussion thread + follow-up event or tool offer
Feedback Loop	Respond to surveys or insight prompts	NPS result triggers strategic update or thank-you
Monetisation Loop	Upgrade, renew, or pay for services	Tiered access based on activity and satisfaction

How to Use the Designer

1. Pick one priority loop (e.g. onboarding → value realisation → renewal)
2. Map the journey using the canvas
3. Identify friction points (e.g. value gaps, drop-off zones)
4. Introduce triggers and enhancements (e.g. nudge emails, micro-rewards)
5. Evaluate loop performance using behavioural metrics (time, return, contribution)
6. Layer loops to build network effects over time

Strategic Applications

- Design platform onboarding pathways
- Optimise renewal and contribution cycles
- Embed into Member Co-Creation Canvas and Heatmap
- Link to Engagement KPIs in the *Measuring What Matters* chapter

Output Example (Visual Summary)

New member → CPD → publishes insight → earns badge → invited to mentor → joins expert forum → becomes advocate

Each touchpoint increases value and deepens commitment, forming a self-reinforcing engagement engine.

Tool 13: Ecosystem Orchestrator Checklist

This checklist helps boards evaluate their current capabilities and identify areas for development when assuming the orchestrator role in a platform-based association.

Table 18-1 Ecosystem Orchestrator Checklist

Orchestrator Capability Area	Key Question for the Board	Current Readiness (Low / Moderate / High)
Strategic Alignment	Have we explicitly positioned orchestration as a strategic pillar in our platform vision?	
Stakeholder Clarity	Do we clearly understand the different participant groups in our ecosystem and their respective needs and incentives?	
Interaction Governance	Have we defined the rules, norms, and value exchange protocols between participants?	
Network Value Measurement	Do we have mechanisms to evaluate the quality and impact of interactions across the platform (e.g. match rates, satisfaction, contribution metrics)?	
Incentive Design	Are we using tailored incentives (e.g. reputation, data access, rewards) to encourage ecosystem participation and alignment?	
Trust and Legitimacy	Are we seen as a neutral, credible, and inclusive actor by ecosystem participants?	
Governance Architecture	Do we have the governance structures needed to manage decentralised decision-making and stakeholder input (e.g. advisory councils, data ethics committees)?	
Technology Enablement	Does our platform infrastructure support modular interactions, peer collaboration, and third-party integration?	
Partnership Strategy	Are we actively cultivating strategic partnerships that extend the value of the	

Orchestrator Capability Area	Key Question for the Board	Current Readiness (Low / Moderate / High)
	ecosystem (e.g. credential providers, employers, educators)?	
Board Capability	Does the board understand its role in overseeing complex, dynamic ecosystems, not just internal performance?	

Scoring Guidance:
High (8–10 "High" ratings) – Strong orchestration readiness – you're well placed to scale an ecosystem approach.

Moderate (5–7 "High" ratings) – Emerging orchestration capability – key pillars are in place, but some gaps may hinder ecosystem scaling.

Low (<5 "High" ratings) – Foundational work needed – invest in strategic design, governance architecture, and board education.

Tool 14: Commercialisation Board Reflection Questions

To be used in commercial strategy discussions, planning workshops, or as part of annual strategy and risk reviews.

Strategic Fit and Purpose

- How does this commercial initiative align with our mission and member value proposition?
- Are we solving a problem for our members, partners, or ecosystem, or just chasing revenue?
- Are we clear on whether we are delivering value or enabling others to create value (platform role clarity)?

Governance and Oversight

- Has the board explicitly endorsed the commercial risk appetite for this initiative?
- What governance mechanisms (e.g. delegations, reporting lines, conflict registers) are in place?
- Are our oversight processes different when commercial and mission-driven operations intersect?

Stakeholder Trust and Reputation

- How might this initiative affect trust among members, regulators, or partners?
- Are we using our brand to endorse, curate, or simply monetise? Do we understand the difference?
- Have we stress-tested reputational risk scenarios (e.g. partner failure, data breach, misaligned values)?

Market and Delivery Readiness

- Have we validated real market demand, or are we relying on internal assumptions?
- Are our systems, staff, and delivery mechanisms platform-ready, scalable, modular, and participatory?
- Have we planned for pilot testing, iteration, and feedback loops?

Mission Protection and Long-Term Impact

- Could this initiative unintentionally displace or diminish our core public or member value?
- Are we clear about exit strategies or decision points if this initiative underperforms or drifts?
- How will we measure success, beyond financial return, to include mission, trust, and platform health?

Tool 15: Monetisation Governance Charter (Template)

Purpose

This Charter establishes the principles, safeguards, and governance processes through which the association evaluates, approves, and oversees monetisation activities. It supports value creation that is aligned with purpose, trusted by members, and transparent to stakeholders.

Foundational Principles

Principle	Definition
Mission Alignment	All monetisation activity will have to reinforce the association's strategic purpose.
Member Trust	Monetisation will have to not compromise the trust, autonomy, or expectations of members.
Transparency	Revenue sources and practices will be clearly disclosed to members and stakeholders.
Ethical Integrity	Member data, community contributions, and institutional reputation are protected.
Shared Value	Where members generate value, the association considers fair benefit distribution.

Scope of Monetisation

This Charter applies to all revenue-generating activities, including but not limited to:

- Membership tiers and benefits
- Continuing professional development (CPD)
- Events and learning programs
- Job boards and career services
- Sponsorships and advertising
- Member-generated content
- Affinity partnerships and licensing
- Data insights and analytics
- Platform services or commissions

Governance Processes

Activity	Governance Requirement
New revenue stream proposal	Reviewed by Executive and approved by Board or relevant Committee
Risk and reputation assessment	Conducted with Monetisation Decision Matrix
Member input and consultation	Required for revenue models involving peer content, data use, or ethical sensitivity
Legal and compliance review	Required for data, contracts, sponsorship, or co-branding arrangements
Pilot phase (if applicable)	All new streams launched with limited scope, evaluation points, and exit criteria
Annual review and reporting	Monetisation portfolio reviewed annually for financial performance, alignment, and risk

Ethical Safeguards

Red Line	Policy
Member data use for commercial purposes	No sale of identifiable member data. Anonymised, aggregate use requires opt-in and transparency.
Undisclosed sponsored content	All sponsored content will have to be clearly marked and reviewed for alignment with member expectations.
Pay-to-participate governance	Leadership, awards, and committees will have to not be monetised or restricted to paying tiers.
Reputational misalignment with partners	Sponsorship or advertising relationships will have to be aligned with organisational values.

Roles and Responsibilities

Role	Responsibility
Board	Oversees alignment with mission and risk appetite
CEO/Executive	Implements strategy, ensures compliance and operational delivery
Monetisation Review Panel *(optional)*	Cross-functional group to assess new proposals and stakeholder impacts
Finance/Audit Committee	Reviews portfolio performance and approves strategic changes
Members	Informed via reporting; consulted where trust or data ethics are implicated

Member Engagement and Feedback

- Members have a right to know how the organisation generates revenue.
- Feedback loops (e.g. surveys, consultation forums) will have to be used for major changes in monetisation approach.
- Feedback will be reported annually alongside financial performance.

Review Cycle

This Charter will be:

- Reviewed annually by the Board and Executive
- Updated to reflect changes in regulatory, digital, or strategic context
- Published in the association's governance documentation and available to all members

Tool 16: Pricing Model Maturity

Pricing Model Maturity: Levels and Characteristics

Table 18-2 **Levels and Characteristics**

Level	Approach	Key Characteristics
1. Inadequate	Flat Pricing	• Single-tier or uniform pricing • No differentiation across segments • Ignores cost or market demand
2. Basic	Simple Tiered Pricing	• 2–3 tiers (e.g. Basic, Premium) • Based on static assumptions • Simplistic segmentation
3. Intermediate	Dynamic Tiered Pricing	• Uses user data to refine tiers • Adjusts for demand or competitor benchmarks • Emerging personalisation
4. Advanced	Data-Driven Tiered Pricing	• Combines demand elasticity and cost models • Factors in variable costs and segment WTP • Increased sophistication
5. Robust	Predictive Pricing Models	• Uses AI/ML to optimise pricing • Adjusts real-time for behaviour and trends • Adaptive and contextual

Pricing Model Maturity: Limitations and Improvement Strategies

Table 18-3 **Limitations and Improvement Strategies**

Level	Key Limitations	Features of Improved Strategy
1. Inadequate	• Over/undercharging • Missed revenue • Member dissatisfaction	• Start segmentation • Align pricing with basic demand and cost trends
2. Basic	• Static pricing logic • No elasticity insights • Rigid to change	• Use Cu (Cost per User) • Analyse WTP across user types
3. Intermediate	• Manual updates • Limited testing • Hard to scale	• Run pricing A/B tests • Build cross-side value logic into tiers
4. Advanced	• Operational complexity • Tooling dependency	• Automate tier adjustments • Move toward micro-targeted pricing structures
5. Robust	• Costly and complex • Risk of algorithmic opacity	• Use live behavioural data • Blend predictive models with governance guardrails

The companion book, *Ecosystem Economics for Modern Associations* provides significantly more detail on this important topic.

Chapter 19. Toolbox for Enabling Rollout and Execution

Tool 17: ROPI Readiness Checklist

Purpose

To evaluate whether a proposed platform-related investment (e.g. a new member hub, CPD platform, marketplace, or data infrastructure) is ready to proceed, based on strategic alignment, co-creation potential, governance capacity, and monetisation maturity.

This ensures that ROPI is not just an **economic metric**, but a **decision filter**.

Checklist Categories and Criteria

Category	Key Criteria	Status	Notes / Actions
Strategic Fit	Initiative is clearly aligned with APSF pillars (e.g. Member Co-Creation, Adaptive Capability)		
	Advances the organisation's shift toward Association 2.0 or 3.0		
	Supports cross-functional goals (e.g. education, policy, insight)		
Member Value Logic	Members will experience tangible value uplift within 6–12 months		
	Contribution pathways for members are embedded in the design		
	Value exchange is clearly modelled (not just passive consumption)		
Revenue & Monetisation	Monetisation model is defined (direct, indirect, hybrid)		
	Pricing or access strategy has been validated with member segments		
	Revenue forecasts reflect engagement assumptions, not just uptake		
Platform Readiness	Tech architecture is scalable, modular, and API-compatible		
	CRM or LMS integration points are scoped		

Category	Key Criteria	Status	Notes / Actions
	Pilot or MVP pathway has been defined with iteration loops		
Governance & Oversight	Board understands the platform model and investment logic		
	Clear decision rights and exit strategy are in place		
	Risk oversight includes ethics, data, and ecosystem dependency		

Scoring Guidance

- Tick or rate (1–5) each item
- Identify any Red Flags (e.g. lack of member-tested value, missing governance alignment)
- Assign a Readiness Tier based on results:

Score / Insight	ROPI Readiness Tier
Fully met across all domains	☑ Investment Ready – Proceed with confidence
Minor gaps, mitigation possible	⚠ Pilot Ready – Validate assumptions and iterate
Major uncertainty or misalignment	⬤ Not Ready – Reassess strategy or structure

When to Use

- **Before board approval** of major tech or program spend
- As part of a **business case template** or **initiative gating process**
- During a **retreat or strategic sprint** for digital transformation
- In combination with:
    - **Monetisation Readiness Matrix**
    - **Exit Strategy Design Canvas**
    - **Insight Ecosystem Diagnostic**
    - **Platform Maturity Spectrum**

The companion book, *Ecosystem Economics for Modern Associations* provides significantly more detail on this important topic.

Tool 18: Technology Alignment & Procurement Framework for Associations

Purpose

This tool helps associations assess, select, and govern technology investments in alignment with strategic priorities and the *Association Platform Success Framework*. It offers a practical reference for evaluating technology categories, solution options, and governance considerations across five key capability areas.

Technology is no longer a back-office utility, it is a strategic enabler of engagement, trust, and innovation. This framework ensures associations treat technology selection as a strategic governance process, not an operational afterthought.

Technology Capability Map

The following tables match core association functions with best-practice Australian solutions and Microsoft Power Platform capabilities, enabling associations to tailor digital investments to their strategy and size.

Membership Management & Engagement

Technology Need	Purpose	Solutions (AU) (examples only)	Microsoft Power Platform
Membership CRM & Database	Manage renewals, engagement, payments	Membes, iMIS, Wild Apricot, 360 Membership	Power Apps, Dataverse
Automated Communications	Trigger emails, SMS, personalised flows	HubSpot, ActiveCampaign, Mailchimp	Power Automate
Community Platforms	Enable forums, peer networking	Higher Logic, Vanilla Forums, Hivebrite	Power Virtual Agents
Event Management	Manage virtual/hybrid events	EventsAIR, Cvent, Eventbrite	Power Automate

Learning & Professional Development

Technology Need	Purpose	Solutions (AU) (examples only)	Microsoft Power Platform
Learning Management System (LMS)	Deliver CPD, certification	Moodle, Go1, Totara Learn, LearnDash	Power BI, Power Apps
Virtual Learning	Webinars and live training	Zoom, GoToWebinar, BigMarker, MS Teams	Power Automate
Microcredentials & AI Learning	Personalised learning pathways	OpenLearning, DeakinCo., Accredible	AI Builder, Power Automate

Finance & Revenue Management

Technology Need	Purpose	Solutions (AU) (examples only)	Microsoft Power Platform
Membership Payments	Automate subscriptions, reminders	Ezypay, Stripe, Xero Payments	Power Automate, Power Apps
Fundraising	Donations and campaign tracking	Raisely, Blackbaud Raiser's Edge	Power BI
Sponsorship & Reporting	Track revenue sources	Xero, MYOB, SAP Concur	Power BI, Power Automate

Governance & Compliance

Technology Need	Purpose	Solutions (AU) (examples only)	Microsoft Power Platform
Board Management	Secure, streamlined board workflows	Diligent, BoardPro, GovTeams	Power Automate, Power BI
Cybersecurity & Compliance	Data privacy, legal risk	Microsoft Purview, AvePoint, OneTrust	Microsoft Defender
Risk Management	ERM, conflict registers, dashboards	Protecht, Resolver, SAI360	Power BI, Power Automate

AI & Data Analytics

Technology Need	Purpose	Solutions (AU) (examples only)	Power Platform & OpenAI
AI Chatbots	Self-service member help	Power Virtual Agents, ChatGPT	Power Virtual Agents
Predictive Analytics	Churn risk, segmentation	Power BI, SAS, Tableau	AI Builder, ChatGPT
Document Automation	Meeting summaries, insights	ChatGPT, Jasper AI	Power Automate, OpenAI

APSF Alignment Guide

APSF Pillar	Technology Alignment	Examples
Member-Centric Design	AI-enhanced CPD, personalised engagement	Chatbots, adaptive learning hubs
Scalable Digital Infrastructure	Cloud-based, API-ready platforms	CRM-LMS integrations, data warehouses
Governance & Trust	Cybersecurity, AI ethics, policy compliance	Risk analytics dashboards, ISO-aligned vendors

Five Steps for Strategic Tech Adoption

Step	Action	Key Question
1. Audit	Identify current gaps and bottlenecks	Where are we limited by manual or legacy tools?
2. Prioritise	Focus on high-impact systems	Will this tool scale and integrate easily?
3. Integrate	Ensure system interoperability	Does it connect to our core platforms (CRM, LMS)?
4. Pilot	Test before full rollout	How can we trial this with minimal disruption?
5. Build Capability	Train staff, boards, and members	Is everyone ready to use and govern the tech well?

Technology Governance Checklist

Use this checklist before major technology procurement decisions:

- Aligned to Delegations of Authority and procurement policy
- Cybersecurity and privacy risks assessed (e.g. ISO 27001)
- Integrates with existing systems
- Financial review conducted (TCO and ROI)
- Legal contracts reviewed (SLAs, IP, data rights)
- Ethical use of AI or automation is assured
- Stakeholder consultation conducted (where appropriate)

Tool Use Case

This tool can be applied by:

- **Boards** during strategic planning or investment approval.
- **CEOs or CIOs** during vendor selection, system implementation, or budget forecasting.
- **Digital transformation working groups** to prioritise and map capabilities.

Technology Implementation

Step 1 – Conduct a Technology Audit

Assess current tools and identify gaps in digital infrastructure.

Key Question – Where are manual processes slowing engagement or limiting revenue opportunities?

Step 2 – Prioritise Strategic Technology Investments

Focus on high-impact technologies that enhance engagement, governance, or revenue generation.

Key Question – Will this technology scale with future needs, or will it be outdated in two years?

Step 3 – Ensure Seamless Integration

Avoid fragmented tech ecosystems by ensuring that CRM, LMS, and event platforms integrate smoothly.

Key Question – Does this tool connect with existing systems, or will it require costly workarounds?

Step 4 – Adopt a Phased Approach

Implement in small, testable phases rather than launching large-scale digital overhauls.

Key Question – How can we pilot new technology with minimal risk before full adoption?

Step 5 – Build Digital Literacy Across the Organisation

Ensure that staff, board members, and members understand the new technology and its value.

Key Question – Are training and support systems in place to drive adoption?

Tool19: Executive Checklist for Board Reporting on Commercial Initiatives

Use this tool to prepare briefing papers, proposals, or performance updates to the Board.

Strategic Alignment

- Does the initiative align with the organisation's strategic plan and value proposition?
- Have we clearly articulated how this supports platform logic (e.g. enabling value exchange, multi-stakeholder benefit)?
- Have we included a logic model or theory of change outlining member and ecosystem value?

Governance and Oversight

- Has this initiative been reviewed under the Board's agreed commercial risk appetite?
- Are delegations of authority and accountability structures for this initiative clearly documented?
- Are conflict of interest declarations updated for all involved executives and directors?

Financial and Risk Analysis

- Have we included a detailed business model and pricing structure?
- Have we provided sensitivity analysis (e.g. optimistic, realistic, and risk-adjusted scenarios)?
- Have risk and mitigation strategies been reviewed, including reputational, legal, and operational risks?

Stakeholder and Brand Considerations

- Has there been engagement with members, partners, or other stakeholders in design or validation?
- Are brand and endorsement implications (including use of the association's logo, credibility, or standard-setting role) clearly assessed?
- Have privacy, data use, and ethical considerations been addressed?

Platform Capability and Scalability

- Are technology systems, platforms, or delivery infrastructure suitable for scale and adaptability?
- Are there mechanisms for user feedback, data collection, and continuous improvement?

- Have we considered partnerships or shared delivery options to extend reach and sustainability?

Measurement and Evaluation

- Are clear success metrics identified across financial, member value, and trust domains?
- Are reporting intervals and review checkpoints aligned to Board expectations?
- Is there a process in place for post-implementation review or sunset/exit planning?

Optional Add-on:

Include a **one-page dashboard** summary with key project information:

- Strategic Purpose
- Target Market
- Financial Forecast
- Governance Owner
- Board Decision Points
- Next Milestone / Reporting Date

Tool 20: Aligning APSF with Digital Strategy

To ensure technology supports strategic growth, associations should align digital investments with the *Association Platform Success Framework*.

Table 19-1 Aligning APSF with Digital Strategy

APSF Pillar	How It Relates to Technology	Examples
Member-Centric Design	AI-driven engagement, personalised CPD pathways.	AI-curated networking recommendations, interactive learning hubs.
Scalable Digital Infrastructure	API-driven platforms, cloud-based management systems.	Integrated membership CRM, e-learning platforms, event automation tools.
Governance & Trust	Data security, AI ethics, transparent governance.	Cybersecurity policies, AI-driven compliance tracking, privacy frameworks.

How to Apply – Before adopting technology, map the digital strategy against APSF's Design Pillars to ensure investments are strategically aligned rather than just operational upgrades.

Tool 21: Companion Risk Assessment Process

Developed for associations pursuing revenue diversification, platform enablement, and value innovation

Overview and Purpose

Commercialisation brings opportunities for financial sustainability and strategic expansion, but also introduces risks that, if not well understood, can undermine trust, member value, and mission integrity.

This risk assessment process supports:

- Pre-implementation planning
- Board-level decision-making
- Ongoing risk monitoring and mitigation planning

It complements your Risk Management Framework but is tailored to the unique risks of platform-based commercial activity in associations.

Step 1 – Identify Risk Categories

Use a structured brainstorming or planning session to identify risks across these eight commercialisation-specific domains:

Category	Examples
Strategic Misalignment	Drift from mission, value conflict with core member expectations
Governance and Oversight	Inadequate delegation, Board disengagement, lack of transparency
Financial Exposure	Revenue shortfalls, sunk cost overruns, unrealistic projections
Reputation and Trust	Brand dilution, backlash from perceived commercialisation of public value
Stakeholder and Member Impact	Reduced trust, inequity in access, member disengagement
Legal and Compliance	IP risks, unfair competition, contract disputes, consumer protection issues
Operational Capability	Inadequate systems, resourcing gaps, failure to scale or deliver reliably
Technology and Data	Platform failure, cyber risks, privacy breaches, misuse of member data

Step 2 – Assess Risk Likelihood and Impact

Use a standard risk matrix (likelihood x consequence) or your organisational rating system.

Suggested scale:

Rating	Likelihood	Consequence
Low	Rare	Minimal operational disruption or member impact
Medium	Possible	Noticeable delays, dissatisfaction, or cost overruns
High	Likely	Strategic, reputational, or financial damage
Critical	Almost certain	Severe governance, brand, or legal implications

For each identified risk, ask:

- What is the **inherent risk** (if left unmanaged)?
- What controls or mitigation strategies are already in place?
- What is the **residual risk** after applying controls?

Step 3 – Apply Platform-Specific Risk Filters

In addition to traditional risk lenses, apply platform risk filters, which focus on emergent risks unique to associations operating in a platform model:

- **Two-sided value failure** – Will both member and partner/user sides extract and contribute value?
- **Disintermediation risk** – Will external actors bypass or undermine the association's role?
- **Governance externality** – Will the platform's operations introduce governance risks (e.g. bias, unequal access, trust asymmetry)?
- **Scaling risk** – Can the model scale without eroding quality or trust?

Step 4 – Develop Mitigation and Oversight Plans

For each risk rated Medium or above, develop a mitigation plan:

Risk	Mitigation Strategy	Responsible Officer	Review Frequency
Brand dilution	Board-approved brand use policy and ethical endorsement framework	Head of Marketing	Quarterly
Data privacy	Data governance policy + DPA in supplier contracts	CTO / Privacy Officer	Monthly
Revenue overestimation	Require dual-path forecasts and board-reviewed sensitivity analysis	CFO	Board review at investment stage

Include risk ownership, monitoring frequency, and thresholds for escalation to the Board or Audit & Risk Committee.

Step 5 – Integrate with Governance Reporting

Embed the commercial risk register or summary into:

- New initiative proposals and business cases
- Board reporting dashboards
- Internal audit and assurance reviews
- Strategic planning updates
- Use a red flag escalation model where residual risks exceed accepted thresholds.

Outputs & Tools Provided

To accompany this process, you might include:

- Template commercialisation risk register (Excel or board-ready Word format)
- Pre-launch risk checklist for executives
- Board summary table for inclusion in board packs.

Example 1 – Brand Dilution through Commercial Partnership

Risk:

Brand dilution or erosion of trust arising from poorly aligned commercial partnerships (e.g. third-party course bundling or discount platforms).

Category:

Reputation and Trust

Inherent Risk Rating:

High

Controls / Mitigation:

- Develop and board-approve a Brand Use and Endorsement Policy
- Require all partnerships to undergo a Strategic Alignment Assessment
- Introduce a review committee with delegated authority for partnership approval

Residual Risk Rating:

Medium

Responsible Officer:

Executive Director, Marketing and Partnerships

Review Frequency:

Quarterly, or when new partnership proposals arise

Example 2 – Platform Scaling Risk in Member Marketplace

Risk:

Inability to scale a member services platform (e.g. job board, referral marketplace), leading to poor user experience, reputational harm, and unmet expectations.

Category:

Operational Capability / Technology and Data

Inherent Risk Rating:
High

Controls / Mitigation:

- Run *pilot programs* with limited user groups before full launch
- Conduct *load testing* and *usability audits*
- Implement a *tiered rollout strategy* with early feedback loops
- Engage a *platform advisor or product strategist* for technical review

Residual Risk Rating:
Medium

Responsible Officer:
Head of Digital Delivery

Review Frequency:
Monthly during development and post-launch for 6 months

Example 3 – Revenue Overestimation and Cost Recovery Shortfall

Risk:
Commercial project (e.g. new credential or data product) fails to reach revenue targets due to flawed market assumptions or optimistic pricing.

Category:
Financial Exposure

Inherent Risk Rating:
High

Controls / Mitigation:

- Require a *dual-path financial model* (realistic and risk-adjusted)
- Obtain *independent market validation* and member/user testing before board sign-off
- Introduce a *staged investment model* with milestone-based checkpoints
- Ensure a *board-approved exit strategy* or *sunset criteria* is documented pre-launch

Residual Risk Rating:
Medium–High

Responsible Officer:
Chief Financial Officer (CFO)

Review Frequency:
At each quarterly board meeting and project milestone reviews

Chapter 20. Toolbox - Monitoring, Learning, and Exit

Tool 22: Digital Trust Dashboard

Purpose

To provide governance visibility into how trust is being maintained, challenged, or eroded across digital touchpoints, platform interactions, AI use, and data systems. This is essential for any association transitioning toward **Association 3.0**, where **trust replaces control** as the central governance currency.

Dashboard Framework

The dashboard tracks ***five domains of digital trust***. Each includes key indicators, risk thresholds, and governance cues.

Domain	Key Indicators	Sample Metric / Cue	Board Questions
Data Ethics & Consent	% of members who opt-in to data sharing; clarity of privacy settings	Consent click-through rates; data access audit scores	Are we earning consent, or assuming it?
AI & Automation Use	Use of algorithms in decision-making or content delivery	Audit trails; flagged bias incidents; fairness reviews	Where is AI shaping experience, and is it explainable?
Platform Safety & Moderation	Reports of harmful content; unresolved complaints	Member incident logs; time-to-resolution benchmarks	Are we safeguarding members without over-moderating?
Reputation & Transparency	Member trust score; complaints; reputational signals in media or forums	NPS for trust; social listening trends; policy transparency	What drives member trust, and how do we respond to breaches?
Feedback & Voice Loops	Volume, quality, and diversity of member feedback integrated into design	% of programs changed based on member feedback	Is our insight loop responsive, or performative?

Scorecard Template (Board-Level Format)

Domain	Current Status (RAG)	Trend	Notes / Actions
Data Ethics & Consent	◍ / ◍ / ◍	↑ / → / ↓	
AI & Automation			
Safety & Moderation			
Reputation & Transparency			
Feedback Integration			

RAG Key:

◍ = Trust indicators strong and improving

◍ = Acceptable but attention needed

◍ = Active risk or trust deterioration

Use Cases

- **Quarterly board reporting** on platform trust health
- **Audit and risk committee dashboards**
- **AI ethics and data governance oversight**
- **Member-facing transparency** (trust signals in UX, annual reports)

Implementation Tips

- Integrate with:
    - CRM dashboards (for opt-ins, complaints, feedback loops)
    - AI oversight processes (model audits, bias testing logs)
    - Moderation platforms (flagged content rates, resolution SLAs)
- Pair with:
    - **Digital Ethics Charter**
    - **AI Governance Checklist**
    - **Insight Ecosystem Diagnostic**

Strategic Framing

- Trust is now a **core strategic asset,** not just a compliance issue
- Associations should treat trust metrics as seriously as financial indicators
- As platform complexity increases, **trust drift** becomes a governance risk
- This dashboard allows the board to **intervene early**, not react late.

Tool 23: Ecosystem Metrics Dashboard

Purpose:

- Track how the association performs across **multi-sided value exchanges** and **ecosystem activation**
- Evaluate **outward-facing platform impact**, not internal insight capability

Key Metrics Include:

Focus Area	Example Metric
Sector Outcomes	Workforce access, sustainability, policy influence
Member Access	Job placements, mentoring, CPD opportunities
Value Co-Creation	Jointly produced research, tools, or services
Network Activation	Number/diversity of ecosystem contributors
Ecosystem Influence	Policy wins, reputation signals, media visibility

This dashboard helps you **move from ecosystem mapping to outcome tracking**.

Tool 24: Ecosystem Impact Measurement Tool

Purpose

To help associations measure and govern their ecosystem-level impact as they evolve into platform orchestrators. This tool enables evidence-based partnership strategy, supports outcome tracking, and reinforces shared-value thinking.

Tool Components

1. Ecosystem Partnership Typology

Use this table to classify current and potential partnerships:

Partnership Type	Example Partners	Primary Purpose
Knowledge Co-Creation	Universities, think tanks	Thought leadership, innovation
Platform Integration	EdTech, data providers	Seamless digital services, analytics
Market Enablement	Employers, intermediaries	Member access to jobs, projects, clients
Collective Impact	Government, NGOs, councils	Systemic change, workforce policy, equity

2. Ecosystem Performance Scorecard

Evaluate outcomes across five focus areas. Use a 1–5 scale to assess performance and identify opportunities.

Focus Area	Sample Metrics	Score (1–5)	Comments / Evidence
Sector Outcomes	Workforce participation, sustainability targets		
Member Access	Jobs, mentors, CPD, cross-sector pathways		
Value Co-Creation	Tools, services, or research created jointly		
Network Activation	No. and diversity of ecosystem actors engaged		
Ecosystem Influence	Policy impact, media visibility, trust indicators		

Scoring Guide:

1 = Not evident; 2 = Emerging; 3 = Developing; 4 = Effective; 5 = Sector-leading

3. Partnership Evaluation Canvas

Use this template to assess new or existing ecosystem partnerships.

Dimension	Key Question	Rating (1–5)	Notes
Strategic Fit	Does this align with our platform goals?		
Shared Value	What can we only achieve together?		
Risk & Governance	Are risks shared and responsibilities defined?		
Cultural Alignment	Do our values and operating styles complement each other?		
Exit Readiness	Are exit mechanisms clear and mutually acceptable?		

How to Use This Tool

Step 1: Map your current partners into the Partnership Typology.

Step 2: Complete the Ecosystem Performance Scorecard with your leadership team.

Step 3: Use the Partnership Evaluation Canvas to:

- Vet new strategic partnerships
- Review existing collaborations annually
- Inform contract terms and review cycles

Step 4: Feed summary scores into your Boardroom Dashboard or Transformation Review Cycle.

Tool 25: Annual Performance Review

Most associations treat performance reporting as a compliance routine, focused on outputs rather than outcomes, and historical performance rather than future direction. But in a platform-based model, **annual performance reviews will have to evolve** into strategic sense-making sessions that use real-time metrics to guide investment, capability building, and governance reform.

The following Sample Annual Performance Review Agenda shows how the *Association Platform Performance Scorecard (APPS)* can be embedded into boardroom routines. It transforms the review process from an administrative check-in to a critical governance function, one that aligns data with risk, strategy, and sustainable value creation.

Sample Agenda – Annual Performance Review – Platform Governance Context

Meeting Title – Annual Performance Review and Strategy Alignment
Facilitator – CEO / Strategy Lead
Attendees – Board of Directors, Executive Team, Committee Chairs
Duration – 3 hours (suggested), split into strategic blocks

Scorecard Review – Briefing (30 mins)

Presented by Executive Leads with dashboard visuals

Table 20-1 APPS Dashboard

Domain	Lead Presenter	Focus Areas
Engagement & Network Activation	Member Services	Participation, contribution, engagement churn
Financial Sustainability	CFO	Revenue mix, recurring income, product ROI
Governance Agility & Integrity	Company Secretary	Decision velocity, delegation use, ethical oversight
Platform Operations & Innovation	CTO or Ops Lead	Uptime, innovation cycle time, user experience metrics

Strategic Reflection (30 mins)

What trends are emerging across the four domains?

What surprised us?

Where are we underperforming strategically despite operational metrics?

Risk Horizon and Scenario Review (30 mins)

Leading indicators from scorecard – emerging risk signals

"What if" scenario flash exercise using insight (e.g. sponsorship shortfall, member churn)

Alignment with board's risk appetite and APSF-based governance maturity

Committee Accountability Check-in (20 mins)

Each committee reports back on:

Use of insight in decision-making

Alignment with APSF performance goals

Any capability or structural gaps

Strategic Adjustments & Capability Planning (30 mins)

What initiatives need to be re-prioritised or resourced?

What board/executive capability investments are needed?

Are our KPIs still aligned to our strategy?

Wrap-Up and Forward Actions (10 mins)

Summary of key insights

Governance follow-ups

Planning for next performance cycle

Tool 26: Exit Strategy Design Canvas

Purpose

To support associations in designing responsible, strategic, and pre-agreed exit plans for initiatives, partnerships, and commercial ventures. This avoids mission drift, minimises reputational risk, and reinforces platform accountability.

Canvas Structure

Dimension	Key Prompts
Strategic Fit	Under what conditions does this initiative no longer serve our platform goals?
Success Thresholds	What measurable indicators define minimum viability or value contribution?
Trigger Points	What events or metrics would activate an exit review?
Stakeholder Impact	Who will be affected by this exit, and how will we engage or support them?
Knowledge Capture	What learning will have to be captured before the exit?
Governance Pathway	Who owns the decision? What is the board's role?
Exit Options	What are our strategic choices? (e.g. sunset, spin-out, transfer)
Communication Plan	How will the exit be communicated to members, partners, and the public?
Brand & Trust Impacts	What risks to credibility will have to be managed through the exit?

How to Use It

1. **Embed at Launch**
    - Use the canvas as part of initial project or partnership approval.
    - Attach to business cases or pilot proposals as a board expectation.
2. **Review Periodically**
    - Integrate into quarterly reviews or board cycles for live initiatives.
    - Use trigger point reviews to pre-empt drift or underperformance.
3. **Facilitate Exit Workshops**
    - Use collaboratively to support non-political, learning-focused exit planning.
    - Include external advisors if required for sensitive initiatives.

Benefits

- Prevents emotional or political overcommitment to underperforming initiatives
- Builds a culture of disciplined innovation and adaptive governance

- Aligns with ISO 37000 principles of stewardship, transparency, and responsiveness
- Protects member value and mission integrity during strategic pivots

Tips for Implementation

- Pair with the Commercialisation Readiness Diagnostic or Partnership Evaluation Canvas.
- Include as a standard section in project briefs or new venture templates.
- Report against exit thresholds in the boardroom alongside impact metrics.

Tool 27: APSF Full Implementation Checklist

Organised by the three APSF pillars and implementation enablers, this checklist can be used in planning, workshops, and board reporting.

I. Member Co-Creation

#	Checklist Item	Status	Notes / Actions
1	Member personas or segments have been clearly defined		
2	We offer flexible membership pathways or modular products		
3	Members co-create programs (e.g. CPD, mentoring, policy input)		
4	Member experience is personalised via data or preferences		
5	We measure and report on engagement depth, not just volume		
6	Member contribution is recognised (e.g. badges, discounts, visibility)		
7	Member voice is embedded into governance or advisory groups		

II. Adaptive Capability

#	Checklist Item	Status	Notes / Actions
8	Strategic plans are agile and reviewed quarterly or iteratively		
9	Pilot programs are used before full implementation		
10	Staff are empowered to test ideas and act on insight		
11	Governance supports experimentation (e.g. delegated authority)		
12	We have clear criteria for scaling, sunsetting, or pivoting programs		
13	Continuous improvement is part of team culture		
14	We use insight dashboards to inform real-time decisions		

III. Ecosystem Thinking

#	Checklist Item	Status	Notes / Actions
15	We have mapped our stakeholder ecosystem (members, partners, regulators)		
16	Strategic partnerships are in place to co-deliver or co-create value		
17	Our business model includes indirect value flows (e.g. via partners)		
18	Ecosystem impact is measured through outcomes (not just activity)		
19	We participate in or lead ecosystem coalitions or collective action		
20	Data-sharing agreements and trust protocols are in place		
21	Members are connected to external opportunities through our platform		

IV. Implementation Enablers

A. Governance Alignment

#	Checklist Item	Status	Notes / Actions
22	Board understands platform logic and APSF pillars		
23	Governance is agile (e.g. dynamic agendas, strategic framing)		
24	Risk and ethics are built into monetisation and tech use		
25	Board regularly reviews APSF-aligned metrics (engagement, agility, trust)		

B. Technology & Data Readiness

#	Checklist Item	Status	Notes / Actions
26	CRM, LMS, and data platforms are integrated		
27	Personalisation and automation are in place		
28	Member data informs program design and content delivery		
29	AI or predictive analytics are governed ethically		

C. Culture & Capability

#	Checklist Item	Status	Notes / Actions
30	Teams are trained in platform thinking and agile delivery		
31	Leadership champions experimentation and co-creation		
32	Communication reinforces strategic priorities and platform role		
33	Performance conversations include APSF-aligned goals		

V. Execution Planning

#	Checklist Item	Status	Notes / Actions
34	We've conducted an APSF Readiness Assessment		
35	Priorities are mapped across a transformation roadmap (assess → align → pilot → scale)		
36	Member Engagement Heatmap and Contribution Canvas are in use		
37	Regular board and executive reviews track implementation progress		

How to Use This Checklist

- Use in strategy offsites or implementation sprints.
- Run as a RAG rating (Red–Amber–Green) with cross-functional teams.
- Link to the Governance Capability Heatmap and Digital Maturity Matrix for deeper alignment
- Share quarterly updates with the board as part of transformation tracking.

Associations Platform Success Framework

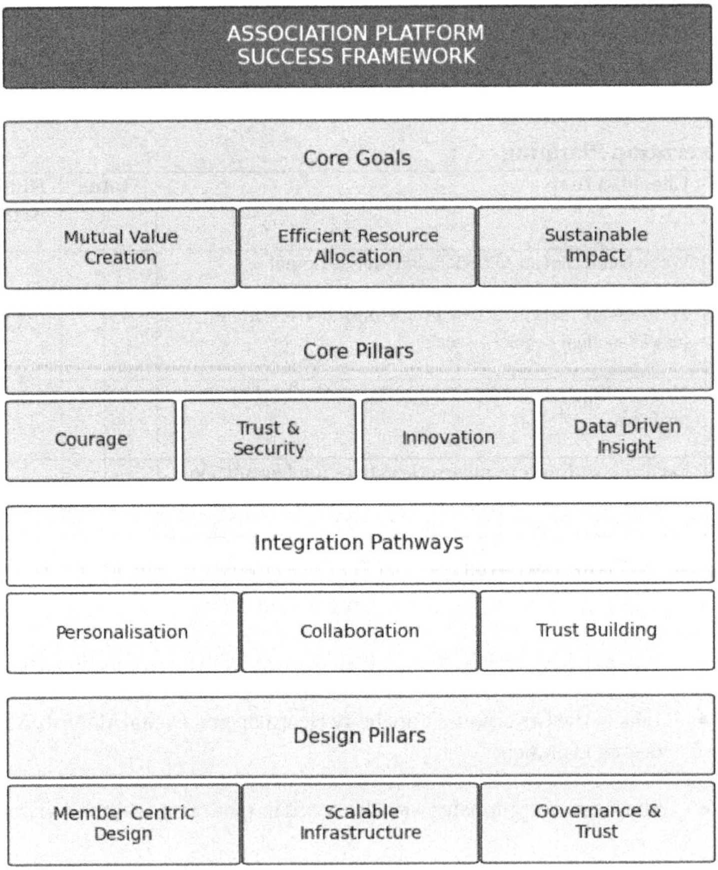

Appendices

Appendix A. Building Your Business Model Before You Monetise

Introduction: Strategy Before Revenue

Associations are under pressure to diversify revenue, monetise digital offerings, and demonstrate financial resilience. Yet, many leap to monetisation without first clarifying the business model that underpins it. The result is predictable: misfires that damage trust, fragment engagement, and misalign governance.

This annex provides a structured approach to building your business model before you monetise. It draws on platform economics, value co-creation, and association governance to help leaders design for sustainability, trust, and member participation. It consolidates tools and insights from both *The Modern Association Playbook* and *Ecosystem Economics for Modern Associations*, offering a bridge between strategy and revenue, intention and implementation.

Why Business Model Alignment Matters

Monetisation decisions are not merely commercial. They are strategic expressions of how your association creates, facilitates, and governs value.

Too often, associations fall into common traps:

- Introducing paywalls that suppress participation.
- Pursuing sponsorship without strategic alignment.
- Launching new services without understanding who actually creates the value.

A well-formed business model acts as a blueprint for alignment across three domains:

- **Value**: What is created, for whom, and how.
- **Revenue**: How value is monetised, ethically, fairly, and sustainably.
- **Governance**: Who decides, who benefits, and how risks are managed.

Without this clarity, monetisation strategies risk undermining engagement, trust, or long-term impact.

Key Principles for Model–Monetisation Alignment

Modern associations are not just service providers. They are platforms enabling value exchange. This shift has profound implications for business model design.

Principle 1: Participation Before Monetisation: Engagement is a prerequisite to revenue. Contribution signals commitment. Design early-stage experiences that invite participation, discussion, content sharing, and co-design, before seeking financial commitment.

Principle 2: Map Value Flows, Not Just Benefits: Understand how value is created within your system: by staff, by members, by partners. Who contributes insights, facilitates learning, or activates networks? Value capture (monetisation) should follow value creation, not precede it.

Principle 3: Monetisation is Governance: Revenue decisions, what to charge for, who pays, what's open or gated, are ethical decisions. They will have to be stewarded with board oversight, using frameworks that assess risk, equity, trust, and purpose alignment.

Tool: Platform-Enhanced Business Model Canvas

Adapt the traditional Business Model Canvas to include:

- Multi-actor value propositions (e.g. members, employers, partners).
- Participation channels, not just delivery channels.
- Trust and governance assumptions (data use, representation, consent).
- Revenue flows from both sides of the platform.

Use this canvas to visualise how value is created *between* actors, not just *by* the association.

Tool: Contribution Mapping Before Commercialisation

Ask:

- Who is creating value in our current system?
- Where are contributions happening that we're not recognising or enabling?
- What is the perceived vs actual value from different actors?

This mapping avoids the common mistake of monetising services members helped to build, without recognition or shared benefit.

Tool: Monetisation Decision Matrix

Evaluate any new revenue idea against five key lenses:

Table A.1 **Monetisation Decision Matrix**

Lens	Question
Strategic Fit	Does this support our mission and platform model?
Member Impact	Will members perceive this as fair, beneficial, and inclusive?
Scalability	Can this model grow sustainably without excessive complexity?
Technology and Ethics Readiness	Do we have the systems, data policies, and consent infrastructure in place?

Risk and Reputational Fit	Could this backfire, bias participation, or damage trust?

Use this as a board-level checkpoint before launching new income streams.

Common Pitfalls of Monetising Too Early

Table A.2 **Common Pitfalls of Monetising Too Early**

Pitfall	Impact
Monetising before mapping value flows	Suppresses organic engagement
Gatekeeping community interaction	Undermines trust and network effects
Assuming one-size-fits-all pricing	Ignores diversity of member preferences and ability to pay
Ignoring contributor labour	Creates perceived inequity or exploitation
Failing to test member appetite	Leads to adoption failure and reputational risk

Avoid these by sequencing design: *build engagement logic → map contribution → design value → test pricing.*

Model–Monetisation–Governance Alignment Map

Table A.3 **Monetisation–Governance Alignment Map**

Model Type	Value Dynamic	Monetisation Pattern	Governance Focus
Knowledge Hub	Curated insight + member-generated content	Tiered access, sponsorship, premium tools	Data ethics, editorial standards
Peer Network	Member-to-member learning	Freemium, membership tiers, partner support	Trust infrastructure, moderation, equity
Credentialing Platform	Skills recognition + learning pathways	CPD bundles, stackable micro-credentials	Standards governance, regulatory alignment
Marketplace Enabler	Members as providers or solvers	Transaction fees, promotion services	Fairness, risk distribution, transparency
Advocacy Platform	Collective voice, influence building	Core funding, outcome-based investment	Representation, legitimacy, inclusion

This map helps boards align each model type with revenue logic and its governance implications.

Example 69. Case Illustrations

PNA *- Pivoted from bundled dues to modular offerings, using contribution mapping to design CPD and events. Early monetisation pilots were run with opt-in contributors before scaling to paid options.*

AHRI *- Built digital certification as a platform product. Ensured standards governance via an independent council. Monetised progression, not access, and anchored fees to long-term sector value.*

ACS *- Transformed into a multi-sided credentialing and digital capability platform. Revenue flows from members, partners, and government, governed by cross-sector logic, not just internal structures.*

Strategic Board Questions

- Have we defined our core value logic before deciding how to monetise?
- Are we designing for interaction, or delivering services?
- Do our monetisation ideas deepen participation, or restrict it?
- What contribution are we capturing without reward?
- Are we governing monetisation with the same rigour as compliance?

Conclusion: Lead with the Model

Before you monetise, model. Your business model is not just an operational plan, it's an ethical, economic, and governance commitment.

Revenue is not neutral. It shapes participation, trust, and legitimacy. Get the business model right, and monetisation becomes a natural extension of value. Get it wrong, and even well-intentioned revenue strategies can undermine your platform's potential.

Use this annex as your foundation for alignment, and as a boardroom guide to monetising with purpose, not just urgency.

Appendix B. Platform Economics: A Primer

From Pipelines to Platforms

As associations navigate a rapidly shifting landscape, traditional revenue and service models are under pressure. In their place, platform-based models are emerging, not just as digital upgrades, but as a fundamental transformation in the economics of value creation and exchange. This annexure introduces the core principles of platform economics and their relevance to association strategy and governance.

In essence, a platform business model facilitates interactions between two or more distinct but interdependent groups, typically via a shared digital infrastructure. The goal is not merely to deliver services, but to orchestrate an ecosystem where participants co-create value.

Why Platform Economics Matters

For boards and executives, platform economics offers a framework to:

- **Drive sustainable growth**: Platform models enable scale without proportional increases in overhead.
- **Diversify revenue**: Associations can move beyond traditional reliance on dues and event income by introducing transaction fees, tiered access, partner integrations, and data-driven products.
- **Engage beyond members**: Platform thinking enables associations to reach and monetise broader audiences, including future members, industry partners, and public stakeholders.
- **Respond to changing behaviours**: Today's professionals want personalised, peer-driven, and real-time learning and networking experiences, preferences well-served by platform models.

Associations that embrace these dynamics can transform their economic logic, while those that cling to traditional models risk becoming irrelevant as their members migrate to alternative digital communities and learning ecosystems.

Examples in Practice

- LinkedIn Learning integrates peer networks, personalised learning pathways, and professional credentials, all monetised through subscriptions, B2B contracts, and advertising.
- SEEK connects job seekers and recruiters in a classic two-sided market, using data and visibility to drive monetisation.

These are not merely corporate success stories, they offer valuable strategic insights for associations reimagining their purpose, reach, and resilience.

Governance Implications

Platform economics also raises new questions for boards:

- How should pricing be structured across different user groups?
- What governance is needed to manage co-creation and data ethics?
- How do you balance member control with commercial partnerships?
- How do you measure value creation when members are also producers?

Understanding these dynamics equips governance leaders to make informed decisions about investment, design, risk, and oversight.

Platform economics shifts the role of associations from service providers to value enablers. This approach allows associations to leverage multi-sided markets, network effects, and data as strategic assets to create scalable, member-driven ecosystems.

This is the *economic rationale* behind the *Association Platform Success Framework*, providing the foundational logic for building a sustainable, interaction-led model of value creation.

A Structured Approach to Transformation

Across the association sector, signs of structural strain and friction are no longer isolated, they are systemic. Declining membership, stagnant revenue, and disjointed engagement strategies are not anomalies; they are symptoms of a broader misalignment between how associations operate and how value is created in a digital economy.

Digital initiatives abound, new websites, member portals, apps, webinars. But without a cohesive strategic model, these efforts risk becoming tactical fragments rather than building blocks of long-term transformation. Associations are not short on intent; they are short on integration.

Many executives and boards know they will have to evolve, but the path forward can feel unclear.

- Should the focus be on technology upgrades?
- Rethinking governance?
- Monetisation strategies?
- Member experience design?

The danger lies in pursuing isolated solutions without a unifying logic, leading to wasted investment, disengaged members, and missed opportunities for systemic renewal.

To address this, a structured, strategic model is essential, one that aligns purpose, technology, governance, and engagement into a coherent platform-based approach. This is where the *Association Platform Success Framework* comes in.

Rather than prescribing a one-size-fits-all template, the APSF provides a modular, flexible framework tailored to the complexity of modern associations. It connects vision to capability, and capability to application, ensuring that digital transformation is not just a collection of projects, but a coordinated shift in how the organisation creates and sustains value.

The APSF is grounded in a core premise: the future association is not a service provider, but an *orchestrator of ecosystems*. It facilitates continuous interaction between members, partners, and the wider sector, enabled by technology, fuelled by insight, and governed with transparency.

In the sections that follow, we unpack the components of the APSF, which provides comprehensive roadmap for associations ready to move from incremental improvements to systemic transformation.

Associations face strategic risk without a coherent roadmap. The APSF provides a layered structure that aligns digital transformation with member engagement, governance, and revenue sustainability.

Platform Economics and the Strategic Role of Associations

As associations navigate a rapidly shifting landscape, traditional revenue and service models are under pressure. In their place, platform-based models are emerging, not as a digital upgrade, but as a fundamental shift in the economics of value creation and exchange. This annex introduces the core economic principles of platform models and their implications for association strategy, sustainability, and governance.

From Pipelines to Platforms

Traditional associations operate like **pipelines**: value flows in one direction, from the organisation to the member, via conferences, publications, and professional development. In contrast, **platforms** facilitate value exchange in many directions. Members, partners, learners, employers, and even non-members interact, contribute, and benefit through shared infrastructure.

Table B.1 Pipeline v Platform Models

Feature	Pipeline Association	Platform Association
Value Flow	Linear: Org → Member	Multi-directional: Member ↔ Org ↔ Partner
Revenue Logic	Dues + Events	Interaction + Data + Ecosystem Services
Scale	Constrained by service delivery	Scales with participation and engagement
Risk Profile	Stable but stagnant	Dynamic, but resilient with network effects
Economic Goal	Efficient service provision	Orchestrated value creation

Why Platform Economics Matters for Associations

Boards and executive teams will have to grapple with declining retention, disaggregated professional development, and fragile revenue portfolios. Platform models offer a compelling alternative, enabling associations to:

- **Drive sustainable growth** through network effects and digital scalability
- **Diversify revenue** beyond dues via data products, multi-sided access, and ecosystem services
- **Engage beyond members** by reaching learners, partners, clients, or regulators
- **Respond to changing behaviours** with flexible, co-designed value pathways

Core Principles of Platform Economics

Table B.2 Core Principles of Platform Economics

Concept	Association Relevance
Network Effects	Each additional member or partner adds value for all users, e.g., CPD forums, peer review systems
Multi-Sided Markets	Serve more than one group: members, employers, educators, funders
Cross-Side Subsidies	Provide low-cost access to one group (e.g. students) to attract others (e.g. sponsors, mentors)
Marginal Cost Reduction	Digital scaling avoids linear cost growth seen in events or staffing
Data as Asset	Member data enables segmentation, insight, and monetisation through benchmarking, targeting, or APIs

Return on Platform Investment (ROPI): A Better ROI Frame

Traditional ROI focuses on short-term financial returns. But platform-based investments also generate intangible, networked, and alignment-based benefits.

ROPI = (Total Platform Benefits – Alignment Costs*) ÷ Total Investment

* e.g. costs of integration, stakeholder engagement, policy adjustments, or change management.

ROPI captures:

- **Engagement Uplift**: e.g. increased CPD usage, retention, referrals
- **New Revenue**: e.g. from digital CPD, partner access, or sponsorship
- **Strategic Alignment**: e.g. policy impact, workforce uplift
- **Efficiency Gains**: lower cost of service delivery through automation
- **Intangible Trust Returns**: when platform design reinforces legitimacy, transparency, and purpose

Board Reflection: Have we evaluated our digital or engagement investments using a multi-dimensional model like ROPI? If not, are we missing key forms of value?

Monetisation Readiness Matrix

Use this diagnostic to assess the strategic and ethical fitness of new revenue opportunities.

Table B.3 Monetisation Readiness Diagnostic Matrix

Revenue Idea	Member Impact	Ecosystem Fit	Scalability	Ethical Risk	Readiness Score
Tiered CPD Model	High	Medium	High	Low	4.5
Employer Subscriptions	Medium	High	High	Medium	4.0
Data Benchmarking Tools	Low	High	High	High	3.0
Sponsored Ecosystem Events	Medium	Medium	Medium	Medium	3.5

Tip: Use this matrix at executive or board level to compare monetisation options through strategic, not just financial, lenses.

Governance Implications of Platform Economics

Platform economics demands a new governance posture. Boards will have to oversee not only financial performance but co-creation, digital ethics, and member data use.

Key Board-Level Questions:

- Are our pricing models fair across user types?
- Who sets the rules of participation (moderation, visibility, contribution rights)?
- How is trust earned, measured, and protected in platform interactions?

- Do our delegations of authority cover AI, algorithms, or user data policy?

ISO 37000 Alignment: Platform-based governance will have to align with principles of *ethical purpose, stakeholder responsiveness, inclusion,* and *transparency.* This means monetisation, technology, and engagement decisions will have to reflect values, not just viability.

Conclusion: Embedding Economics in Strategy & Governance

Platform economics is not just a new way to make money, it is a new way to think about value creation, participation, legitimacy, and sustainability. Associations that grasp this shift can reimagine themselves not as content or service providers, but as ecosystem enablers, trusted convenors, and adaptive institutions.

Strategic Prompt for Boardroom Reflection

"Where is value currently being created in our association, and by whom? What would change if we reimagined our business model through the lens of platform economics, co-creation, and network activation?"

Summary of Value Added by These Enhancements

- Bridges strategy with economic decision-making
- Strengthens board utility through practical diagnostics
- Aligns tightly with *Ecosystem Economics for Modern Associations*
- Enables integration into board packs, diagnostics, or CPD

Associations that grasp this shift can reimagine themselves not just as service providers, but as ecosystem enablers, shaping professions, sectors, and society through collaborative infrastructure, data stewardship, and member-led innovation.

Appendix C. Platform KPI Reference Guide

This appendix offers detailed explanations of KPIs that modern associations can utilise to measure performance across four critical dimensions: Engagement and Network Activation, Financial Sustainability, Governance Agility and Integrity, and Platform Operations and Innovation. Each KPI is defined with its purpose, significance, and practical application.

Engagement and Network Activation

Table C.1 Engagement and Network Activation

Metric	Purpose	Application
Net Promoter Score (NPS) or Member Trust Index	Assesses member loyalty and satisfaction by measuring the likelihood of members recommending the association to others.	Regularly survey members to gauge satisfaction and identify areas for improvement.
Peer-to-Peer Connection Rate	Tracks the frequency of interactions between members on digital platforms.	Encourage community engagement by facilitating networking opportunities and monitoring interaction metrics.
Member Content Contribution Rate	Measures the proportion of members actively contributing content, such as articles, forum posts, or resources.	Foster a culture of knowledge sharing by recognising and promoting member contributions.
Return Visits to Platform per Month	Indicates the average number of times a member returns to the association's digital platform within a month.	Enhance platform value by regularly updating content and features to encourage repeat visits.
First-Year Renewal Rate by Cohort	Evaluates the percentage of new members who renew their membership after the first year, segmented by joining cohort.	Identify onboarding effectiveness and tailor engagement strategies for new members.

Financial Sustainability

Table C.2 Financial Sustainability

Metric	Purpose	Application
Share of Revenue from Non-Dues Sources	Represents the proportion of total revenue generated from sources other than membership dues.	Diversify income streams through events, publications, sponsorships, and other services.
Cost of Member Acquisition (CAC) vs Lifetime Value (LTV)	Compares the cost of acquiring a new member to the projected revenue that member will generate over time.	Optimise marketing strategies to ensure sustainable growth and return on investment.
Ratio of Fixed vs Recurring Income	Analyses the stability of income by comparing fixed (one-time) revenues to recurring (ongoing) revenues.	Aim to increase recurring income for financial predictability and stability.
Financial Risk Exposure by Revenue Stream	Assesses the potential risk associated with reliance on specific revenue sources.	Mitigate financial risks by balancing revenue streams and developing contingency plans.

Governance Agility, Integrity and Innovation

Table C.3 Governance Agility and Integrity

Metric	Purpose	Application
Time from Insight to Decision	Measures the duration between identifying a significant insight and making a corresponding decision	Streamline decision-making processes to respond promptly to emerging trends and data.
Delegation Rate (% of Decisions Pushed to Executive or Agile Teams)	Quantifies the proportion of decisions delegated from the board to operational teams.	Empower teams by delegating appropriate decisions, fostering agility and responsiveness.
AI Usage Oversight (Audit Frequency, Fairness Checks)	Monitors the governance of artificial intelligence applications, including audit frequency and fairness evaluations.	Ensure ethical AI deployment by implementing regular audits and bias assessments.
Digital Tool Adoption Rates Across Teams	Assesses the uptake of digital tools among staff and volunteers.	Promote digital literacy and adoption through training and support initiatives.

Use of Real-Time Dashboards in Board Packs	Evaluates the integration of up-to-date data visualisations in board meeting materials.	Enhance transparency and informed decision-making by providing real-time data to board members.
Diversity and Inclusion in Governance Bodies	Assesses the representation of diverse groups within the association's leadership and committees.	Promote inclusive practices by actively seeking diverse perspectives in governance roles.
AI Usage Oversight (Audit Frequency, Fairness Checks)	Monitors the governance of artificial intelligence applications, including audit frequency and fairness evaluations.	Ensure ethical AI deployment by implementing regular audits and bias assessments.
Time to Market for New Service Releases	Tracks the duration from concept initiation to the launch of new services.	Accelerate innovation cycles by refining development and approval processes.
Percentage of Platform Usage by Members Each Month	Measures the proportion of members actively engaging with the digital platform monthly.	Increase platform engagement through user-friendly design and relevant content offerings.
Feedback Loop Cycle Time (e.g. from Idea to Pilot)	Evaluates the time taken to implement feedback, from initial suggestion to pilot testing.	Enhance responsiveness by establishing efficient feedback mechanisms and pilot programs.
Innovation Conversion Ratio (Ideas Trialled vs Adopted)	Compares the number of ideas tested to those successfully implemented.	Foster a culture of experimentation by tracking and learning from innovation outcomes.

Table C.4 **Detailed Metrics for Governance & Trust**

Metric	Description	Rationale
Data Security Score	Measures the robustness of data protection protocols (e.g. ISO 27001 compliance, encryption standards, breach frequency).	Members and partners need confidence that their data is secure in a digital ecosystem.
Policy Compliance Rate	Percentage of internal and partner operations that align with governance policies (e.g. code of conduct, privacy policy, risk frameworks).	Indicates the effectiveness of governance systems in ensuring consistent behaviour.
Transparency Index	Availability and accessibility of key policies, decisions, financials, and performance reports.	Enhances stakeholder confidence and reduces perception of opacity or centralised control.

Metric	Description	Rationale
Board & Committee Engagement	Attendance, participation, and strategic contribution of governance leaders.	Demonstrates active and informed leadership in a rapidly evolving environment.
Member Trust Score	Derived from surveys or net trust scores assessing how much members trust the organisation's integrity, fairness, and responsiveness.	A direct signal of reputational capital and relationship quality.
Issue Resolution Time	Average time to address complaints, disputes, or governance breaches.	Reflects responsiveness and accountability in the governance framework.
Diversity and Inclusion Metrics	Representation across governance structures (board, committees, speakers).	Supports legitimacy and alignment with social and generational expectations.
Audit Outcomes	Results from financial, operational, and IT audits.	Formal assurance of good governance and risk management practices.

Boardroom Application Guide

Table C.5 KPI Format Example

Metric	Purpose	Suggested Scoring	Data Source	Accountable Owner
Net Promoter Score (NPS) or Member Trust Index	Assesses member loyalty and satisfaction	Red: <30, Amber: 30–50, Green: >50	Member surveys, CRM	Head of Strategy / CX
Peer-to-Peer Connection Rate	Tracks member-to-member engagement	Red: <15%, Amber: 15–30%, Green: >30%	Community platform analytics	Digital Engagement Manager
Member Content Contribution Rate	Measures how many members contribute resources or posts	Red: <5%, Amber: 5–15%, Green: >15%	LMS, CMS, forum data	Knowledge Manager
Return Visits to Platform per Month	Indicates stickiness of digital experience	Red: <1.5 visits, Amber: 1.5–3, Green: >3	Web analytics, LMS logs	Head of Digital
First-Year Renewal Rate by Cohort	Evaluates onboarding success	Red: <50%, Amber: 50–70%, Green: >70%	CRM / Membership DB	Membership Lead

Scoring Dashboard Option

Table 20.6

Domain	KPI Average	Weighted Score	Maturity Level
Engagement & Network Activation	3.8 / 5	76%	Emerging Platform Performer
Financial Sustainability	4.2 / 5	84%	Financially Resilient
Governance Agility & Integrity	3.5 / 5	70%	Agile but Inconsistent
Platform Operations & Innovation	3.0 / 5	60%	Developing Capability

Example Data Sources Legend

- **CRM** = Customer/Constituent Relationship Management platform
- **LMS** = Learning Management System
- **CMS** = Content Management System (e.g. for member contributions)
- **DMS** = Document Management System
- **Pulse Surveys** = Monthly or quarterly micro-surveys
- **Analytics** = Web or platform usage tracking tools (e.g. Google Analytics, Mixpanel)

Boardroom Application Guide

Putting the Platform KPI Framework into Practice

To support modern, agile, and platform-oriented governance, associations should not only define KPIs, they will have to also embed them into a regular performance and decision-making rhythm. This guide offers a practical approach for boardroom use of the KPI framework outlined in Annexure B.

1. Apply Red–Amber–Green (RAG) Thresholds to Assess KPI Health

Each KPI domain can be monitored using a traffic light system:

Rating	Interpretation	Board Response
Red	Below target; performance is misaligned or deteriorating	Request corrective action plan, deeper root cause analysis
Amber	Acceptable but requires improvement; trend unclear or mixed	Monitor closely, consider resource allocation or pilot programs
Green	On target or exceeding expectations	Continue and scale; extract lessons and document enablers

Boards should agree on specific thresholds during strategy or risk workshops and update them annually.

2. Assign Responsibility and Data Sources

Boards should ensure every KPI has:

- **An accountable owner** (typically at executive or GM level)
- **A verified data source** (CRM, LMS, analytics, surveys, audit logs)
- **A reporting frequency** aligned to board rhythms (e.g. quarterly)

Example:
"Return Visits to Platform per Month", Owner: Head of Digital; Source: Google Analytics; Reported: Monthly to Executive, Quarterly to Board.

3. Use KPI Domains as Strategic Performance Pillars

The four domains support governance aligned to platform-era strategy:

Table 20.6

KPI Domain	Governance Use
Engagement & Network Activation	Member value, community health, platform growth
Financial Sustainability	Risk exposure, business model diversification, margin resilience
Governance Agility & Integrity	Ethical oversight, responsiveness, stakeholder legitimacy
Platform Operations & Innovation	Strategic delivery, transformation effectiveness, capability maturity

Boards may consider assigning **sub-committees or advisory panels** to oversee each domain, especially during transformation periods.

4. Integrate into Dashboards and Board Packs

Boards should receive **quarterly or biannual dashboards** structured around these domains. These can include:

- **Trend graphs** (e.g. member retention over time)
- **Pulse indicators** (e.g. last 90 days of platform engagement)
- **Red–Amber–Green summaries**
- **Narrative insights** (e.g. explanation of deviations, corrective actions)

Tip: Link KPI discussions to key agenda items, especially budget planning, risk reviews, or strategy updates.

This appendix serves as a practical reference for associations aiming to modernise their performance measurement frameworks. By adopting these KPIs, organisations can better align their strategies with contemporary challenges and opportunities.

Glossary

Adaptive Governance: A governance approach that enables rapid, insight-informed decision-making in complex and changing environments. Emphasises learning, agility, and cultural responsiveness. *See also: Agile Governance; Governance Capability*

Agile Governance: A model of governance that prioritises responsiveness, transparency, and ethical oversight. It replaces rigid oversight structures with dynamic mechanisms for real-time risk management and participatory input. *See also: Governance Maturity; Trust Infrastructure*

APPS Scorecard: The Association Platform Performance Scorecard is a diagnostic tool for assessing an association's platform maturity across core domains: infrastructure, insight, governance, and engagement. *See also: Platform Readiness; Diagnostic Tools*

***Association Platform Success Framework*:** A foundational model introduced in Chapter 2 that integrates five design pillars: scalable infrastructure, data insight, modular experience, participation strategy, and governance/trust. *See also: Platform Thinking; Enabling Layers*

Behavioural Governance: Focuses on how decisions are made, examining trust, board dynamics, values, and leadership culture. One of the three governance capability domains. *See also: Governance Capability; Culture Maturity*

Boardroom Capability: Refers to the skills, digital fluency, and adaptive leadership required at board level to govern complex, platform-based associations. *See also: Capability Domain; Governance Maturity*

Business Model Innovation: The process of reimagining how value is created, delivered, and captured. In platform-based associations, this includes transitioning to multi-sided models and non-linear revenue flows. *See also: Monetisation Models; Platform Economics*

Capability Domain: One of the three governance capability domains. Focuses on the skills, confidence, and digital readiness of the board and executive team. *See also: Structure Domain; Behavioural Governance*

Co-Design: A participatory design method where members, users, and stakeholders collaborate in developing services, policies, or platforms. *See also: Participation Strategy; Member Experience Lab*

Crowd Contribution: Value generated through user input, peer learning, co-creation, or member-generated content. A key feature of scalable platform engagement. *See also: Marketplace Model; Network Effects*

Data-Driven Insight: The use of analytics, segmentation, and predictive modelling to inform strategy and improve member experiences. One of the APSF pillars. *See also: Insight Maturity; Strategic Data Capability*

Diagnostic Continuum: The tool for assessing Governance Friction, from Harmony through Friction to Conflict and Collapse. Supports early intervention and realignment. *See also: Governance Friction; Adaptive Governance*

Digital Risk Threshold: A governance mechanism that defines acceptable risk boundaries for digital tools, AI systems, and data practices. *See also: Ethical AI; Scenario Testing*
Dynamic Risk Intelligence: A real-time, adaptive capability that enables organisations to sense, interpret, and respond to emerging risks across complex systems and digital environments. It integrates predictive analytics, scenario modelling, and human judgment to anticipate friction points, detect weak signals, and enable timely governance interventions. Supports decision-making under uncertainty by fusing structured data with contextual insight. *See also: Diagnostic Continuum; Scenario Testing; Adaptive Governance*
Ecosystem
A dynamic network of interconnected organisations, individuals, platforms, and resources that collaboratively create and exchange value. In the context of associations, ecosystems extend beyond traditional member-service models to include partners, platforms, funders, beneficiaries, and data contributors, often operating under shared governance or aligned purpose. Well-designed ecosystems enable adaptability, co-creation, and scale by leveraging network effects and shared infrastructure. See also: *Ecosystem Leverage; Platform Orchestration; Participation Strategy*
Ecosystem Leverage: Using partnerships, networks, and third-party contributors to scale impact and value creation. Central to the platform mindset. *See also: Platform Orchestration; Multi-Sided Models*
Enabling Layers: Refers to the infrastructure, governance frameworks, and technical capabilities that allow platform associations to scale responsibly. *See also: Enabling Capabilities; Strategic Infrastructure*
Ethical AI: The design and governance of artificial intelligence systems that align with ethical standards, transparency, and human oversight. *See also: ISO 42001; Trust Infrastructure*
Foresight Capability: A board's ability to anticipate emerging risks, opportunities, and signals through scenario planning and horizon scanning. *See also: Future Readiness; Strategic Risk Intelligence*
Freemium Model: A monetisation strategy that offers free baseline access with optional paid upgrades. Common in content, CPD, and community platforms. *See also: Monetisation Pathways; Subscription Models*
Future Readiness Radar: A visual diagnostic tool for assessing preparedness across digital, economic, and governance dimensions. *See also: APPS Scorecard; Scenario Testing*
Governance Capability: A multi-dimensional measure of a board's ability to govern effectively. Includes structure, behaviour, and capability. *See also: ISO 37004; Governance Maturity*
Governance Friction: The tension or misalignment that emerges when governance structures are no longer fit-for-purpose in changing environments. *See also: Diagnostic Continuum; Friction-to-Function Model*
Governance Maturity: The evolution of governance systems from compliance-based to strategic and adaptive. Often measured using tools like the Maturity Matrix. *See also: Agile Governance; Capability Domains*
Insight Maturity: Describes an association's capacity to turn raw data into decision-ready insight. A key enabler of strategic agility. *See also: Strategic Data Capability; Dashboards*
ISO 37000 Series: A suite of international standards on governance, including ISO 37000 (principles), ISO 37004 (maturity models), and ISO 37005 (governance indicators). *See also: Capability Domains; Governance Assessment*
Marketplace Model: A business model in which the association acts as a platform enabling transactions between users (e.g. CPD courses, services, mentoring). *See also: Multi-Sided Revenue; Platform Ecosystem*
Member Experience Lab: A method for involving members in the co-design and testing of new services and engagement strategies. *See also: Co-Design; Participation Architecture*

Modular Design: Designing content, services, and systems in flexible, customisable units that can be recombined or scaled across use cases. *See also: Product Strategy; Freemium Models*

Monetisation Pathways: The range of strategies available for generating revenue, direct and indirect, member- and partner-based. *See also: Platform Revenue Model Matrix; Business Model Innovation*

Multi-Sided Revenue: Income derived from multiple sources beyond members, such as sponsors, advertisers, partners, and data clients. *See also: Network Effects; Platform Economics*

Network Effects: The phenomenon where the value of a platform increases as more users participate. Includes both direct and indirect effects. *See also: Platform Economics; Ecosystem Leverage*

Participation Strategy: A deliberate approach to designing how members and stakeholders engage, contribute, and create value within the platform. *See also: Ecosystem Participation; Value Co-Creation*

Platform Economics: An economic model where value is co-created by users, marginal costs decline with scale, and growth is driven by network effects. *See also: Multi-Sided Revenue; Value Multiplication*

Platform Orchestration: The strategic role of an association in enabling and managing multi-party interactions within an ecosystem. *See also: Ecosystem Leverage; Governance and Trust*

Platform Posture: An association's overall orientation to platform strategy, including how it designs for value exchange, openness, and strategic growth. *See also: APSF; Business Model Transformation*

Risk Appetite: The amount and type of risk an organisation is willing to accept in pursuit of its goals. It guides decision-making and sets boundaries for strategic and operational risk-taking. See also: *Governance Capability; Risk Management Framework*

Risk Management Framework: A structured approach to identifying, assessing, mitigating, and monitoring risks across an organisation. It ensures risk is managed consistently and transparently in line with strategic objectives.: See also: *Governance Maturity; Scenario Testing*

Scenario Testing: A practice used by boards to explore future risks and decisions through hypothetical but plausible situations. *See also: Risk Intelligence; Simulation Tools*

Trust Infrastructure: The frameworks, policies, and behaviours that ensure ethical oversight, data integrity, and reciprocal value exchange. *See also: Governance and Trust; Ethical AI*

Detailed Table of Contents

Tables of Tables

Table of Figures

Table of Cases

Bibliography

26 DX. (2024, October 9). *From publisher to digital pioneer: CIPD's smart content evolution*. Retrieved May 9, 2025, from https://26-dx.com/blog/from-publisher-to-digital-pioneer-cipd-s-smart-content-evolution/

Accenture. (2023). Future of work: Reimagining work, workers, and workplaces. Accenture. https://www.accenture.com/

Aagaard, A. & Tucci, C. (2024). AI-Driven Business Model Innovation: Pioneering New Frontiers in Value Creation. In A. Aagaard (Ed.), Business Model Innovation: Game Changers and Contemporary Issues (pp. 295–329). Palgrave Macmillan. https://doi.org/10.1007/978-3-031-57511-2_10

Aagaard, A. (2024). Business model innovation: Game changers and contemporary issues. Palgrave Macmillan.

Aagaard, A. (2024). Introducing Business Model Innovation and the Game Changers of Tomorrow. In A. Aagaard (Ed.), Business Model Innovation: Game Changers and Contemporary Issues (pp. 1–26). Palgrave Macmillan. https://doi.org/10.1007/978-3-031-57511-2_1

Accounting Times (2024, April) CPA Australia axed 121 staff, services for internal revamp: report. Retrieved from https://www.accountingtimes.com.au/profession/cpa-australia-axed-121-staff-services-in-wake-of-internal-revamp

Adner, R. (2017). Ecosystem as structure: An actionable construct for strategy. Journal of Management, 43(1), 39–58. https://doi.org/10.1177/014920631667845 1

Aged Care Workforce Industry Council. (2022). *Workforce Planning Tool*. Retrieved July 9, 2025, from https://www.agedcareworkforce.com.au/workforce-planning-tool

Aged Care Workforce Strategy Taskforce. (2018). *A matter of care: Australia's aged care workforce strategy*. Australian Government Department of Health. Retrieved July 9, 2025, from https://oia.pmc.gov.au/sites/default/files/posts/2021/09/A-matter-of-care-australia-s-aged-care-workforce-strategy.pdf

Agrawal, A. Gans, J. & Goldfarb, A. (2018). Prediction Machines: The Simple Economics of Artificial Intelligence. Harvard Business Review Press.

AHRI (Australian HR Institute). (2023). Annual Transparency Report. www.ahri.com.au

AHRI Annual Report 2022; AHRI Capability Framework. https://www.ahri.com.au/certification-and-training/the-australian-hr-capability-framework

Allen, D. W. E. Berg, C. & Davidson, S. (2023). The Exchange Theory of Web3 Governance. *Kyklos*, *76*(4), 659-675

Allen, D. W. E. Berg, C. Davidson, S. Gettler, L. Kane, E. Lane, A. M. & Potts, J. (2020). So, You Run a University?

American Institute of Architects. (2023). *AIA Year in Review 2023*. The American Institute of Architects. Retrieved May 9, 2025, from https://www.aia.org/year-review-2023

American Institute of Architects. (2024). *AIA Knowledge Communities*. The American Institute of Architects. Retrieved May 9, 2025, from https://classic.aia.org/pages/4856-aia-knowledge-communities

American Institute of Architects. (2020). *AIA Strategic Plan 2021–2025* [PDF]. The American Institute of Architects. Retrieved May 9, 2025, from https://content.aia.org/sites/default/files/2020-12/EX20_StrategicPlan-2021-2025_RJ_v06.pdf

American College of Cardiology. (2023). Our Mission and Vision. Retrieved from https://www.acc.org/About-ACC

American College of Cardiology. (2023) Annual Report. Retrieved from https://www.acc.org/About-ACC/Annual-ReportC

American College of Cardiology. (2023) Annual Report: 75 Years of Collective Action. Retrieved from https://www.acc.org/About-ACC/Annual-Report/75-Years-of-Driving-Collective-Action

American Marketing Association. (2024). *Weekly Perks for Members*. Retrieved May 9, 2025, from https://www.ama.org/membership-perk/

American Marketing Association. (2024). *About AMA*. Retrieved May 9, 2025, from https://www.ama.org/about-ama/

AMI (Australian Marketing Institute). (2023). Flexible Membership Models for a Changing Market. Retrieved from https://ami.org.au/membership

Austin, J. E. & Seitanidi, M. M. (2012). Collaborative Value Creation: A Review of Partnering Between Nonprofits and Businesses. Nonprofit and Voluntary Sector Quarterly, 42(5), 739–768. https://doi.org/10.1177/0899764012454685

Australia Council for the Arts. (2021). *Digital Culture Strategy 2021–24*. Retrieved May 9, 2025, from https://camd.org.au/ausco-digital-culture-strategy-2021-24/

Australia Council for the Arts. (2023). *Digital case studies*. Retrieved May 9, 2025, from https://australiacouncil.gov.au/resources/digital-case-studies?opportunity_type=Digital+case+study

Australian Ageing Agenda. (2023, June 15). *New tool helps providers build workforce planning capability*. Retrieved July 9, 2025, from https://www.agedcareguide.com.au/talking-aged-care/industry-body-releases-new-workforce-planning-tool

Australian Digital Health Agency. (2025, March 19). *Expanded investment in Allied Health to accelerate connected care*. https://www.digitalhealth.gov.au/newsroom/media/expanded-investment-in-allied-health-to-accelerate-connected-care

Australian Government Department of Health and Aged Care. (2024). *Workforce planning in aged care*. Retrieved July 9, 2025, from https://www.agedcarequality.gov.au/resource-library/workforce-planning-aged-careAustralian HR Institute. (2024). AHRI Certification and Professional Development. https://www.ahri.com.au/certification-and-training/ahri-certification

Australian HR Institute. (2023). Annual Report 2022–2023. https://www.ahri.com.au/wp-content/uploads/2022-AHRI-Annual-Review.pdf

Australian HR Institute. (2022). *National Certification Council: Governance and Standards Overview.*

Australian Institute of Architects. New Online CPD Platform. Received from https://www.architecture.com.au/archives/news_media_articles/new-online-cpd-platform

Australian Institute of Architects. New Member Networking Platform. Retrieved from https://www.architecture.com.au/archives/news_media_articles/introducing-community-your-new-member-networking-platform

Australian Institute of Architects. ABIC Contracts Done Digital. Retrieved from ABIC Digital Contracts - Australian Institute of Architects

Australian Institute of Company Directors (AICD). (2023). Governing through uncertainty: Lessons for boards on transformation and risk. https://aicd.companydirectors.com.au

Australian Marketing Institute. (2024). *Annual Report.* https://ami.org.au/about-us/annual-report/

Australian Marketing Institute. (2025). *Membership.* https://ami.org.au/membership/

Australian Marketing Institute. (2025). *Corporate Membership.*

https://ami.org.au/corporate-membership/

Australian Medical Association (2021) AMA's free CPD Tracker for Australian Doctors is now on Topbar. Retrieved from : https://www.ama.com.au/media/amas-free-cpd-tracker-australian-doctors-now-topbar-and-matched-new-legislation

Australian Psychological Society. (2025). *CPD and events: Professional learning and standards for psychologists*. Retrieved May 9, 2025, from https://psychology.org.au/training-events/events-calendar

Australian Red Cross. (2023). Annual Report 2022–2023: Strengthening communities through partnership. https://www.redcross.org.au/

BoardSource. (2021). Leading with intent: BoardSource index of nonprofit board practices. https://boardsource.org/research-critical-issues/leading-with-intent/

Brynjolfsson, E. & McAfee, A. (2017). Machine, Platform, Crowd: Harnessing Our Digital Future. W. W. Norton & Company.

Bryson, J. M. (2018). Strategic planning for public and nonprofit organizations: A guide to strengthening and sustaining organizational achievement (5th ed.). Jossey-Bass.

Budden, P. & Murray, F. (2022). Strategically engaging with innovation ecosystems. MIT Sloan Management Review, 64(1), 38-43. https://mitsloan.mit.edu/

Budden, P. & Murray, F. (2025). Accelerating Innovation: Competitive Advantage through Ecosystem Engagement. MIT Press.

Camplify Holdings Limited. (2021). Prospectus. https://chl.global/wp-content/uploads/2023/06/Camplify-Prospectus.pdf

Camplify Holdings Limited. (2023). Camplify Holdings Limited: ASX Broker Report. https://www.asx.com.au/content/dam/asx/broker-reports/2023/chl-ordminnett-initiation-270123.pdf

Camplify. (n.d.). Camplify Global: AU, UK, NZ & ES. https://www.camplify.com

Chait, R. P. Ryan, W. P. & Taylor, B. E. (2005). Governance as Leadership: Reframing the Work of Nonprofit Boards. Wiley.

Carr, A. (2023). *Growing our community and working together*. Chartered Institute of Personnel and Development. Retrieved May 9, 2025, from https://community.cipd.co.uk/cipd-blogs/b/the_people_profession_now_and_for_the_future/posts/growing-our-community-and-working

Chartered Institute of Personnel and Development (2022). Annual Report and Accounts 2021–22. https://www.cipd.co.uk/about/annual-report

Chartered Institute of Personnel and Development. (2025). *CIPD Learning Hub*. Retrieved May 9, 2025, from https://shop.cipd.org/catalog?pagename=Learning-Hub

Chartered Institute of Personnel and Development. (2025). *Passion for learning: Introductory programme*. Retrieved May 9, 2025, from https://shop.cipd.ie/product?catalog=IE-Passion-for-Learning-Introductory-Programme

Chesbrough, H. (2006). Open Innovation: The New Imperative for Creating and Profiting from Technology. Harvard Business Review Press.

CIPD (Chartered Institute of Personnel and Development). (2021). Member Value Index: Segmented Engagement Framework. www.cipd.co.uk

Coase, R. H. (1937). The Nature of the Firm. Economica, 4(16), 386-405.

Commerce Commission New Zealand. (2021). Camplify Co (NZ) Limited and Tourism Holdings Limited and TH2connect LP Clearance application. https://comcom.govt.nz/__data/assets/pdf_file/0028/274816/Camplify-Co-NZ-Limited-and-Tourism-Holdings-Limited-and-TH2connect-LP-Clearance-application-23-December-2021.pdf

Cornforth, C. (2003). The Governance of Public and Non-Profit Organizations: What Do Boards Do? Routledge.

Corney, S. (2021). "Measuring Member Value: Beyond Satisfaction Scores." CIPD Insights Retrieved from https://memberwise.org.uk/ever-wondered-members-really-thinking-quantifying-cipd-brand/

Creative Australia. (2024, March 18). *Think planning, think strategy, think digital*. ArtsHub. Retrieved May 9, 2025, from https://www.artshub.com.au/news/sponsored-content/think-planning-think-strategy-think-digital-2724835/

Creative Australia. (2025). *Think Digital: Resources for the arts sector*. Retrieved May 9, 2025, from https://creative.gov.au/resources/think-digital

Cusumano, M. A. Gawer, A. & Yoffie, D. B. (2019). The Business of Platforms: Strategy in the Age of Digital Competition, Innovation, and Power. Harper Business.

Davidson, S. De Filippi, P. & Potts, J. (2018). Blockchains and the economic institutions of capitalism. Journal of Institutional Economics, 14(4), 639–658. https://doi.org/10.1017/S1744137417000200

Davidson, S. Novak, M. & Potts, J. (2018). The Cost of Trust: A Pilot Study on Blockchain Governance. Journal of Institutional Economics, 14(6), 1065-1087.

De Filippi, P. & Wright, A. (2018). Blockchain and the Law: The Rule of Code. Harvard University Press.

Deloitte Global Risk Advisory. (2022). The connecting force: Risk intelligence platforms enabling decisions (Issue 2). Deloitte. Retrieved from https://www.deloitte.com

Deloitte. (2020). The Boardroom Frontier: Redefining Governance in the Digital Age. Retrieved from www.deloitte.com

Deloitte. (2023). CEO Survey: Ecosystems and platforms for growth. Deloitte Insights. https://www2.deloitte.com/

Digital Health Cooperative Research Centre. (2024). *2023–2024 Annual Report*. https://digitalhealthcrc.com/wp-content/uploads/2024/11/DHCRC-Annual-Report-2023-2024_Final-1.pdf

Dribbble. (2025). How Dribbble Works. https://dribbble.com/about

Dribbble. (2025). *Pro Membership & Hiring*. https://dribbble.com/pro

Drucker, P. F. (1990). Managing the nonprofit organization: Principles and practices. HarperBusiness.

Ebrahim, A., & Rangan, V. K. (2014). What Impact? A Framework for Measuring the Scale and Scope of Social Performance. *California Management Review, 56*(3), 118-141. https://doi.org/10.1525/cmr.2014.56.3.118

Eckerson, W. W. (2010). *Performance dashboards: measuring, monitoring, and managing your business*. John Wiley & Sons.

Edelman. (2024). Edelman Trust Barometer 2024. https://www.edelman.com/trust-barometer

Edelman. (2025). Edelman Trust Barometer 2025: The precipice of a grievance-based society. Edelman. https://www.edelman.com/trust/2025/trust-barometer

Edmondson, A. C. (2019). The fearless organization: Creating psychological safety in the workplace for learning, innovation, and growth. Wiley.

Elkington, J. (1997). Cannibals with Forks: The Triple Bottom Line of 21st Century Business. Capstone Publishing.

Engineers Australia. (2022). *Annual Report 2021–2022.*

Engineers Australia. (2023). Strategic Plan 2023–2027.

Eric von Hippel. (2005). Democratizing innovation. MIT Press.

European Commission. (2021). Proposal for a Regulation Laying Down Harmonised Rules on Artificial Intelligence (AI Act).

European Data Protection Board. (2020, March 3). *Dutch DPA fines Tennis Association*. Retrieved May 9, 2025, from https://www.edpb.europa.eu/news/national-news/2020/dutch-dpa-fines-tennis-association_nl

Evans, D. S. & Schmalensee, R. (2008). Catalyst Code: The Strategies Behind the World's Most Dynamic Companies. Harvard Business Review Press.

Evans, D. S. & Schmalensee, R. (2011). Platform Economics: Essays on Multi-Sided Businesses. Competition Policy International.

Evans, D. S. & Schmalensee, R. (2016). Matchmakers: The New Economics of Multisided Platforms. Harvard Business Review Press.

Evans, D. S. Schmalensee, R. Noel, M. D. Chang, H. H. & Garcia-Swartz, D. D. (2011). Platform Economics: Essays on Multi-Sided Businesses. Competition Policy International.

Evans, P. C. & Gawer, A. (2016). The Rise of the Platform Enterprise. A Global Survey. Center for Global Enterprise.

Fenwick, M. & Vermeulen, E. P. (2018). Technology and Corporate Governance: Blockchain, Crypto, and Artificial Intelligence. SSRN Electronic Journal. https://doi.org/10.2139/ssrn.3285524

Freeman, R. E. (1984). Strategic management: A stakeholder approach. Pitman Publishing.

Frumkin, P. (2002). On being nonprofit: A conceptual and policy primer. Harvard University Press.

Gawer, A. & Cusumano, M. A. (2014). Industry Platforms and Ecosystem Innovation. Journal of Product Innovation Management, 31(3), 417–433.

Gawer, A. Cusumano, M. A. & Yoffie, D. B. (2023). The Platform Organization. In C. Snow & Ø. Fjeldstad (Eds.), Designing Modern Organizations. Cambridge University Press.

Gawer, A. (2020). Digital Platforms' Boundaries: The Interplay of Firm Scope, Platform Sides, and Digital Interfaces. Long Range Planning, 54(5), 102045. https://doi.org/10.1016/j.lrp.2020.102045

Governance Institute of Australia. (2024). Micro-credentials and digital badges. Retrieved April 20, 2025, from https://www.governanceinstitute.com.au/education/micro-credentials/

Guild Group. (n.d.-a). Our story. Retrieved May 9, 2025, from https://guildgroup.com.au/about/our-story

Guild Group. (n.d.-b). Guild Insurance. Retrieved May 9, 2025, from https://guildgroup.com.au/companies/guild-insurance-2

Hagiu, A. & Wright, J. (2015). Marketplace or Reseller?. Management Science, 61(1), 184–203.

Halamka, J. & Cerrato, P. (2020). The digital reconstruction of health care. NEJM Catalyst Innovations in Care Delivery, 1(6).

Hansmann, H. (1980). The role of nonprofit enterprise. The Yale Law Journal, 89(5), 835–901. https://doi.org/10.2307/796089

Harrison, Y. & Pipas, J. (2017). Membership Essentials: Recruitment, Retention, Roles, Responsibilities, and Resources. ASAE & The Center for Association Leadership.

Heifetz, R. Grashow, A. & Linsky, M. (2009). The practice of adaptive leadership: Tools and tactics for changing your organization and the world. Harvard Business Press.

Hein, A. Schreieck, M. Wiesche, M. & Krcmar, H. (2016). Multiple-Case Analysis on Governance Mechanisms of Multi-Sided Platforms. Journal of Information Technology, 31(2), 1–10.

Herman, R. D. & Renz, D. O. (2008). Advancing nonprofit organizational effectiveness research and theory: Nine theses. Nonprofit Management and Leadership, 18(4), 399–415. https://doi.org/10.1002/nml.195

Iansiti, M. & Levien, R. (2004). The Keystone Advantage: What the New Dynamics of Business Ecosystems Mean for Strategy, Innovation, and Sustainability. Harvard Business Review Press.

IndieHackers. (2025). About Indie *Hackers*. https://www.indiehackers.com/about

IndieHackers. (2025). *Community Guidelines*. https://www.indiehackers.com/community-guidelines

Inside Ageing. (2023, August 10). *Transforming aged care workforce readiness through microcredentials*. Retrieved July 9, 2025, from https://insideageing.com.au/transforming-aged-care-workforce-readiness-through-microcredentials/

International Organization for Standardization (ISO). (2021). ISO/IEC 27001:2021: Information Security, Cybersecurity and Privacy Protection: Information Security Management Systems. Geneva: ISO.

International Organization for Standardization (ISO). (2023). ISO 37000:2023: Governance of Organizations. Geneva: ISO.

International Organization for Standardization (ISO). (2023). ISO/IEC 42001:2023 - Artificial Intelligence - Management System. Geneva, Switzerland: ISO.

International Organization for Standardization (ISO)(2018). ISO 31000:2018 Risk Management: Guidelines. International Organization for Standardization.

IRM (2024). Setting the Risk Agenda: Exploring the Future of the Risk Management Profession. Institute of Risk Management.

IWRA (International Water Resources Association). (2024). Membership Categories and Benefits. Retrieved from https://www.iwra.org/membership-categories

International Water Resources Association. (2024). *IWRA Membership Structure Presentation*. Retrieved May 9, 2025, from https://www.iwra.org/wp-content/uploads/2021/02/Membership-Structure-Presentation-Town-Hall.pdf

International Water Resources Association. (2024). *IWRA Membership Grant Recipients 2024*. Retrieved May 9, 2025, from https://www.iwra.org/mg-recipients-2024/

Jacobides, M. G. Cennamo, C. & Gawer, A. (2018). Towards a Theory of Ecosystems. Strategic Management Journal, 39(8), 2255–2276. https://doi.org/10.1002/smj.2904

Jacobs, C. & Goddard, M. (2020). Adaptive Governance: The Next Frontier for Board Effectiveness. Journal of Governance & Accountability Studies, 14(2), 215-238.

Jobin, A. Ienca, M. & Vayena, E. (2019). The Global Landscape of AI Ethics Guidelines. Nature Machine Intelligence, 1(9), 389-399.

Kania, J. & Kramer, M. (2011). Collective Impact. Stanford Social Innovation Review, 9(1), 36–41.

Kaplan, R. S. & Norton, D. P. (1996). The Balanced Scorecard: Translating Strategy into Action. Harvard Business Review Press.

Kegan, R. & Lahey, L. L. (2009). Immunity to change: How to overcome it and unlock the potential in yourself and your organization. Harvard Business Press.

Kenney, M., Bearson, D., & Zysman, J. (2021). The platform economy matures: Measuring pervasiveness and exploring power. *Socio-economic review, 19*(4), 1451-1483.

Lepaya. (2024). Evolution of skills 2030: Preparing organisations for the future. https://www.lepaya.com/

Lewin, K. (1947). Frontiers in Group Dynamics: Concept, Method and Reality in Social Science; Social Equilibria and Social Change. Human Relations, 1(1), 5-41V 2.7

Markova, G. Ford, R. C. Dickson, D. R. & Bohn, T. M. (2013). Professional associations and members' benefits: What's in it for me? Nonprofit Management and Leadership, 23(4), 491–510. https://doi.org/10.1002/nml.21075

Marty, F. & Warin, T. (2023). Multi-Sided Platforms and Innovation. Harvard Business Review.

Mayer, R. C. Davis, J. H. & Schoorman, F. D. (1995). An integrative model of organizational trust. Academy of Management Review, 20(3), 709–734.

McCrindle Research. (2023). The future of education, employment and engagement in Australia. https://mccrindle.com.au/

MCI Group. (2024). Global association benchmarking report. https://www.mci-group.com/

McKinley Advisors. (2022). Association viewpoint: An age of acceleration. McKinley Advisors. https://www.mckinley-advisors.com

McKinsey & Company. (2023). Skill shift: Automation and the future of the workforce. https://www.mckinsey.com/

McKinsey & Company. (2024). Rewired: The Future of Digital Transformation. McKinsey Digital.

Medical Technology Association of Australia. (2023). Ethical AI in Medical Technology: Position Paper. Retrieved April 20, 2025, from https://www.mtaa.org.au/news/ethical-ai-medtech-position-paper

Miehé, L. & Gassmann, O. (2024). New Venues for Collaborative Business Model Innovation Through Ecosystems. In A. Aagaard (Ed.), Business Model Innovation: Game Changers and Contemporary Issues (pp. 57–87). Palgrave Macmillan. https://doi.org/10.1007/978-3-031-57511-2_3

Mihelich, J. (2023, April 12). *The Future of Association Membership: Why Subscription-Based Models Are Here to Stay*. LinkedIn. Retrieved May 9, 2025, from https://www.linkedin.com/pulse/future-association-membership-why-subscription-based-models-mihelich

Mintzberg, H. Ahlstrand, B. W. & Lampel, J. (1998). Strategy safari: A guided tour through the wilds of strategic management. Free Press.

Moore, B. (2024). *Evolving association membership models*. Strategic Membership Solutions. https://smsonline.net.au/blog/new-whitepaper--evolving-association-membership-models

Moore, B. (2025). *Purpose under pressure: Global association trends in 2025*. Strategic Membership Solutions / Global Association Research Initiative. https://smsonline.net.au

Mopoke Cloud. (2021, August 23). Camplify: Why the AirBnb for Caravans has a long way to run. https://www.mopokecloud.com/p/camplify-deep-dive

Neely, A., Gregory, M., & Platts, K. (1995). Performance measurement system design: A literature review and research agenda. *International journal of operations & production management, 15*(4), 80-116.

NIST. (2018). Framework for Improving Critical Infrastructure Cybersecurity (Version 1.1). National Institute of Standards and Technology.

OECD. (2021). Collaborative innovation: Transforming public sector ecosystems. https://www.oecd.org/

OECD. (2023). Good governance for critical infrastructure resilience. OECD Publishing. https://doi.org/10.1787/3f4a2f31-en

Osterwalder, A. & Pigneur, Y. (2010). Business Model Generation: A Handbook for Visionaries, Game Changers, and Challengers. Wiley.

Parker, G. G., Van Alstyne, M. W., & Choudary, S. P. (2016). *Platform revolution: How networked markets are transforming the economy and how to make them work for you*. WW Norton & Company.

Parmenter, D. (2012). *Key performance indicators for government and non profit agencies: Implementing winning KPIs*. John Wiley & Sons.

Petrie, N. (2014). Future trends in leadership development. Center for Creative Leadership. https://www.ccl.org/wp-content/uploads/2020/04/futureTrends.pdf

Pharmaceutical Society of Australia (2024). "PSA and Audirie mark first year of partnership, announcing expansion of AI-powered education simulations in 2025. Retrieved from: https://www.psa.org.au/psa-and-audirie-mark-first-year-of-partnership-announcing-expansion-of-ai-powered-education-simulations-in-2025/

Porter, M. E. (2011). Creating Shared Value. Harvard Business Review, 89(1/2), 62–77.

Potts, J. (2025). von Hippel innovation. Prometheus, 40(2), 74-91.

Potts, J. (2025). Von Hippel Innovation: Innovation as Infrastructure. In Wennberg, K. & Sandström, C. (Eds.), Questioning the Entrepreneurial State. Springer.

Professional Advantage. (2023, September 21). Governance Institute of Australia: Going all-in on cloud to focus on members. Retrieved April 20, 2025, from https://www.pa.com.au/client-success/governance-institute-of-australia/

Putnam, R. D. (2000). Bowling Alone: The Collapse and Revival of American Community. Simon & Schuster.

PwC. (2023). Workforce of the future: The competing forces shaping 2030. https://www.pwc.com/

Queensland Audit Office. (2024). *Responding to and recovering from cyber attacks (Report 12: 2023–24).*

Ray, P. P. (2023). Web3: A Comprehensive Review on Background, Technologies, Applications, Zero-Trust Architectures, Challenges, and Future Directions. Internet of Things and Cyber-Physical Systems, 3, 213–248.

Reim, W. Sjödin, D. & Parida, V. (2023). Enabling Collaboration on Digital Platforms: A Study of Digital Twins. Journal of Business Research.

Re:Members. (2024, August 7). *Tiered Membership Models to Consider for Your Association*. Retrieved May 9, 2025, from https://www.remembers.com/blog/tiered-membership-models-to-consider-for-your-association/

Ritala, P. & Jovanovic, M. (2024). Platformizers, Orchestrators, and Guardians: B2B Models for Digital Ecosystems. Working Paper.

Ritala, P. & Jovanovic, M. (2024). Platformizers, Orchestrators, and Guardians: Strategies for Managing Multi-Sided Platform Ecosystems.

Ritala, P. & Jovanovic, M. (2024). Platformizers, orchestrators, and guardians: Three archetypes for digital platform business models. California Management Review, 66(2), 78–96.

Ritala, P. & Jovanovic, M. (2024). Platformizers, Orchestrators, and Guardians: Three Types of B2B Platform Business Models. In A. Aagaard & C. Nielsen (Eds.), Business Model Innovation: Game Changers and Contemporary Issues (pp. 75–91). Palgrave Macmillan.

Rochet, J. C. & Tirole, J. (2003). Platform Competition in Two-Sided Markets. Journal of the European Economic Association, 1(4), 990–1029.

Rochet, J.C. & Tirole, J. (2006). Two-sided markets: A progress report. RAND Journal of Economics, 37(3), 645–667.

Royal Australasian College of Surgeons. (2023). *MALT Licensing and Partnerships*. Retrieved May 9, 2025, from https://www.surgeons.org/research-audit/malt/licensing-partnerships

Royal Australasian College of Surgeons. (2024). *Annual Report*. Retrieved May 9, 2025, from https://www.surgeons.org/about-racs/annual-report

Royal Australasian College of Surgeons. (2025). *Morbidity Audit and Logbook Tool (MALT)*. Retrieved May 9, 2025, from https://www.surgeons.org/research-audit/morbidity-audit-logbook-tool

Rumelt, Richard. (2022). The crux: How leaders become strategists. Profile Books.

Saadatmanesh, H. (2022). AI-enabled: Transforming Digital Business Models. Technological Forecasting and Social Change, 183, 121912.

Saadatmanesh, H. (2022). AI-Enabled Dynamic Capabilities for Transforming Digital Business Models to Smart Business Models. University of Oulu

Salamon, L. M. (1999). America's nonprofit sector: A primer. Foundation Center.

Sankur, A. et al. (2024). True Customer-Centricity: An Operating Model for Competitive Advantage. McKinsey & Company.

Sattlegger, A. & Bharosa, N. (2024). Beyond principles: Embedding ethical AI risks in public sector risk management practice. Proceedings of the 25th Annual International Conference on Digital Government Research (DGO 2024), Taipei, Taiwan, June 11–14, 2024. ACM. https://doi.org/10.1145/3657054.3657063

Schrepel, T. (2019). Collusion by Blockchain and Smart Contracts. Harvard Journal of Law & Technology, 33(2), 1–44. https://doi.org/10.2139/ssrn.3242860

Schumpeter, J. A. (1942). Capitalism, Socialism, and Democracy. Harper & Brothers.

Senge, P. M. (1990). The fifth discipline: The art and practice of the learning organization. Doubleday.

Srnicek, N. (2017). Platform Capitalism. Polity Press.

Stack Overflow. (2024). Developer survey 2024. https://survey.stackoverflow.co/2024/

Staykova, K. S. & Damsgaard, J. (2015). A Typology of Multi-Sided Platforms: The Core and the Periphery. European Conference on Information Systems (ECIS).

Susskind, R. & Susskind, D. (2015). The future of the professions: How technology will transform the work of human experts. Oxford University Press.

Switch Labs. (2024). *Seamlessly sync WordPress users with Mailchimp using Zapier*. Retrieved May 9, 2025, from https://www.switchlabs.dev/resources/seamlessly-sync-wordpress-users-with-mailchimp-using-zapier

Szabo, N. (1997). Formalizing and Securing Relationships on Public Networks. First Monday, 2(9).

Teece, D. J. (2010). Business Models, Business Strategy and Innovation. Long Range Planning, 43(2–3), 172–194.https://doi.org/10.1016/j.lrp.2009.07.003

Tejero, A. Márquez, J. A. & Dodero, J. M. (2020). University as a Platform: An Evolutionary Process Towards an Open Educational Ecosystem in Europe. Open Science Framework

The Pharmacy Guild of Australia. (n.d.). The Guild: Structure and governance. Retrieved May 9, 2025, from https://www.guild.org.au/__data/assets/pdf_file/0015/5226/guild-structure.pdf

The Treasury. (2023). Camplify. https://treasury.gov.au/sites/default/files/2023-01/c2021-176975-camplify.pdf

Tiwana, A. (2014). Platform Ecosystems: Aligning Architecture, Governance, and Strategy. Morgan Kaufmann.

Tucci, C. L. Afuah, A. & Viscusi, G. (2018). Creating and capturing value through digital platforms. MIT Sloan Management Review, 60(1), 21–27.

Tuckman, H. P. & Chang, C. F. (1991). A Methodology for Measuring the Financial Vulnerability of Charitable Nonprofit Organizations. Nonprofit and Voluntary Sector Quarterly, 20(4), 445-460.

Universities Australia. (2020). *Submission to the Royal Commission into Aged Care Quality and Safety: Workforce*. Retrieved July 9, 2025, from https://www.universitiesaustralia.edu.au/wp-content/uploads/2020/01/UA-Submission-to-the-Royal-Commission-into-Aged-Care-Quality-and-Safety-Workforce.pdf

von Hippel, E. (2005). Democratizing Innovation. MIT Press.

Waringarri Aboriginal Arts. (2022). *Case Study: Waringarri Arts digital transformation*. Retrieved May 9, 2025, from https://static1.squarespace.com/static/62d4a4c5b3745161454a15e2/t/62fdf0bcfd71002c4aac4c6e/1730844078074/EK_Case+Study_Waringarri+Arts.pdf

Weisbrod, B. A. (1988). The nonprofit economy. Harvard University Press.

West, M. A. (2021). Compassionate leadership: Sustaining wisdom, humanity and presence in health and social care. Swirling Leaf Press.

Williamson, B. (2019). Policy Networks, Performance Metrics, and Platform Markets. Journal of Economic Policy Research.

Williamson, O. E. (1975). Markets and Hierarchies: Analysis and Antitrust Implications. Free Press

Williamson, O. E. (1981). The Economics of Organization: The Transaction Cost Approach. American Journal of Sociology, 87(3), 548-577.

World Economic Forum. (2020). The board's guide to artificial intelligence. https://www.weforum.org/whitepapers/the-board-s-guide-to-artificial-intelligence

World Economic Forum. (2024). Future of Jobs Report 2024. https://www.weforum.org/reports/future-of-jobs-report-2024

Yablonsky, S. A. (2019). Multi-Sided Platforms: Current State and Future Research. Russian Management Journal, 17(4), 519–546.

Young, D. R. (2007). Financing nonprofits: Putting theory into practice. Rowman & Littlefield.

Companion Book: Ecosystem Economics for Modern Associations

In the companion book to this I have set out *Ecosystem Economics for Modern Associations: How Participation, Governance, and Platform Thinking Reshape Value Creation* to enable the refinement to sustainable and viable business model.

This companion is written for readers who want to go deeper:

- **Strategic directors and board members** managing structural reform.
- **Policy designers and economists** grappling with how to fund and govern collective value.
- **Executives and consultants** tasked with designing monetisation models or evaluating impact.
- **Readers of the Playbook** who want to understand the 'engine room' behind the strategic frameworks.

It assumes a working familiarity with association operations, but no prior economic training. The goal is clarity, not complexity.

If *The Modern Association Playbook* is the architect's field manual, then this book is the technical blueprint. It explains:

- The economic rationale behind platform-enabled associations
- How trust, participation, and value co-creation are governed and monetised
- Why some models scale, and others collapse
- Where the limits of traditional business thinking apply to non-market ecosystems

It provides theoretical depth, strategic nuance, and an analytical toolkit to stress-test assumptions and guide design decisions.

You don't need to read it cover to cover. Each part is modular, useful on its own or in sequence.

- **Parts I–II** introduce platform economics and value architecture for associations
- **Part III** explores governance and risk in multi-sided, participatory systems
- **Part IV** bridges these models to policy and sector-wide reform
- **Part V** offers real-world tools, formulas, and models to support application

Each chapter includes reflection prompts, application examples, and risk insights. Tools are included to support diagnostic and design use in real-world settings, from boardrooms to sector briefings.

Sean M Johnson

Lakefield Drive Publishing

Books:

The Modern Association Playbook: Reimagining Strategy, Governance, and Value Creation

Ecosystem Economics for Modern Associations: How Participation, Governance, and Platform Thinking Reshape Value Creation

Lakefield Drive Pty Ltd
Australia
info@lakefielddrive.co
https://lakefielddrive.co/

lakefield drive

Made in United States
Orlando, FL
04 November 2026

90206774R00213